The Gay & Lesbian Address Book

THE EDITORS OF OUT MAGAZINE

A Perigee Book

Every effort has been made to provide the most current mailing addresses. Addresses, however, do change, and neither the publisher nor OUT magazine is responsible for misdirected or returned mail.

A Perigee Book
Published by The Berkley Publishing Group
200 Madison Avenue
New York, NY 10016

Editorial director: Elise Harris
Book design: Debi Farmer and Yvette Robinson
Cover design: James R. Harris

First edition: May 1995
Published simultaneously in Canada.

Library of Congress Cataloging-in-Publication Data

The gay and lesbian address book / the editors of OUT magazine.—1st ed.
p. cm.
"A Perigee book."
ISBN 0-399-51933-5
1. Gays—United States—Dictionaries. 2. Gays—Services for—United States—Directories. I. OUT (New York, NY)
HQ76.25.G3765 1995
305.9'0664'03—dc20 94-44475 CIP

Printed in the United States of America

10 9 8 7 6 5 4 3 2 1

Dedicated to all the openly gay and lesbian people in the public eye who inspire and lead the way for all of us.

ACKNOWLEDGMENTS

This book is a list of names and addresses, but it is also a record of a community that has organized itself over the last twenty-five years. Many gay and lesbian organizations generously shared their lists and their specialized knowledge with us.

An initial source of information was provided courtesy of the National Coalition for Gay, Lesbian and Bisexual Youth, from QueerAmerica, the national database of lesbian and gay resources. Christopher Kryzan of that organization was kind enough to send us his resources.

In addition, we would like to thank City College of New York's Center for Gay and Lesbian Studies for their directory of gay and lesbian academics; the American Library Association for their list of gay and lesbian archives; the American Booksellers Association for their gay booksellers list. Countless religious organizations such as the Metropolitan Community Church, Dignity, Integrity, and the World Congress of Gay and Lesbian Jewish Organizations shared their information.

The Working Group on Funding Lesbian and Gay Issues publishes an invaluable directory of foundations, and the National AIDS Fund and Funders Concerned About AIDS were generous in pointing us in the right direction for AIDS grantmakers. The *You Are Not Alone* guide published by the Hetrick-Martin Institute for gay and lesbian youth in New York City was invaluable for our youth chapter, which will soon be available from them in an updated version. The U.S. Conference of Mayors publishes the most thorough national guide to AIDS service organizations, although within high-incidence areas, major AIDS service providers tend to publish even more complete local lists.

Deb Schwartz and Tara Sutton made great contributions to this book, which could not have been completed without the dedication of Nick Boston. Thanks also to Ariel Kaminer for late nights of uncompensated labor. The book's elegant design was crafted by Debi Farmer and Yvette Robinson.

Finally, OUT is grateful to the editors at Perigee, especially John Duff, for making this happen.

—Elise Harris, editorial project director

CONTENTS

INTRODUCTION

This book is a guide to the brave, prominent gay men and lesbians who excel in their fields (such as Martina Navratilova, k.d. lang and David Geffen) and to the leading organizations and individuals in, or of interest to, the gay community. Not all individuals listed in this book are gay, lesbian or bisexual, nor are groups or associations exclusively gay . . . but each is of particular interest to the gay community.

To that end, this guide was designed to serve both the fan who wants to send a thank-you note to Greg Louganis, and the experienced activist who needs to find the movers and shakers or put together a specialized mailing list.

The format within each chapter depends on its topic. Where entries have particular regional appeal, chapters are sorted geographically: first by state, then by city, then by the name or organization. All other chapters are sorted by name alone, to facilitate quick identification of the address you want.

No address reference book can be entirely comprehensive. Nine hundred and fifty AIDS service organizations seem like a lot to include—until we found out that there are two thousand in New York City alone. But this is a start—a start for the rest of you out there to finish.

—Michael Goff, Editor and President, OUT magazine

Academics

Henry Abelove
Department of English
Wesleyan University
Middletown, CT 06459
Editor, The Lesbian and Gay Studies Reader

Alaska Gay & Lesbian Association
(AGLA)
University of Alaska, Fairbanks
Fairbanks, AK 99775-0123

Tomas Almaguer
Oakes College
University of California
Santa Cruz, CA 95064

Ana Maria Alonso
Department of Anthropology
University of Arizona
Tucson, AZ 85721

American Federation of Teachers, National Gay and Lesbian Caucus
P.O. Box 190983
Miami Beach, FL 33119
Steve Severance & Merry Overholzer

The American University Gay, Lesbian & Bisexual Community
American University
Mary Graydon Center, Rm. 217
4400 Massachusetts Ave. N.W.
Washington, DC 20016

Amherst Lesbian, Bisexual & Gay Alliance
Amherst College
Box 1731, P.O. Box 5000
Amherst, MA 01002-5000

Amherst GALA
Box 102
6 University Dr.
Amherst, MA 01002

Antioch College Gay & Lesbian Student Union
Antioch College
Yellow Springs, OH 45389

Lourdes Arguelles
Professor and MacArthur Chair
Women's Studies Department
Pitzer College
1050 N. Mills Ave.
Claremont, CA 91762
Co-editor, Second Lesbian issue of Signs

Auburn Gay & Lesbian Association
Auburn University
P.O. Box 821
Auburn, AL 36831-0821

Michele Barale
Department of English
Amherst College
Amherst, MA 01002

Jerry Battey
Eagle Center
7051 Santa Monica Blvd.
Los Angeles, CA 90038
Founder

Bay Area Network of Gay and Lesbian Educators
Contra Costa
2970 Graymont Ct.
Concord, CA 94518
Professional organization

Bay Area Network of Gay and Lesbian Educators
East Bay
1246 King Dr.
El Cerrito, CA 94530
Professional organization

Bay Area Network of Gay and Lesbian Educators
San Francisco
P.O. Box 460545
San Francisco, CA 94146-0545
Professional organization

Bay Area Network of Gay and Lesbian Educators
South Bay
175 Stockton Ave.
San José, CA 95126
Professional organization

Evelyn Torton Beck
Professor of Women's Studies
2101 Woods Hall
University of Maryland
College Park, MD 20742-4521
Editor, Nice Jewish Girls: A Lesbian Anthology

Paula Bennett
Associate Professor of English
Department of English
Southern Illinois University
Carbondale, IL 62901
Author, Emily Dickinson: Woman, Poet

Bobbi Bernstein
HRCF - Student Outreach
10421 Beach Mill Rd.
Great Falls, VA 22066

Mark Blasius
Associate Professor
Political Science Department
CUNY, LaGuardia
31-10 Thompson Ave. E-235
Long Island City, NY 11101
Author, "Sexuality, Subjectivity, and Collective Identity," in Lesbian and Gay Political Behavior in the U.S.

Boston Latin School Lesbian / Gay / Bisexual Alumni Group
Boston Latin School Foundation
101 Arch St., 9th Fl.
Boston, MA 02117

Boston College University Committee on Sexual Diversity and Personal and Community Development
Boston College
McElroy 233
Chestnut Hill, MA 02167-3805

Boston University Lesbian, Gay & Bisexual Association
775 Commonwealth Ave.
Boston, MA 02215

Bowdoin Gay, Lesbian & Straight Alliance
c/o Student Activities
Bowdoin College
Brunswick, ME 04011

Nan Jenese Boyd
Assistant Professor of Women's Studies
University of Colorado
Boulder, CO 80309
Author (dissertation), "A History of Gender in San Francisco's Lesbian and Gay Communities, 1950-1965"

The Bridge
c/o Student Activities
Colby College
Waterville, ME 04901

Brown Lesbian, Gay & Bisexual Alliance
Box 1930 SAO
Brown University
Providence, RI 02912

Bryn Mawr / Haverford BGALA
P.O. Box C-1725
Bryn Mawr College
Bryn Mawr, PA 19010

Charlotte Bunch
Director, Center for Women's Global Leadership
Douglass College
27 Clifton Ave.
New Brunswick, NJ 08903

Judith Butler
Professor of Rhetoric
University of California
Berkeley, CA 94720
Author, Gender Trouble: Feminism and the Subversion of Identity

Cal. State, Fresno Gay, Lesbian & Bisexual Student Alliance
Student Programs Officer
California State University, Fresno
Fresno, CA 93740

Cal-Aggie Gay, Lesbian, Bisexual Alumni Association
P.O. Box 72804
Davis, CA 95617

Cal. State, Los Angeles Gay & Lesbian Association
51514 State University Dr., #227
California State University, LA
Los Angeles, CA 90032

California Polytechnic Gay and Lesbian Student Association
(GLSU)
California Polytechnic State University (Pomona)
3108 W. Temple Ave.
Pomona, CA 91768

California State University - Domingez Hills GLSU
1000 E. Victoria St.
Carson, CA 90747

California State University - Fullerton GLSU
University Center 243, Box 67
Fullerton, CA 92701

California State University - Long Beach GLSU
1250 Bellflower Blvd.
Long Beach, CA 90804

California State University - Northridge LAGA
18111 Nordhoff St.
Northridge, CA 91330

Claudia Card
Professor of Philosophy
University of Wisconsin
600 N. Park St.
Madison, WI 53706
Author, Lesbian Choices and Values

Carolina Gay & Lesbian Association
University of North Carolina (Chapel Hill)
P.O. Box 39, Carolina Union
CB#5210
Chapel Hill, NC 27514

Sue-Ellen Case
Professor of English
University of California
Riverside, CA 92521
"Towards a Butch-Femme Aesthetic" *in* Making a Spectacle

Catholic University Organization for Lesbian & Gay Students
The Catholic University of America
UCW 200
Washington, DC 20064

George Chauncey
Assistant Professor of History
University of Chicago
1126 E. 59 St.
Chicago, IL 60637
Author, Gay New York: Gender, Urban Culture and the Making of the Gay Male World, 1890-1940.

Chico State Gay & Lesbian Union
California State University–Chico
1st and Normal Sts.
Chico, CA 95926-0247

Clemson Lambda Society
Clemson University
P.O.Box 5795
University Station
Clemson, SC 29632

City College of San Francisco Department of Gay & Lesbian Studies
Box L169
50 Phelan Ave.
San Francisco, CA 94112

City College of San Francisco Gay & Lesbian Alliance
City College of San Francisco
50 Phelan St., Box A48
San Francisco, CA 94112

Danae Clark
Department of Communication
1117 Cathedral of Learning
University of Pittsburgh
Pittsburgh, PA 15260

Cathy Cohen
Assistant Professor
African-American Studies
Yale University
P. O. 203388, Yale Station
New Haven, CT 06520
Political science and African-American studies

Colgate Lesbian, Gay & Bisexual Advocates
c/o Student Activities
Colgate University
Hamilburg, NY 13346

Columbia Gay & Lesbian Alliance
Columbia University
Earl Hall
New York, NY 10027

Columbia Law Gay & Lesbian Law Student Association
Columbia Law School
435 W. 16th St.
New York, NY 10011

Connecticut College Gay Straight & Bisexual Alliance
Connecticut College
Box 1295
New London, CT 06320

Blanche Wiesen Cook
Professor of History
John Jay College
The Graduate School, CUNY
33 W. 42nd St.
New York, NY 10036
Author, Eleanor Roosevelt, Volume I

Cornell Gay & Lesbian Alumni
New York Law School
57 Worth St.
New York, NY 10013

Cornell Gay, Lesbian & Bisexual Coalition
207 Willard Straight Hall
Cornell University
Ithaca, NY 14853

Cornell University Graduate Minor in Gay, Lesbian, and Bisexual Studies
c/o Department of German Studies
183 Goldwin Hall
Cornell University
Ithaca, NY 14853-320
Biddy Martin, Coordinator

Louie Crew
Professor of English
Rutgers University at Newark
P.O. Box 30
Newark, NJ 07107
Interests: images of lesbians / gays within versus outside the canon

Douglas Crimp
139 Fulton St., #912
New York, NY 10038

Margaret Cruikshank
Department of Gay and Lesbian Studies
City College of San Francisco
Box A25, 50 Phelan Ave.
San Francisco, CA 94112

CUNY People
CUNY Graduate Center
33 W. 42nd St.
New York, NY 10036

John D'Emilio
Professor and Director of Graduate Studies,
Department of History
University of North Carolina
Greensboro, NC 27412
Author, Sexual Politics, Sexual Communities: The Making of a Homosexual Minority in the United States, 1940-1970.

Dartmouth Area Gay, Lesbian & Bisexual Organization
Hinman Box 5057
Dartmouth College
Hanover, NH 03755

Dartmouth GALA
208 W. 13th St.
New York, NY 10011-7702

Robert Dawidoff
Professor of History
Claremont Graduate School
Claremont, CA 91711
At work on book on gay men in American culture, especially contributions of gay writers, artists, critics, etc.

Delta Lambda Phi Fraternity / Arizona State University
Student Development Office
Box 16, ASU
Tempe, AZ 85287-3001

Delta Lambda Phi Fraternity / University of California, Davis
Student Activities, Box 424
Davis, CA 95616

Delta Lambda Phi Fraternity / National Offices
1008 10th St., Suite 374
Sacramento, CA 95814
1-800-988-2783
Lou Camera

Delta Lambda Phi
CSU / Student Activities
6000 "J" St., Box 59
Sacramento, CA 95819-6009
Brian Berkuylen

Delta Lambda Phi Fraternity / San Diego
P.O. Box 87239
San Diego, CA 92138-7239

Delta Lambda Phi Fraternity / San Diego State University
Box 17, Aztec Center, SDSU
San Diego, CA 92182

Delta Lambda Phi Fraternity / San Francisco State University
P.O. Box 14741
San Francisco, CA 94114

Delta Lambda Phi Fraternity / San José State University
45 N. 1st St., Suite 75
San José, CA 94003

Delta Lambda Phi Fraternity / Boise State University
Student Activities
Box 145, BSU
1910 University Dr.
Boise, ID 83725

Delta Lambda Phi Fraternity / Purdue University
P.O. Box 3171
West Lafayette, IN 47906

Delta Lambda Phi Fraternity / Baltimore
1008 10th St., Suite 374
Sacramento, CA 95814

Delta Lambda Phi Fraternity / University of Minnesota
P.O. Box 13122
Dinkytown Station
Minneapolis, MN 55414

Delta Lambda Phi Fraternity / Appalachian State University
P.O. Box 5520
Boone, NC 28607

Delta Lambda Phi/ UNLV
P.O. Box 70972
Las Vegas, NV 89160

Delta Lambda Phi Fraternity / University of Portland
c/o 1008 10th St., Suite 374
Sacramento, CA 95814

Delta Lambda Phi Fraternity / University of Houston
4800 Calhoun, Box #219
Houston, TX 77204-0001

Delta Lambda Phi Fraternity / University of Wisconsin, Madison
Box 513, Memorial Union
880 Langdon St.
Madison, WI 53706

Delta Lambda Phi Fraternity / University of Wisconsin, Milwaukee
2200 E. Kenwood, P.O. Box 413
Union Box 51
Milwaukee, WI 53201

Denver University Gay, Lesbian and Bisexual Alliance
University of Denver
Denver, CO 80208-0362

Jonathan Dollimore
Cultural & Community Studies
Arts Building
Sussex University
Brighton BN1 9QN England

Martin Duberman
Center for Lesbian & Gay Studies at CUNY
33 W. 42nd St., Rm. 404N
New York, NY 10036-8099
Co-editor, Hidden from History: Reclaiming the Gay and Lesbian Past

Lisa Duggan
Assistant Professor of American Studies
New York University
715 Broadway, Room 445
New York, NY 10012
Author, Sapphic Slashers: Love, Murder and Lesbian Subjectivities, 1890-1910

Duke Bisexual, Gay and Lesbian Alumni
P.O. Box 61026
Durham, NC 27715-1026

Duke Gay & Lesbian Caucus for the Modern Languages
P.O. Box 90021
Duke University
Durham, NC 27708-0021
Shelton Waldrep, publishes Lesbian & Gay Studies Newsletter

Duke Association of Gay and Lesbian Alums / DC Area
2114 "N" St. N.W,. #14
Washington, DC 20037

Eagle Center
7051 Santa Monica Blvd.
Hollywood, CA 90038
Jerry Battey, Founder

Lee Edelman
Department of English
Tufts University
Medford, MA 02155

Emory Lesbian & Gay Organization
Box 23515
Emory University
Atlanta, GA 30322

Jeffrey Escoffier
Independent scholar
Editorial consultant
332 Bleecker St., Box K27
New York, NY 10014
Author, John Maynard Keynes

Paula Ettelbrick
Adjunct lecturer,
University of Michigan
Law School
625 S. State St.
Ann Arbor, MI 48109
Author, "Who Is a Parent?" New York Law School Journal of Human Rights 513, Spring 1993

Lillian Faderman
Department of English
5245 N. Backer Ave.
California State University
Fresno, CA 93740-0098
Author, Chloe Plus Olivia

Florida Institute of Technology Gay & Lesbian Alliance for Student Support
Student Activities Center
150 W. University
Melbourne, FL 32901-6988

Florida State University Gay & Lesbian Student Union
U. Box 5914
Florida State University
Tallahassee, FL 32313

Estelle Freedman
Professor of History
Stanford University
Stanford, CA 94305
Co-author, Intimate Matters: A History of Sexuality in America

Marilyn Frye
Department of Philosophy
Michigan State University
East Lansing, MI 48824

Ft. Hays State University, Western Gay & Lesbian Services
Ft. Hays State University
600 Park St.
Hays, KS 67601

Charlotte Furth
California State University
Long Beach, CA 90840

Diana Fuss
Assistant Professor
Department of English
Princeton University
22 McCosh Hall
Princeton, NJ 08544
Editor, Inside/Out:Lesbian Theories, Gay Theories

Gay, Lesbian & Bi Independent School Caucus
232-A Hartford St.
San Francisco, CA 94114

GALE Network
P.O. Box 930
Amherst, MA 01004-0930

Eric Garber
166 Fell St.
San Francisco, CA 94117
Editor, San Francisco Lesbian & Gay Historical Society Newsletter

Marjorie Garber
Professor and Director, Center for Literary & Cultural Studies
61 Kirkland St.
Harvard University
Cambridge, MA 02138
Author, Vested Interests: Cross Dressing and Cultural Anxiety

Gay & Lesbian Alliance for Resources and Education
Box 65, Emporia State University,
1200 Commercial St.
Emporia, KS 66801

Gay & Lesbian Union
P.O. Box 710
Medical Education Bldg. U.P.
Philadelphia, PA 19104-7021

Gay, Lesbian, and Straight Teachers Network
Kevin Jennings, P.O. Box 390526
Cambridge, MA 02139

Gay & Lesbian Association of Durango
P.O. Box 1656
Durango, CO 81302-1656
Helpline

Gay / Lesbian Educators Assoc. of Michigan
P.O. Box 271
Royal Oak, MI 48068

Gay / Lesbian University of Seattle
P.O. Box 20771
Seattle, WA 98102
Support services

Gays and Lesbians United for Education
P.O. Box 19856
Cincinnati, OH 45219

Gays & Lesbians of Notre Dame
St. Mary's College
University of Notre Dame
South Bend, IN 46615

Gays & Lesbians of Rice University
P.O. Box 1892
Houston, TX 77251

George Mason Gay, Lesbian & Bisexual Student Association
George Mason University
4400 University D.
MS: 2D6-GLBSA
Fairfax, VA 22030

Georgetown Law Bisexual, Lesbian & Gay Association
Georgetown University Law Center
600 Jersey Ave.
Washington, DC 20001

Georgia State Gay Student Alliance
Georgia State University
1 University Plaza, Box 506
Atlanta, GA 30303

Georgia State University Alliance of Lesbian, Gay and Bisexual Students
Georgia State University
P.O.Box 1817, University Plaza
Atlanta, GA 30303

Georgia Tech Gay & Lesbian Alliance Program Area,
Student Center
Georgia Institute of Technology
225 North Ave. N.W.
Atlanta GA 30032-0001

Sander Gilman
Cultural Studies Department
Cornell University
914 Golwin Smith Hall
Ithaca, NY 14853
Author, Sexuality: An Illustrated History

Allen Ginsberg
Distinguished Professor of English
Graduate School & Brooklyn College, CUNY
33 W. 42nd St.
New York, NY 10036

GLB Community
UC 224—Volunteer Services Center
University of Miami
Coral Gables, FL 33124

GLQ
2 Gateway Center
Newark, NJ 07102
Alfred Vander Marck, Editor

Judith Halberstam
Assistant Professor, Department of Literature
University of California, San Diego
La Jolla, CA 92093
Author, "F2M: The Making of the Female Masculinity", in The Lesbian Postmodern

Stuart Hall
Faculty of Social Sciences
The Open University
Walton Hall
Milton Keynes, Mk7 6AA
England

David Halperin
Professor of Literature
Massachusetts Institute of Technology
14N-432
Cambridge, MA 02139
Co-editor, The Lesbian and Gay Studies Reader

Hamilton Gay, Lesbian & Bisexual Student Association
Hamilton College
198 College Hill Rd.
Student Activities Center
Clinton, NY 13323

Bert Hansen
Office of the President
Baruch College
Box 334
17 Lexington Ave.
New York, NY 10010
Author, "American Physicians' 'Discovery' of Homosexuals, 1880-1900: A New Diagnosis in a Changing Society"

Ellis Hanson
Assistant Professor
Sarah Lawrence College
Bronxville, NY 10708

Harvard Divinity Lesbian & Gay Caucus
c/o Harvard Divinity School
45 Francis
Cambridge, MA 02138

Harvard GALA
95 Grand St., #5
New York, NY 10013

Harvard Gay & Lesbian Review
P.O. Box 1809
Cambridge, MA 02238
Journal of the Harvard Gay & Lesbian Caucus

Harvard-Radcliffe Bisexual, Gay, Lesbian (Transgender and Friends) Student Association
Harvard University
P.O.Box 382852
Cambridge, MA 02238-2852

Harvard-Radcliffe GLB Issues Network
197 Memorial Hall
Harvard University
Cambridge, MA 02138

Harvey Milk School
Christopher Rodriguez, Coordinator
2 Astor Place, 3 Fl.
New York, NY 10003
Institute for gay and lesbian youth

Gloria T. Hull
University of California
Santa Cruz, CA 95064

Hunter College Gay Men's Alliance / Woman Rising
Hunter College
695 Park Ave., Box 297 USG
New York, NY 10021

Joyce Hunter
Independent Scholar:
HIV Center for Clinical & Behavioral Studies
722 W. 168th St., Box 29
New York, NY 10032
Co-author, "Adolescents and AIDS: Coping Issues" in Living and Dying with AIDS

Institute of Gay and Lesbian Education
626 N. Robertson Blvd.
West Hollywood, CA 90069

Iowa Gay / Lesbian Educators
John Lynch
1534 47th St.
Des Moines, Iowa 50311

Karla Jay
Professor of English
Pace University
1 Pace Plaza
New York, NY
Author, The Amazon and the Page: Natalie Clifford Barney and Renee Vivien

JCCC Alternatives
Johnson County Community College
College & Quivera
Overland Park, KS 662210

Johns Hopkins University—Bisexual, Gay & Lesbian Association
3400 N. Charles St.
SAC Office Levering Hall
Baltimore, MD 21218

Robin G. Joseph
Experiential Learning Coordinator
CB #5140,
211 Hanes UNC-Chapel Hill
Chapel Hill, NC 27599

Arnie Kantrowitz
Professor of English
College of Staten Island
Department of English, Room 2S222
2800 Victory Blvd.
Staten Island, NY 10314
Author, Walt Whitman: A Biography

Jonathan Katz
Instructor in Gay and Lesbian Studies
City College of San Francisco
50 Phelan Ave., Box 169
San Francisco, CA 94112
Author, Andy Warhol

Jonathan Ned Katz
c/o D. Cleaver
55 5th Ave.
New York, NY 10003
Author, Gay American History: Lesbians and Gay Men in the USA

Kellogg Gay and Lesbian Management Association
Northwestern University
Kellogg Graduate School of Management
2001 Sheridan Rd.
Evanston, IL 60201

KGLF Alumni Club
Kent State University
P.O.Box 1983
Kent, OH 44240

Kevin Kopelson
Assistant Professor
Department of English
University of Iowa
308 EPB
Iowa City, IA 52242
Author, Love's Litany: The Writing of Modern Homoerotics

Maria Teresa Koreck
American Studies
University of Michigan
Ann Arbor, MI 48104

Kansas State University, Bisexual & Gay & Lesbian Society
Box 63,
Kansas State University
Manhattan, KS 66506

Frances Kunreuther
National Advocacy Coalition for Lesbian and Gay Youth
The Hetrick Martin Institute
2 Astor Pl., 3rd Fl.
New York, NY 10003

Lambda Alumni Association
University of Southern California
University Park Campus
Los Angeles, CA 90089-0911

Joan Larkin
Assistant Professor, English Department
Brooklyn College
2900 Bedford Ave.
Brooklyn, NY 11210
Co-editor, Gay and Lesbian Poetry in Our Time: An Anthology

Teresa de Lauretis
History of Consciousness
University of California
Santa Cruz, CA 95064

Arthur Leonard
Professor of Law,
New York Law School
57 Worth St.
New York, NY 10013
Author, Sexuality and the Law: An Encyclopedia of Major Cases

Lesbian, Gay and Bisexual Issues in Education: A Network of the Association for Supervision & Curriculum Development (AscD)
P.O. Box 27527
Oakland, CA 94602
Advocacy organization

Lesbian, Gay and Bisexual Student Association
c/o Office of Campus Life
221 Goodison Hall
Ypsilanti, MI 48197

Lesbian & Gay Teachers Assoc. of N.Y.
P.O. Box 021052
Brooklyn, N.Y. 11202-0023

Simon LeVay
Institute of Gay and Lesbian Education
626 N. Robertson Blvd.
West Hollywood, CA 90069
Chairperson, IGLE; author, "A Difference in Hypothalmic Structure Between Heterosexual and Homosexual Men," Science 253

Christopher Looby
Assistant Professor
Department of English
Science Building, Rm. 320
University of Chicago
Chicago, IL 60628
Author, "'As Thoroughly Black as the Most Faithful Philanthropist Could Desire': Erotics of Race in Higginson's Army Life in a Black Regiment," in Race and the Subject of Masculinites

Loyola Lesbian & Gay Law Union
Loyola Law School
1441 W. Olympic Blvd.
Los Angeles, CA 90015

Mankato State University, Alternative Lifestyles Program
Mankato State University
Box 4
Mankato, MN 56001

Jordan Marsh
Wisconsin Student Association
511 Memorial Union
Madison, WI 53706

Mary Washington Gay, Lesbian & Bisexual Student Association
Mary Washington College, Box 603
Fredericksburg, VA 22401-4666

Mount Holyoke Lesbian & Bisexual Alliance
Mount Holyoke College
P.O. Box 2253
South Hadley, MA 01075

Biddy Martin
Associate Professor
Department of German Studies
Goldwin Smith Hall
Cornell University
Ithaca, NY 14853
Author, Woman and Modernity: The Lifestyles of Lou Andreas-Salome

Elena Martinez
Assistant Professor of Modern Languages
Baruch College
17 Lexington Ave.
Modern Language Department
Box G-1224
New York, NY 10010
Interests: Latina lesbian writings; Author, Onctti: estrategias textuales y operaciones del lector

Deborah E. McDowell
University of Virginia
Charlottesville, VA 22903

D.A. Miller
Columbia University
Department of English
New York, NY 10027

Oscar Montero
Associate Professor,
Romance Languages,
Lehman College and The
Graduate Center, CUNY
Center for Lesbian & Gay Studies
33 W. 42nd St.
New York, NY 10036
Author, "Latino Queers and National Identity", in Radical America

Michael Moon
Department of English
Duke University
Box 90015
Durham, NC 27708
Author, Disseminating Whitman: Revision and Corporeality in Leaves of Grass

George Mosse
A.D. White Professor at Large
Department of History
Cornell University
Ithaca, NY 14853
Author, Nationalism and Sexuality

Jose Muñoz
American Studies
New York University
715 Broadway, Rm. 445
New York, NY 10003

Serena Nanda
John Jay College of Criminal Justice
CUNY
New York, NY 10019

National Advocacy Coalition for Lesbian and Gay Youth
The Hetrick Martin Institute
2 Astor Pl., 3 Fl.
New York, NY 10003
Frances Kunreuther

National Education Association Gay and Lesbian Caucus
2917 McGee Wy.
Olmey, MD 20832
Bonnie Cullison & Jim Testerman

National Education Association Gay and Lesbian Caucus
P.O. Box 3559
York, PA 17402-0559
Bonnie Cullison & Jim Testerman

National Education Association, Human and Civil Rights Division
1201 16th St. N.W.
Washington, DC 20036
Ron Houston, Senior Professional Associate

National Institute for Gay, Lesbian, Bisexual, and Transgender Concerns in Education
55 Glen St.
Malden, MA 02148
Karen Harbeck, Executive Director

Joan Nestle
Lecturer in English
SEEK Department
Queens College, CUNY
65-63 Kissena Blvd.
Flushing, NY 11367
Editor, The Peristent Desire: A Femme-Butch Reader

NetGALA Network of Gay and Lesbian Alumni
P.O. Box 53188
Washington, DC 20009
Chuck Edwards, Board Chair

Network of Gay & Lesbian Alumni / ae Assns.
P.O. Box 15141
Washington, D.C. 20003

New Mexico State University Gay & Lesbian Student Association
New Mexico State University
P.O. Box 3CC
Las Cruces, NM 88003

Esther Newton
Professor of Anthropology
Division of Social Science
SUNY Purchase
Purchase, NY 10577
Author, Cherry Grove, Fire Island

New York University Lesbian, Bisexual & Gay Union
New York University
566 La Guardia Pl. #810
New York, NY 10003

Vivien Ng
Associate Professor
History Department
455 W. Lindsey -Room 406
University of Oklahoma
Norman, OK 73019
Author, Madness in Late Imperial China: From Illness to Deviance

NGLTF Campus Project
6030 Wilshire Blvd., Suite 200
Los Angeles, CA 90036
Curtis Shepard

North Carolina State University Lesbian and Gay Student Union
North Carolina State University
Box 7314-NCSU
Raleigh, NC 27695-7314

Northwestern University Gay & Lesbian Alliance
Northwestern University
1999 Sheridan Rd., Norris Rm.
Evanston, IL 60201

Northwestern Lesbian & Gay Law Students' Alliance
Northwestern Universtiy
School of Law
357 E. Chicago Ave.
Chicago, IL 61821

Notre Dame Gay and Lesbian Alumni
(GALA/ND)
Notre Dame University
P.O. Box 194
Notre Dame, IN 46556

Jeff Nunokawa
Professor of English
Princeton University
McCosh 22
Princeton, NJ 08554
Author, "All the Sad Young Men: The Work of Mourning in the Age of AIDS"

NYU Law Lesbian & Gay Law Students
New York University Law School
33 Washington Square W.
New York, NY 10010

Oberlin Lesbian, Gay & Bisexual Alumni
Oberlin College
Alumni Association,
Bosworth Hall
50 W. Lorain St.
Oberlin, OH 44074-1089

Occidental College BGALA
1600 Campus Rd., Box 205
Los Angeles, CA 90041

Office of Gay, Lesbian and Bisexual Concerns
University of Massachusetts (Amherst)
Crampton House, S.W.
Amherst, MA 01003

Ohio University Student Senate-Lesbian, Gay & Bisexual Commission
Ohio University
308 Baker Center
20 E. Union St.
Athens, OH 45701

Old Dominion University Gay & Lesbian Student Union
Old Dominion University
Webb Center
Student Activities Office
Norfolk VA 23508

Oklahoma Gay, Lesbian & Bisexual Community Association
Oklahoma State University
040 Student Union, Box 601
Stillwater, OK 74078

Onodaga Community College Gay & Lesbian & All Student Association
Onodaga Community College
Route 173
Syracuse, NY 13215

Oregon State Gay & Lesbian Association
Oregon State University
Student Activities Center
M.U.E.
Corvallis, OR 97331

OUT: Indiana University's Gay, Lesbian & Bisexual People's Union
Indiana University
P.O. Box 11213
South Bend, IN 46634

Camille Paglia
University of the Arts
320 S. Broad St.
Philadelphia, PA 19102
Academic/Cultural Critic

Cindy Patton
Temple University
849 S. 7th St.
Philadelphia, PA 19147

Pennsylvania State Lesbian, Gay & Bisexual Student Association
Pennsylvania State University
310 Hetzel Union Building
University Park, PA 16802-6601

People for Lesbian, Gay & Bisexual Concerns
University of Illinois
319 Illini Union
Urbana, IL 61821

Shane Phelan
Department of Political Science
University of New Mexico
Albuquerque, NM 87131
Author, Getting Specific: Postmodern Lesbian Politics

Minnie Bruce Pratt
The Graduate School
The Union Institute
440 E. MacMillan
Cincinatti, OH 45206-1947
Author, Crime Against Nature

Princeton Bisexual, Lesbian and Gay Alliance of Princeton
Princeton University
306 Aaron Burr Hall
Princeton, NJ 08544

Program for Gay, Lesbian & Bisexual Students
Crampton House, S.W./N.
University of Massachusetts
Amherst, MA 91003

Program for the Lesbian, Gay and Bisexual Community at Penn
University of Pennsylvania
3537 Locust Walk, 3rd Fl.
Philadelphia, PA 19104-6225

Project 10
Fairfax High School
7850 Melrose Ave.
Los Angeles, CA 90046
Virginia Uribe

Project 10 East
Cambridge Rindge and Latin School
459 Broadway
Cambridge, MA 02138
Al Ferreira

Project 21
GLAAD San Francisco/Bay Area
514 Castro, Suite B
San Francisco, CA 94114
Jessea Greenman

Project 21 Central States
4600 N. Winchester Ave.
Kansas City, MO 64117
Rob Birle

Quinnipiac Lesbian and Gay Law Student Association
Quinnipiac College School of Law
303 University Ave.
Bridgeport, CT 06604-3769

Louise Rafkin
Box 1010
Truro, MA 02666
Author, Queer and Pleasant Danger

Rensselaer Gay, Lesbian & Bisexual Association
Rensselaer Polytechnic Institute
P.O. Box 146
Troy, NY 12181-0146

B. Ruby Rich
1736 Stockton
San Francisco, CA 94133
Author, "When Difference Is (More Than) Skin Deep," in Queer Looks

Adrienne Rich
Center for Study of Women & Gender
Stanford University
Stanord, CA 94305

RIT Bisexual, Gay & Lesbian Association
Rochester Institute of Technology
c/o Student Directorate/RITreat
1 Lomb Memorial Drive
Rochester, NY 14623

Amy Robinson
Assistant Professor
Department of English
Georgetown University
37th and "O" Sts. N.W.
Washington, DC 20057

Ruthann Robson
Professor, School of Law
CUNY Box 814
Nyack, NY 10960
Author, Lesbian (Out)Law

Christopher Rodriguez
Harvey Milk School
2 Astor Pl., 3 Fl.
New York, NY 10003
Coordinator

Gayle Rubin
Box 31452
San Francisco, CA 94131
Author, "The Traffic in Women" in Toward an Anthropology of Women, *"The Catacombs: Temple of the Butthole," in* Leatherfolk

Leila Rupp
Department of History
Ohio State University
230 W. 17th Ave.
Columbus, OH 43210
Co-author, "Women's Culture and Lesbin Feminist Activism: A Reconsidering of Cultural Feminism," in Signs

Rutgers University Lesbian & Gay Alliance
Rutgers Student Center
College Ave. Campus
New Brunswick, NJ 08903

Rutgers University Peer Counseling and Information Line
Rutgers University
Student Activities Center Box 146
New Brunswick, NJ 08903

San Diego State Lesbian, Gay & Bisexual Student Association
Aztec Center, Box 45
San Diego State University
San Diego, CA 92182

San Francisco Art Institute Lesbian & Gay League
San Francisco Art Institute
800 Chestnut St.
San Francisco, CA 94133

San José State University Continuing Education
1 Washington Square
San José, CA 95192-0135
Information

Sarah Lawrence Lesbian, Gay & Bisexual United
Sarah Lawrence College
One Mead Way
Bronxville, NY 10708

Joan W. Scott
School of Social Science
Institute of Advanced Study
Princeton, NJ 08540

Eve Kosofsky Sedgwick
Newman Ivey White
Professor of English
English Dept., Box 90015
Duke University
Durham, NC 27708
Author, Epistemology of the Closet

Daniel L. Seldan
Board of Studies in Literature
University of Santa Cruz
Santa Cruz, CA 95064

Sexual Awareness Group of Appalachian University
Appalachian State University
P.O. Box 8979
Boone, NC 28608

"Sexuality and Society" Brown University
A Concentration
Professor David Savron
Department of English
Box 1852
Brown University
Providence, RI 02912

Smith Lesbian, Bisexual Alliance
Smith College
Stoddard Annex
Northampton, MA 01063

Society for Lesbian, Gay & Bisexual Studies
Kevin Kopelson
Department of English
University of Iowa
308 English/Philosophy Bldg.
Iowa City, IA 52242-1492

Alisa Solomon
Associate Professor of
English/Journalism
Baruch College-CUNY
17 Lexington Ave.
New York, NY 10010
Author, "Notes on Butch: Not Just a Passing Fancy" in Theater; *numerous articles in* The Village Voice

Southern Methodist University Gay & Lesbian Student Organization
Southern Methodist University
SMU Box 172
Dallas, TX 75275

St. Cloud State University Bisexuals United
St. Cloud University
St. Cloud, MN 56301

Stanford Law Bisexual, Gay & Lesbian Law Students
Stanford University
Stanford Law School #45
800 Chestnut St.
Palo Alto, CA 94133

Stanford University Bisexual Gay & Lesbian Alliance
Box 8265
Stanford University
Stanford, CA 94309

Stanford University Lesbian & Gay Alums of Northern California
P.O. Box 460632
San Francisco, CA 94146-0632

Carlton Stansbury
NLGLA
University of Iowa,
College of Law
Iowa City, IA 52242

Stephen F. Austin State University
Gay & Lesbian Student Association
P.O.Box 7121
Nacogdoches, TX 75962

Catherine R. Stimpson
Office of the Dean
Graduate School
Rutgers University
New Brunswick, NJ 08903

STIR
University of San Francisco
Kendrick Hall
2130 Fulton St.
San Francisco, CA. 94117

The Stonewall Coalition
P.O. Box U-5
Grinnell College
Grinnell, IA 50112

Kristina Straub
Associate Professor
Department of English
Carnegie Mellon University
Pittsburgh, PA 15213
Author, Sexual Suspects: Eighteenth-Century Players and Sexual Ideology

St. Edwards University
Gay & Lesbian Student Association
Office of Student Activities
3001 S. Congress Ave.
Austin, TX 78704-6489

SUNY Albany Gay & Lesbian Association
SUNY Albany
1400 Washington Ave., Box 22740
Albany, NY 12222

SUNY Buffalo Gay & Lesbian Association
SUNY Buffalo
207 Talbert Hall
Amherst, NY 14260

SUNY New Paltz, BiGAYla
S.U.B. Rm. 332
New Paltz, NY 12561

Swarthmore Gay, Lesbian & Bisexual Students
Swarthmore College
Swarthmore, PA 19081

Syracuse University Gay, Lesbian & Bisexual Student Association
Syracuse University
750 Ostrom Ave.
Syracuse, NY 13244-4350

Teachers Group: Gays & Lesbians Working in Education
P.O. Box 280346
Lakewood, CO 80228-0346

Temple University Lambda Alliance
P.O. Box 116 SAC
Philadelphia, PA 19122

Ten Percent
UCLA, 112-B Kerckhoff Hall
308 Westwood Plaza
Los Angeles, CA 90024

Ten Percent (10%), Wichita State U
Box 25, Wichita State University
Wichita, KS 67208

Jennifer Terry
361 Dulles Hall
230 W. 17th Ave.
Ohio State University
Columbus, OH 43210
Assistant Professor, Comparative Studies in the Humanities

Texas A&M Gay Student Services
Texas A&M University
MSC Student Finance Center #789
College Station, TX 77844-5688

Texas Woman's University Student Advocates for Lesbian / Gay Affirmation
Texas Woman's University
P.O. Box 22305
Denton, TX 76204

Sasha Torres
Brown University
155 George St.
Providence, RI 02912

Valerie Traub
Assistant Professor,
Department of English
Vanderbilt University
Box 122, Station B
Nashville, TN 37235
Author, Desire and Anxiety: Circulations of Sexuality in Shakepearean Drama

Triangle Coalition
University of Missouri-Columbia
AO22 Brady Commons
Columbia, MO 65211

Randolph Trumbach
Professor of History
Baruch College
Deparment of History
17 Lexington Ave.
New York, NY 10010
Author, "London's Sapphists" in Third Sex, Third Gender: Beyond Sexual Dimorphism in Culture and History

United Council of the University of Wisconsin
122 State St., Suite 500
Madison, WI 53703

United Teachers of Los Angeles
2511 W. 3rd St.
Los Angeles, CA 90057
A gay and lesbian issues committee

University of Alabama Lesbian / Gay Alumni Association
3355 Beech Dr.
Decatur, GA 30032

University of Arizona Bisexual, Gay & Lesbian Association
Association of Students of the University of Arizona
Building 19, Room 215
Tucson, AZ 85721

University of California Berkeley, BLGA
304 Eshleman Hall
UC Berkeley
Berkeley, CA 94720-4500

University of California Berkeley Gay, Lesbian & Bisexual Alliance
UC Berkeley
300 Eshlemann Hall
Berkeley, CA 94720

University of California Berkeley Lesbian & Gay Caucus
UC Berkeley, Boalt Hall
Berkeley, CA 94720

University of California Irvine, GLSU
102 University Center
Irvine, CA 92717

University of California San Diego Lesbian & Gay Organization
UC San Diego
Q-077 B-18
La Jolla, CA 92093

University of California Riverside Lesbian & Gay Student Union
Campus Activities Office
UC Riverside
Riverside, CA 92521

University of California Santa Cruz A-Frame
Redwood Building
Santa Cruz, CA 95064

University of California Los Angeles Lambda Alumni
P.O. Box 24048
Los Angeles, CA 90024

University of California Los Angeles, GALA
500 Kerkoff Hall
308 Westwood Plaza
UCLA
Los Angeles, CA 90024

University of California Los Angeles Lesbian, Gay, Bisexual Interdepartmental Program Task Force
c/o Professor Peter Hammond
Department of Anthropology
405 Hillgard Ave.
Los Angeles, CA 90024-1553

University of Chicago Gay & Lesbian Law Students Association
University of Chicago Law School
1111 E. 60th St.
Chicago, IL 60637

University of Cincinnati Alliance of Lesbian, Gay & Bisexual People
University of Cincinnati
211 Tangeman University Center, ML 136
Cincinnati, OH 45221

University of Colorado (Boulder) Lesbian, Gay and Bisexual Alumni
University of Colorado (Boulder)
Campus Box 287
Boulder, CO 80309

University of Connecticut Bisexual, Gay & Lesbian Association
University of Connecticut
Box U-8, 2110 Hillside Rd.
Storrs, CT 06286

University of Connecticut Lesbian, Gay & Bisexual Alliance
University of Connecticut
School of Social Work
1800 Asylum Ave.
West Hartford, CT 06117

University of Delaware Lesbian, Gay & Bisexual Student Union
201 Perkins Student Center
University of Delaware
Newark, DE 19716

University of Houston Gay & Lesbian Student Alliance
Box 314, University of Houston
Campus Activities
Houston, TX 77004

University of Idaho Lesbian & Gay Student Group
Women's Center
University of Idaho
Moscow, ID 83843

University of Indiana Lesbian and Gay Student Association
University of Indiana
Student Center Box 400
Muncie, IN 47306

University of Iowa Gay & Lesbian Student Outreach
University of Iowa
Room Memorial Union
Ames, IA 50100

University of Iowa Gay People's Union
University of Iowa
Memorial Union
Student Activities Center
Iowa City, IA 52242

University of Louisville Gay & Lesbian Union
University of Louisville
Louisville, KY 40292

University of Massachusetts / Boston Lesbian & Gay Center
University of Massachesetts, Boston
Harbor Campus, 4th Fl., Rm. 127
Boston, MA 02125

University of Michigan, Lesbian & Gay Male Programs Office
University of Michigan
3118 Michigan Union
530 S. State St.
Ann Arbor, MI 48109-1349

University of Minnesota Association of Lesbian, Gay & Bisexual Students
University of Minnesota
230-A Coffman Union
300 Washington Ave. S.E.
Minneapolis, MN 55455

University of Missouri Lesbian & Gay Assoc.
267 University Center
8001 Natural Bridge Rd.
St. Louis, MO 63121

University of Montana Lesbian Students Group
Women's Reource Center
University Center
University of Montana
Missoula, MT 59806

University of New Mexico Gay & Lesbian Student Union
University of New Mexico
Box 100, Student Union Bldg.
Albuquerque, NM 87131

University of New Orleans Gay and Lesbian Alliance
University of New Orleans
Office of Campus Activities
New Orleans, LA 70148

University of North Carolina Gay, Lesbian & Bisexual Student Association
University of North Carolina
(Greensboro)
Box 27, Elliott University Center
Greensboro, NC 27412-5001

University of North Carolina Gay and Lesbian Association
University of North Carolina
(Asheville)
Asheville, NC 28813

University of North Dakota University Gay and Lesbian Community
Marianne Lustgraff
University of North Dakota
P.O. Box 8055,
University Station
Grand Forks, ND 58202

University of Northern Iowa Gay & Lesbian Outreach
University of Northern Iowa
c/o Counseling Center, SSC 213
Cedar Falls, IA 50614-0385

University of Oklahoma Gay & Lesbian Association
303 Ellison Hall
Norman, OK 73019

University of Oregon Gay & Lesbian Alliance
University of Oregon
Suite 319 EMU
Eugene, OR 97403

University of Pennsylvania PRISMA
Office of Students
University of Pennsylvania
Houston Hall CM
3417 Spruce St.
Philadelphia, PA 19104

University of Rhode Island Gay, Lesbian & Bisexual Association
University of Rhode Island
c/o Student Senate,
Memorial Union
Kingston, RI 02881

University of Rochester Gay, Lesbian, Bisexual and Friend's Association
University of Rochester
Wilson Commons, #101J
Rochester, NY 14627-2175

University of South Florida Gay & Lesbian Coalition
University of South Florida
CTR 2466
Tampa, FL 33620

University of Southern California Gay & Lesbian Assembly for Student Support
University Park Campus
Los Angeles, CA 90089-0911

University of Southern California Gay, Lesbian & Bi Assembly
Student Union #409
University of Southern California
Los Angeles, CA 90089-0890

University of Southern California Lambda Alumni Association
830 Childs Way, P.O. Box 28
Los Angeles, CA 90089
Provides financial support for scholarships and links lesbian, gay and bisexual students, alumni, faculty, staff and friends

University of Texas Arlington Gay & Lesbian Association
University of Texas (Arlington)
P.O. Box 19348-77
Arlington, TX 76019

University of Texas at Austin Gay & Lesbian Association
117 12th St. N.E.
Washington, DC 20002

University of Texas, Austin University Lambda
University of Texas (Austin)
3622 Marshacka, #255
Austin, TX 78704

University of Texas Gay & Lesbian Student Association
University of Texas (Pan America)
1201 W. University Dr.
University Center, Rm. 205
Edinburg, TX 78539

University of Texas Gay & Lesbian Association
University of Texas (Dallas)
P.O. Box 83688, SU 21
Richardson, TX 75083-0688

University of Texas Gay & Lesbian Law Students Association
University of Texas, School of Law
727 E. 26th St.
Austin, TX 78705

University of Utah Lesbian & Gay Student Union
234 Olpin Union Building
University of Utah
Salt Lake City, UT 84112

University of Vermont Gay, Lesbian & Bisexual Association
University of Vermont
B-163 Billings
Burlington, VT 05405-0040

University of Virginia Law Lesbian & Gay Law Students Association
c/o UVA Law School
University of Virginia
Charlottesville, VA 22904

University of Virginia Lesbian & Gay Concerns Committee
c/o UVA Student Council
University of Virginia
Charlottesville, VA 22904

University of Washington Gay People's Association
PK-10 Box 96
University of Washington
Seattle, WA 98195

University of Wisconsin (Madison) GLB Alumni Council
765 W. Washington, #207
Madison, WI 53715

University of Wisconsin Gay, Lesbian & Bisexual Alumni Council
University of Wisconsin (Madison)
650 N. Lake St.
Madison, WI 53706

University of Wyoming (Laramie) Lesbian, Gay and Bisexual Association
University of Wyoming (Laramie)
P.O. Box 3625
Laramie, WY 82701

University-Wide Task Force on Lesbian & Gay Issues
Michigan State University
B-325 W. Fee Hall
East Lansing, MI 48824

Virginia Uribe
Friends of Project 10
7850 Melrose Ave.
Los Angeles, CA 90046
Also contact at 213-651-5200. Information and support services for gay, lesbian, and bisexual teens; resources for educators, guidance counselors and school-based care providers.

Valdosta State College Gay 0and Lesbian Association
Valdosta State College
VSC Box 7097
Valdosta, GA 31698

Valparaiso Gay & Lesbian Association
Valparaiso University
Box 20
Valparaiso, IN 46383

Carole Vance
Associate Research Scientist
School of Public Health
Columbia University
600 W. 168th St.
New York, NY 10032
Editor, Pleasure and Danger: Exploring Female Sexuality

Martha Vicinus
Professor, Department of English
University of Michigan
Ann Arbor, MI 48109
Co-editor, Hidden From History: Reclaiming the Gay and Lesbian Past

Virginia Commonwealth Gay & Lesbian Alumni Association
Virginia Commonwealth University & Medical College of Virginia
P.O. Box 7118
Richmond, VA 23221
Alumni organization

Walt Whitman Center
Rutgers University
409 Hickman Hall
New Brunswick, NJ 08903

Michael Warner
Associate Professor of English
Rutgers University
New Brunswick, NJ 08903
Editor, Fear of a Queer Planet: Queer Politics and Social Theory

Washburn Gay & Lesbian Info. Network
Washburn University School of Law
Topeka, Kansas 66621

Simon Watney
Red Hot AIDS Charitable Trust
Suite 32, The Eurolink Centre
49 Effra Rd.
Brixton, London
SW2 IBZ England
Author, Practices of Freedom

West Chester University Lesbian, Gay and Bisexual Association
West Chester University
311 Wayne Hall Student Union
West Chester, PA 19383

Wellesley Lesbians, Bisexuals, & Friends
Wellesley College
Wellesley, MA 02181

Wesleyan Gay Lesbian & Bisexual Alliance
Wesleyan University
190 High St., Box A
Middletown, CT 06457

Western Carolina University Rap Group
Western Carolina University
Counseling & Psychological Services
Cullowhee, NC 28723

Western KS Gay & Lesbian Services
Ft. Hays State University
600 Park St.
Hays, KS 67601

Western Michigan University, Advisor for Lesbian, Bisexual & Gay Men's Issues
Western Michigan University
2117 Faunce Student Services Bldg.
Office of Student Life
Kalamazoo, MI 49008-5074

Wheaton College Gay & Lesbian Alumni Association
369 Montezuma, Suite 209
Santa Fe, NM 87501
Alumni organization

Wheaton Lesbian, Gay & Bisexual Alliance
Wheaton College
Norton, MA 02766

Patricia White
Assistant Professor
Department of English
Swarthmore College
Swarthmore, PA 19081
Author, "Madame X of the China Seas" in Queer Looks

Whitman Gay and Lesbian Association
WGALA Journal
1202 E. Pike St., Suite 1130
Seattle, WA 98122-3934
Alumni organization

William & Mary Alternatives
c/o Office of Student Activities
Campus Center
College of William & Mary
Williamsburg, VA 23185-8795

Monique Wittig
Department of French and Italian
University of Arizona
Tucson, AZ 85721

Yale Gay and Lesbian Alumni of New York
P.O. Box 2119
New York, NY 10185

Yale Gay, Lesbian & Bisexual Co-operative
Yale University
P.O. Box 2031, Yale Station
New Haven, CT 06520

Yvonne Yarbro-Bejarano
Department of Romance Languages & Comparative Literature
University of Washington
Seattle, WA 98195

Bonnie Zimmerman
Women's Studies Department
San Diego State University
San Diego, CA 92182
Author, The Safe Sea of Women: Lesbian Fiction 1969-1989

AIDS/HIV

18th Street Services
217 Church St.
San Francisco, CA 94114
Frank Davis

A.C.E. OUT
103 E. 125 St.
New York, NY 10035
Program for women ex-offenders in transition from prison

A.R.C. AIDS
P.O. Box 70530
Toledo, OH 43607
Geneva J. Chapman

AAPHR Reporter
American Association of Physicians for Human Rights
273 Church St.
San Francisco, CA 941143
Steve Taravella, Editor

ACLU AIDS & Civil Liberties Project
P.O. Box 1161
Philadelphia, PA 19105

ACLU AIDS in Prison Project
National Prison Project
1875 Connecticut Ave. N.W., #410
Washington, DC 20009

ACLU Lesbian & Gay Rights / AIDS Project
132 W. 43rd St.
New York, NY 10036
Ruth Harlow, Associate Director

ACLU Lesbian & Gay Rights / AIDS Project
132 W. 43rd St.
New York, NY 10036
Matt Coles, Project Director

ACT Lexington AIDS Education and Referral
650 Newtown Pike
Lexington, KY 40508
Greg Lee

Act Now
525 Hamilton St.
Toledo, OH 43620
Ann Wayson Locher/Agnes

ACT UP / AIDS Coalition to Unleash Power
135 W. 29th St.
New York, NY 10001

ACT UP Atlanta
44 12th St. N.E.
Atlanta, GA 30309

ACT UP Austin
P.O. Box 13322
Austin, TX 78711
Mack McKaskle

ACT UP Boston
483 Kendle Square Station
Cambridge, MA 02142

ACT UP Columbia
Box 6352
Portland, OR 97228
Catherine Smith

ACT UP Denver
432 Broadway, #100
Denver, CO 80209

ACT UP Golden Gate
519 Castro St., Suite 93
San Francisco, CA 94114
Gdali Braverman

ACT UP Little Rock
1419 S. Taylor
Little Rock, AR 72204

ACT UP Long Beach
5595 E. 7th St., #174
Long Beach, CA 90804

ACT UP Los Angeles
3924 W. Sunset Blvd, #2
Los Angeles, CA 90029

ACT UP Milwaukee
P.O. Box 1707
Milwaukee, WI 53201

ACT UP New York
135 W. 29th St., 10th Fl.
New York, NY 10001

ACT UP Philadelphia
1216 Arch St., 4th Fl.
Philadelphia, PA 19107
Anna Forbes

ACT UP Portland
142 High St., Suite 222
Portland, ME 04101

ACT UP Provincetown
P.O. Box 1619
Provincetown, MA 02657

ACT UP Sacramento
Lambda Community Center
1931 "L" St.
Sacramento, CA 95814
Mike DeeHarg

ACT UP San Francisco
333 Valencia St.
San Francisco, CA 94103

ACT UP Seattle
1202 E. Pike St., Suite 814
Seattle, WA 98122
Randy South

ACT UP Washington DC
1339 14th St. N.W., #5
Washington, DC 20005

Action AIDS, Inc.
1216 Arch St., 4th Fl.
Philadelphia, PA 19107
Anna Forbes

Action for a Better Community
Anthony Jordon Health Center
82 Holland St.
Rochester, NY 14621
Rudy Riviera

ADAPT
552 Southern Blvd.
Bronx, NY 10455
Yolanda Serrano

AEGIS
3817 S.E. 122nd Terrace
Gainesville, FL 32601
Lois Snowden

AEGIS
P.O. Box 540694
Merritt Island, FL 32954
Bill Mitchell

African-American AIDS Network
1307 S. Wabash Ave.
Chicago, IL 60605

Aid for AIDS
8235 Santa Monica Blvd., #311
West Hollywood, CA 90046
Paul Self, Executive Director

AID for AIDS
Box 66414
Houston, TX 77266

Aid for AIDS of Nevada
1111 Desert Ln.
Las Vegas, NV 89102
Greg Durrett

AID Atlanta
1438 W. Peachtree, N.W., Suite 100
Atlanta, GA 30309
Tricia Grindel, Director of Education; Jane Carr, Executive Director

AIDS Action Baltimore
2105 N. Charles St.
Baltimore, MD 21218
Includes buyer's club

AIDS Action Coalition, Inc.
224 Church St., Suite A
Huntsville , AL 35801
Lisa Landers

AIDS Action Committee of Massachusetts
131 Clarendon St.
Boston , MA 02116
Larry Kessler, Executive Director

AIDS Action Council
1875 Connecticut Ave. N.W., Suite 700
Washington, D.C. 20009
Mario Cooper, Chairman

AIDS Activities Coordinating Office
1220 Sansom St., 7th Fl.
Philadelphia, PA 19107
James P. Hymes, Director

AIDS Administration
Center for AIDS Education
201 W. Preston St., Rm. 308
Baltimore, MD 21201
Kathleen Edwards

The AIDS Alliance for Greater Harrisburg
121 State St., P.O. Box 678
Harrisburg, PA 17108
Sandy Pepinsky

AIDS Alliance of Greenwich
Department of Health
101 Field Point Rd.
Greenwich, CT 06836
Wendy Blumenthal

AIDS Alliance of Howard County
5537 Twin Knolls Rd., Suite 433
Columbia , MD 21045
Elaine Patico

AIDS Alliance of Western New York
367 Delaware Ave.
Buffalo, NY 14202
Judy Borton

AIDS Alternative Health Project (AAHP)
4753 N. Broadway
Chicago, IL 60640

AIDS and Cancer Research Foundation
8306 Wilshire Blvd.
Beverly Hills, CA 90211

AIDS and Substance Abuse Speakers Network
P.O. Box 366
Duluth, GA 30136
Advocacy organization

AIDS ARMS Network
Box 190945
Dallas, TX 75219

AIDS Aspen Cares
P.O. Box 4807
Aspen, CO 81612

AIDS Athens
337 S. Village Ave.
Butler Building, Suite 206
Athens, GA 30605

AIDS Benefit Counselors
470 Castro St., Suite 202
San Francisco, CA 94114
John Yarling

AIDS Benefit Foundation of South Carolina
P.O. Box 2403
Columbia, SC 29202

AIDS Buddy Program
American Red Cross Central Iowa Chapter
Des Moines, IA 50312
Jane Brindley

AIDS Call-in Live
TV 21-Chicago Access Corporation
Chicago, IL 60607
Media

AIDS Care Alliance (ACA)
P.O. Box 1342
Oakbrook, IL 60522-1342

AIDS Care and Education
421 W. Church St.
Jacksonville, FL 32206

AIDS Care Connection
4221 Cass Ave.
Detroit, MI 48071
Paula Eblert

AIDS Care Network
221 N. Longwood, Suite 105
Rockford, IL 61107-4172

AIDS Care Program
1631B E. 2nd St.
Austin, TX 78703

AIDS Care Support
Mercy Center
Council Bluffs, NE

AIDS Care Team
P.O. Box 2614
Greenville, SC 29602

The AIDS Center at Hope House
19-21 Belmont Ave., Box 851
Dover, NJ 07802
Michael David-Wilson, Director

AIDS Center of Queens County
175-61 Hillside Ave., Suite 40B
Jamaica, NY 11432

AIDS Center of Queens County (Rego Park)
97-45 Queens Blvd., Suite 1220
Rego Park, NY 11374
Alan R. Sutherland

AIDS Clinic at Bronx Lebanon Hospital
1309 Fulton Ave
Bronx, NY 10456
Risa Denenberg, GYN and primary care provider at AIDS clinic

AIDS Clinical Trial Unit
Stanford University Medical Center
Rm. S-156
Stanford, CA 94305-5107

AIDS Clinical Trial Unit
462 1st Ave.
New York, NY 10016

AIDS Clinical Trial Unit of University Hospitals
2061 Cornell
Cleveland, OH 44106

AIDS Clinical Trials Information Service
800-TRIALS-A

AIDS Clinical Trials Unit
4511 Forest Park, Suite 304
St. Louis, MO 63108
Diana Bose and Sue Wightman

AIDS Clinical Update
Gay Men's Health Crisis
129 W. 20th St.
New York, NY 10011

AIDS Coalition
Shelby Co. Advisory Committee
1400 Central Ave.
Memphis, TN 38104

The AIDS Coalition of Coastal Texas
1419 Tremont
Galveston, TX 77550
Raymond Lewis

AIDS Coalition of Lincoln County
P.O. Box 421
Damariscotta, ME 04543-0421
Lynn Plumb, Chairperson

AIDS Coalition of Pueblo
151 Central Main St.
Pueblo, CO 81003

AIDS Coalition of Southern NJ
900 Haddon Ave., Suite 210
Collingswood, NJ 08108

AIDS Committee of London
343 Richmond St., Suite 200
London, ON N6A 3C2 Canada

AIDS Community Care Team
2114 Lau'ula St., Suite 3B
Honolulu, HI 96815
Marylinda Stawasz

AIDS Community Research Consortium
1048 El Camino Real, Suite A
Redwood City, CA 94063
Stan Deresinski, MD

AIDS Community Residence Association
P.O. Box 13052
Durham, NC 27709
Nat Blevins

AIDS Community Resource Network
P.O. Box 2057
Lebanon, NH 03766

AIDS Community Resources
627 W. Genesee St.
Syracuse, NY 13204
Michael Crinnin, Executive Director

AIDS Community Services of Western New York
121 W. Tupper St.
Buffalo, NY 14201
Ronald T. Silverio, Executive Director

The AIDS Council
2801 Wyandotte, Suite 167
Kansas City, MO 64108
Leslie Caplan

AIDS Council of Erie County Inc.
110 W. 10th St., Suite 214
Erie, PA 16501
Craig Bennett, Executive Director

AIDS Council of Gaston County
P.O. Box 1071
Gastonia, NC 28053
J. Culp

AIDS Council of Northeastern New York
88 4th Ave.
Albany, NY 12202

AIDS Council of Western Virginia
Council of Community Services
P.O. Box 598
Roanoke, VA 24004

AIDS Drug Assistance Program
P.O. Box 2052, Empire Station
Albany, NY 12220

AIDS Education Project
Kapiolani Women/Children Center
1319 Punahou St., 6th Fl.
Honolulu, HI 96826
Jane Waldron

AIDS Education Project
2045 W. Washington
Chicago, IL 60612

AIDS Education / Services for Minorities
P.O. Box 87277
Atlanta, GA 30337

AIDS Emergency Fund
1540 Market St., Suite 320
San Francisco, CA 94102
Rick Salinas, President, Board of Directors

AIDS Foundation Houston, Inc.
3202 Wesleyan Annex
Houston, TX 77027
Joyce E. Yost, Executive Director

AIDS Foundation Miami Valley—A Service & Prevention Organization
P.O. Box 3539
Dayton, OH 45401
William J. Hardy, Executive Director

AIDS Foundation of Chicago
1332 N. Halstead St., Suite 303
Chicago, IL 60622
Karen Fishman, Executive Director
AIDS Information & Referral Service (for healthcare professionals)

AIDS Foundation San Diego
4080 Centre St.
San Diego, CA 92130

The AIDS Fund, Inc.
Tidewater AIDS Crisis Task Force
740 Duke St., Suite 520
Norfolk, VA 23510
Giles R. Norrington

AIDS Health Project
1855 Folsom St., Suite 506
San Francisco, CA 94103

AIDS Healthcare Foundation
1800 N. Argyle, 3rd Fl.
Los Angeles, CA 90028-5219

AIDS Help, Inc.
P.O. Box 4374
Key West, FL 33041
Frank Richards

AIDS Holistic Services
655 N. Main St.
Akron, OH 44312

AIDS Hotline
800-AID-AIDS
Chicago, IL

AIDS Hotline
504-944-AIDS
1407 Decatur St.
New Orleans, LA 70116-2010

AIDS Hotline
910-323-2552
Fayetteville, NC

AIDS Hotline
800-322-2437
Columbia, SC

AIDS Hotline
615-385-AIDS
Tennessee

AIDS Hotline for Women at the Feminist Women's Health Center
580 14th St., N.W.
404-888-9991
Atlanta, GA 30318
Nancy Boothe, Executive Director

AIDS Housing Council
1413 W. 80th St.
Cleveland, OH 44102

AIDS Housing of Washington
93 Pike St., Suite 312
Seattle, WA 98101
Betsy Lieberman

AIDS Housing Project
1000 Howard Ave., Suite 1200
New Orleans, LA 70113

AIDS in Minorities
P.O. Box 1116
1630 4th Ave. N.
Birmingham, AL 35201

AIDS Info Bulletin Board Service
Modem to 415-626-1246
P.O. Box 421528
San Francisco, CA 94142-1528

AIDS Info Line
404-876-9944
800-551-2728
Atlanta, GA

AIDS Information Network
32 N. 3rd St.
Philadelphia, PA 19106
Jean Hofacket, Executive Director

AIDS Information Tape
Chicago Medical Society
312-670-3670

AIDS Institute
New York State Department of Health
ESP Corning Tower
Albany, NY 12237

AIDS Interfaith Ministries
P.O. Box 9576
Canton, OH 44711

AIDS Interfaith Network
100 N. 62nd St.
Omaha, NE

AIDS Interfaith Network
1555 Merrimac St., Suite 218
Fort Worth, TX 76107
Rev. Susan Cockrell

AIDS Interfaith Network, Inc.
2727 Oak Lawn, Suite 1088
Dallas, TX 75219
Sergio Rogina

AIDS Interfaith Network of Colorado
P.O. Box 102051
Denver, CO 80250-2051

AIDS Interfaith Network of Iowa
c/o Ecumenical Ministries of Iowa
3816 36th St.
Des Moines, IA 50310

AIDS Interfaith New York
423 W. 46th St.
New York, NY 10036
Rev. Elice Higginbotham

AIDS Interfaith Residential Services
600 W. North Ave.
Baltimore, MD 21217
Leslie Kayne

AIDS Law Project of Pennsylvania
924 Cherry St., Suite 519
Philadelphia, PA 19107
Nan Feyler, Executive Director

AIDS Legal Assistance
800-828-6417
Austin, TX
Legal Services

AIDS Legal Council of Chicago
220 S. State St., Suite 1330
Chicago, IL 60604-2103

AIDS Legal Referral Panel
114 Sansom St., #1129
San Francisco, CA 94104
Kristin Chambers

AIDS Legal Services
111 N. St. John, #315
San José, CA 95113

AIDS Life Link
P.O. Box 1790
Spokane, WA 99210-1790

AIDS Lodging House
233 Oxford St., P.O. Box 3820
Portland, ME 04104-3820
Rick Bouchard, Program Director

AIDS Manasota
2080 Ringling Blvd, Suite 302
Sarasota, FL 34237
Donna Fruzia; includes buyer's club

AIDS Medical Resource Center
101 W. Grand Ave.
Chicago, IL 60610

AIDS Ministries / AIDS Assistance (N. Indiana)
P.O. Box 11582
South Bend, IN 46634
Michael Beatty, Executive Director

AIDS Ministry - Holy Covenant
Holy Covenant MCC
17 W. Maple
Hinsdale, IL 60521

AIDS Minority Health Initiative
1440 Broadway, Suite 403
Oakland, CA 94612
Mabel Hazard

AIDS National Interfaith Network
110 Maryland Ave. N.E.
Washington, DC 20002
Jacquelyn C. Wilkerson

AIDS National Interfaith Network
475 Riverside Dr., 10th Fl.
New York, NY 10115

AIDS Network of the Tri-State
290 Berkeley Plaza, Suite 5
Martinsburg, WV 25427
Andrew D. Michael, President

AIDS Outreach
112 N. 5th St.
Allentown, PA 18102

AIDS Outreach Center
1125 W. Peter Smith
Fort Worth, TX 76104
Cathy Cochlan

AIDS Outreach of Northern Arizona
1325 N. Beaver, P.O. Box 183
Flagstaff, AZ 86001
Bill Mayes / Robbie Bergman

AIDS Pastoral Care Network
4753 N. Broadway, Suite 800
Chicago, IL 60640
Carol S. Reese, Executive Director

AIDS Pastoral Care Network / DuPage County
Edward Hospital
801 S. Washington St.
Naperville, IL 60566

AIDS Patient Care
1651 3rd Ave.
New York, NY 10128

AIDS Prevention Center
513 Whitehead St.
Key West, FL 33040
Mark Szvrek

AIDS Prevention Program
3305 N. Broadway
Boulder, CO 80304
Walk-in clinic

The AIDS Project
22 Monument Square, 5th Fl.
Portland, ME 04101
Deborah Sheilds, Executive Director

AIDS Project Central Coast
Gay and Lesbian Resource Center
126 E. Haley St., Suite A-17
Santa Barbara, CA 93101
Derek Gordon

AIDS Project Greater Danbury
P.O. Box 91
Newton, CT 06801
James Harlow

AIDS Project / Hartford
30 Arbor St.
Hartford, CT 06105
Judith Fox, Executive Director

AIDS Project: Lambda Legal Defense & Education Fund
666 Broadway
New York, NY 10012-2317

AIDS Project New Haven
P.O. Box 636
New Haven, CT 06503
Jean Hess, Executive Director

AIDS Project of Centre County
301 S. Allen St., Suite 102
State College, PA 16801
Sally Maud Robertson

AIDS Project of Greater New Britain
P.O. Box 1214
New Britain, CT 06053

AIDS Project of the East Bay
565 16th St.
Oakland, CA 94612

AIDS Project of the Ozarks
1722-LL S. Glenstone Ave.
Springfield, MO 65804
Jack McCroskey, Administrator

AIDS Project Worcester, Inc.
305 Shrewsbury St.
Worcester, MA 01604
James A. Voltz, Executive Director

AIDS Referral Services, Inc.
1809 N. Broadway, Suite E
Wichita, KS 67214-1146
Dee Suloboda, Office Manager

AIDS Related Community Services
2269 Sawmill River Rd., Bldg., 1S
Elmsford, NY 10606
Barbara Shannon

AIDS Research Consortium of Atlanta
131 Ponce de Leon Ave., Suite 130
Atlanta , GA 30308
Melanie Thompson/Amy Morris, community program for clinical research on AIDS

AIDS Resource Alliance of North Central Lycoming County
507 W. 4th St.
Williamsport, PA 17701
Nancy West

AIDS Resource Center
1337 14th St. NW
Washington, DC 20005

AIDS Resource Center
P.O. Box 190712
Dallas, TX 75219
Deborah Trott, RN / Nicholas Bellos, MD

AIDS Resource Center
2701 Reagan, P.O. Box 190712
Dallas, TX 75219
John Thomas

AIDS Resource Center, Inc.
275 7th Ave., 12th Fl.
New York, NY 10001
Regina Quattrochi

AIDS Resource Group
Old Court House, Suite 301
201 N.W. 4th St.
Evansville, IN 47708
Randy Dennison, Jr., Executive Director

AIDS Response Effort, Inc.
P.O. Box 3788
Winchester, VA 22604
Hal Palmer, Chairman

AIDS Response Knoxville
P.O. Box 6069
Knoxville , TN 37914
Dawn Nickoloff, Executive Director

AIDS Response Progam
12832 Garden Grove Blvd., Suite A
Garden Grove, CA 92643
Dan Wooldridge

AIDS Rochester
1350 University Ave. #C
Rochester, NY 14607
Paula Silvestrone

AIDS Service Agency of Orange County
P.O. Box 16574
Chapel Hill, NC 27516

AIDS Service Agency of Wake County
P.O. Box 12583
Raleigh, NC 27605
Cullen Gurgannus, Executive Director

AIDS Service Center
557 E. Broad St., P.O. Box 1800
Bethlehem, PA 18016
Robert Roush, Executive Director

AIDS Service Project
Box 3203
Durham, NC 27715
Jill Duvall

AIDS Services Center
P.O. Box 1392
Anniston, AL 36202

AIDS Services Center
810 Barret Ave., #266B
Louisville, KY 40204
Jamie Rittenhouse

AIDS Services for the Monadnock Region
331 Main St., P.O. Box 1473
Keene, NH 03431
Susan Curtis and Susan Lane Shaw

AIDS Services of Austin
P.O. Box 4874
Austin, TX 78765
Janna Zumbrum, Executive Director

AIDS Services of Dallas
PWA Coalition of Dallas
P.O. Box 4338
Dallas, TX 75208
Don Maison

AIDS Southern Kentucky, Inc
P.O. Box 09733
Bowling Green, KY 42102
Dr. Mary Nazzard

AIDS Support Group
The Psychotherapy Center
210 Pulaski St.
Little Rock, AR 72201
Dr. Ralph A. Hyman

AIDS Support Group
214 Rugby Rd.,
Box 2322
Charlottesville, VA 22902
Catherine Drabkin, Director

AIDS Support - Jewish Family Services
1605 Peachtree Rd. N.E.
Atlanta, GA 30309-2410
Support Services

AIDS Support Network of Spartanburg
Box 4796
Spartanburg, SC 29305
Denise Morris/Jim Womack

AIDS Support Program
P.O. Box 12185
Oklahoma City, OK 73112
Diane Persson

AIDS Support Services
Department of Human Services
Jefferson County Urban
Government Center
810 Barrett Ave.
Louisville, KY 40204
Carl L. Enoch, Supervisor

AIDS Survival Project
44 12th St. N.E.
Atlanta, GA 30309

AIDS Task Force
P.O. Box 20983
Winston-Salem, NC 27102

AIDS Task Force, Inc.
2124 Fairfield Ave.
Fort Wayne, IN 46802
John Roach, Executive Director

AIDS Task Force of Alabama
P.O. Box 55703
Birmingham, AL 35255
Randall H. Russell, Executive Director

AIDS Task Force of Philadelphia
1642 Pine St.
Philadelphia, PA 19103
Roger D. Armstrong

AIDS Task Force (Porter County)
P.O. Box 5010
Chesterton, IN 46304

AIDS Task Force Regional Cooperative
P.O. Box 1091
Lima, OH 45802

AIDS Task Force Upper Ohio Valley
P.O. Box 6360
Wheeling, WV 26003
Jay Adams

AIDS Theatre Project
197 E. Broadway, #U2
New York, NY 10002

AIDS Treatment Data Network
259 W. 30th St.
New York, NY 10001
Kenneth Fornataro

AIDS Treatment News
P.O. Box 411256
San Francisco, CA 94141
Also available on the Internet's Queer Resources Directory

AIDS Unit Youngstown Health Department
City Hall Building
26 S. Phelps St.
Youngstown, OH 44503
Kate Wallace

AIDS Upstate
P.O. Box 2507
Greenville, SC 29602

AIDS Volunteers of Cincinnati, Inc.
2183 Central Parkway
Cincinnati, OH 45214
Charles Albrecht, Administrator

AIDS Volunteers of Lexington
214 W. Maxwell St.
Lexington, KY 40508
Kim Berkowitz, Executive Director

AIDS Walk Chicago
909 W. Belmont, Suite 101
Chicago, IL 60657

AIDS Wellness Clinic
811 St. Michaels Dr.
Santa Fe, NM 87501
Donald Romig, MD

AIDS Wellness Program
811 St. Michael Dr.
Santa Fe, NM 87501
Tom Minf

AIDS Work for Tompkins County
DeWitt Office Complex
215 N. Cayuga St.
Ithaca, NY 14850
George Ferrari, Jr.

AIDS-Related Community Services
c/o PCMH
47 Brewster
Carmel, NY 10512

AIDS-Related Community Services
473 Broadway
Newburgh, NY 12550

AIDS-Related Community Services
89 Market St.
Poughkeepsie, NY 12601

AIDS-Related Community Services
228 N. Main St.
Springfield, NY 10977

AIDS / ARC Council of Douglas County
P.O. Box 1146
Roseburg, OR 97470

AIDS / HIV Housing Law Project
c/o Legal Assistance Foundation of Chicago
343 S. Dearborn, Suite 700
Chicago, IL 60604
Legal Services

AIDS / HIV Spiritual Support Group
980 Clarkson
Denver, CO 80218

AIDSCare, Inc.
P.O. Box 14619
Chicago, IL 60614-0619

AIDSLaw
P.O. Box 30203
New Orleans, LA 70170
800-375-5035

The AIDSline
800-851-AIDS
Helpline

AIDSPAC
1775 "T" St.
Washington, DC 20009

Alabama AIDS Hotline
800-228-0469

Alaska AIDS Assistance Association
1057 W. Fireweed
Anchorage, AK 99503
Trish Queen, publishes Alaska Resource Directory

Alaska AIDS Hotline
800-478-2437

Alcohol Treatment Center HIV
2400 Belvedere St.
Waukegan, IL 60085
Ruth Costello

Aliveness Project / PWA Coalition
730 E.38th St.
Minneapolis, MN 55427
Leo J. Teachout, buyer's club

All Saints AIDS Service Center
126 W. Del Mare Blvd.
Pasadena, CA 91105-2508

All Souls Parish Gay & Lesbian AIDS Ministries
3 Angle St., P.O. Box 5978
Asheville, NC 28803
Rev. Joan C. Marshall

ALLGO-PASA
Informe-SIDA
P.O. Box 13501
Austin, TX 78711
Maria S. Limon

ALLIA News
135 E. 15th St.
New York, NY 10003
Newsletter of the Alliance for Inmates with AIDS

American Association of Physicians for Human Rights
273 Church St.
San Francisco, CA 941143

American College Health Association AIDS Task Force
P.O. Box 378
University of Virginia
Charlottesville, VA 22908

American Foundation for AIDS Research
5900 Wilshire Blvd., 23rd Fl.
Los Angeles, CA 90036-5032
Steve Chapman, Deputy Director

American Foundation for AIDS Research (AmFAR)
733 3rd Ave., 12th Fl.
New York, NY 10017-3204
Donald Mochsberger

American Indian AIDS Institute
333 Valencia St., Suite 400
San Francisco, CA 94103
Sacheen Littlefeather

American Institute for Teen AIDS Prevention
6032 Jacksboro Hwy., Suite 100
P.O. Box 136116
Forth Worth, TX 76136
Duane Crumb, Executive Director

American Red Cross AIDS Education Projects
1900 25th Ave. S.
Seattle, WA 98144
Angelique Von Halle

Androscoggin Valley AIDS Coalition
P.O. Box 7977
Lewiston, ME 0423-7977

APLA
1313 N. Vine St.
Los Angeles, CA 90028
Jamie Henderson

Arizona AIDS Hotline
602-420-9396

Arizona AIDS Information Line
4460 N. Central Ave.
Phoenix, AZ 85011

Arizona AIDS Project
4460 N. Central Ave.
Phoenix, AZ 85012
Robert Horton

Arkansas AIDS Foundation
P.O. Box 255007
Little Rock, AR 72205

Arkansas AIDS Hotline
800-448-8305

Asian American AIDS Foundation
P.O. Box 408739
Chicago, IL 60640

Asian Health Services
310 8th St., #200
Oakland, CA 94607
Kevin Fong, AIDS Coordinator

Athens AIDS Task Force
18 N. College St.
Athens, OH 45701
Jeanne Donato, Director

Atlanta AIDS Fund
2221 Peachtree Rd., N.E.
Suite D104
Atlanta, GA 30309
Ava Diamond Suber

Atlanta Buyers Club Foundation
44 12th St.
Atlanta, GA 30309-3979

Atlanta Interfaith AIDS Network
1053 Juniper St.
Atlanta, GA 30309
Robert A. Hudak, Executive Director

Atlanta Lesbian AIDS Project
P.O. Box 5409
Atlanta, GA 30307

Auglaize County AIDS Task Force
Wood & Lima Sts.
Wapokoneta, OH 45895

Auntie Helen's Fluff 'N Fold
4028 30th St.
San Diego, CA 92104

Bailey House
180 Christopher St.
New York, NY 10014

Baltimore Community Research Initiative
22 S. Greene St.
Baltimore, MD 21201
Brenda Woods-Francis

Baltimore Community Research Consortium
22 S. Greene St., Box 243
Baltimore, MD 21201
David Wheeler, MD

David Barr
Gay Men's Health Crisis
129 W. 20th St., 2nd Fl.
New York, NY 10011
Director of Treatment Education & Advocacy

Bay Area AIDS Consortium
266 Swann Ave., Suite 107
Tampa, FL 33609
Dorece Norris, MD

Bay Area HIV Support & Education Services
3135 Courtland Ave.
Oakland, CA 94619
Lee Woo, Director

Bay Area Physicians for Human Rights
4111 18th St., Suite 6
San Francisco, CA 94114
Lisa Capaldini

BEAT AIDS
3923 IH 10 East
San Antonio, TX 78219
Paul B. Mayfield

Being Alive
621 N. San Vicente Blvd.
W. Hollywood, CA 90069

Being Alive: People with HIV/AIDS
3626 Sunset Blvd.
Los Angeles, CA 90026

Berrien County AIDS Coalition
P.O. Box 8822
Benton Harbor, MI 49023
Michael Mortimore

BETA
(Bulletin of Experimental Treatments for AIDS)
Box 2189
Berkeley, CA 94702-0189

Better Existence With HIV
P.O. Box 5171
Evanston, IL 60204
Craig Foley

Bienestar Latino AIDS Project
1169 N. Vermont Ave.
Los Angeles, CA 90029
Oscar de la O

Big Island AIDS Project
308 Kamehameha, Suite 214
P.O. Box 11510
Hilo, HI 96721
John Voorhees, Program Coordinator

Birmingham AIDS Outreach
P.O. Box 550070
Birmingham, AL 35255
Sem Thompson, Executive Director

Black AIDS Project at Large
1525 Josephine
Denver, CO 80206

Blacks Against AIDS
Box 7732
Atlantic City, NJ 08404
Ava C. Brown

Bluelights Campaign
109 Minna St. #125
San Francisco, CA 94105

Body Positive Resource Center, Inc.
175 N.E. 36th St.
Miami, FL 33137
Christine Nolan, Executive Director

Body Positive
2095 Broadway, #306
New York, NY 10023
Michael Stanton

Body Positive / Houston
3415 1/2 Graustard
Houston, TX 77706

Boulder County AIDS Project
2118 14th St.
Boulder, CO 80302-4804
Robin Bohannan, Director

Boulder County AIDS Project
400 E. Simpson St.
Lafayette, CO 80026

Boulder County Health Department's AIDS Prevention Program
3450 Broadway Blvd.
Boulder, CO 80304
Program office

Brake for Lunch
810 Barret Ave., Suite 266B
Louisville, KY 40204
Jamie Rittenhouse

Brattleboro Area AIDS Project
67 Main St., P.O. Box 1486
Brattleboro, VT 05346
Susan Bell, Executive Director

Brazos Valley AIDS Foundation
Box 4209
College Station, TX 77842
Tom Edwards

The Bridge
3232 Lay Springs Rd.
Gadsden, AL 35901
Tim Naugher, Executive Director

Bronx Lebanon Hospital AIDS Division
1276 Fulton Ave., Rm. 223
Bronx, NY 10456
Jerome Ernst/Andrew Wiznia, community program for clinical research on AIDS

Brooklyn AIDS Task Force
465 Dean St.
Brooklyn, NY 11217
Elaine Greeley, Executive Director
Yannick Durand, Education

Broward AIDS Partnership
2601 E. Oakland Park Blvd.
Suite 202
Ft. Lauderdale, FL 33306
Jan Crocker

Brown University AIDS Program
Brown University, Box G-S204
Providence, RI 02912
Kenneth Mayer, MD

Bucks County AIDS Network
P.O. Box 242
Jamison, PA 18929
Sylvia Lefcourt

Butler County Health Center
1618 N. Main St.
Poplar Bluff, MO 63901
Vicki H. Sparkman, RN

California AIDS Hotlines
800-367-2437 (North)
800-922-2437 (South)

California Association of AIDS Agencies
926 "J" St., Suite 803
Sacramento, CA 95814
Geni Cowen, PhD, Executive Director

California Prevention Education Project
630 20th St., 3rd Fl.
Oakland, CA 94612
Gloria Lockett, AIDS education for prostitutes and ex-prostitutes

Cambridge Cares About AIDS, Inc.
678 Massachussetts Ave., Suite 402
Cambridge, MA 02139

Cape Cod AIDS Council
592 Main St. Connection
Hyannis, MA 02601
Jason Schneider

Cara A Cara Latino AIDS Project
3324 Sunset Blvd.
Los Angeles, CA 90026
Arturo Olivas, Director

Marisa Cardinale
Community Research Initiative Against AIDS
275 7th Ave.
New York, NY 10001
Executive Director

CAEAR (Cities Advocating Emergency AIDS Relief)
c/o SFAF
P.O. Box 4126182
San Francisco, CA 94142

Carl Vogel Foundation, Inc.
1413 "K" St. N.W., 3rd Fl.
Washington, DC 20005
Ron Mealy, buyer's club

Carle Comprehensive HIV Clinic
602 W. University Ave.
Urbana, IL 61801
Judy Baker, RN, Clinic Coordinator

Carlos Andarsio AIDS Project
301 S. Fountain Ave.
Springfield, OH 45506

Carmi AIDS Awareness Group
1002 1/2 W. Oak St.
Carmi, IL 62821

Cascade AIDS Project
620 SW 5th Ave., Suite 300
Portland, OR 97204
Mica Smith, Executive Director

CDC AIDS Weekly
P.O. Box 830409
Birmingham, AL 35283

CDC National AIDS Hotline
800-342-AIDS
800-344-SIDA (Spanish access)
800-AIDS-TTY (Deaf access)
24-hour hotline

Cedar AIDS Support System
(CASS)
2101 Kimball, Suite 401
Waterloo, IA 50702

The Center for AIDS Services
5720 Shattuck Ave.
Oakland, CA 94609

Center One /Anyone in Distress
3015 N. Ocean Blvd., Suite 111
Fort Lauderdale, FL 33308
John C. Weatherhead

The Center One in Long Beach, Inc.
2017 E. 4th St.
Long Beach, CA 90814
Richard F. Gaylord

The Center / Lesbian Health Project
P.O. Box 3357
San Diego, CA 92163-3357
Katie Blayda

Central Florida AIDS Unified Resources
(CENTAUR)
741 W. Colonial
Orlando, FL 32804
James Stuckey, Executive Director

Central Illinois Friends of People With AIDS
416 St. Mark's Ct., Suite 403
Peoria, IL 61603
Mary Nash

Central Louisiana AIDS Support Services
824 16th St.
Alexandria, LA 71301

The Central Valley AIDS Team
Gay United Services, Inc.
P.O. Box 4640
Fresno, CA 93744
Tim Reese, Executive Director

Central Virginia AIDS Services & Education
1627 Monument Ave.
Richmond, VA 23220
Fred Wilson, Executive Director

Central Wisconsin AIDS Network
1200 Lakeview Dr., Suite 200
Wasau, WI 54403

Charleston AIDS Network
Box 1024
Charleston, WV 25324
Brian Henry

Chattanooga CARES
701 Cherokee Rd., P.O. Box 4497
Chattanooga, TN 37405
John D. McGee III, Executive Director

Chester AIDS Coalition
20 East 5th St., P.O. Box 356
Chambersburg, PA 17201

Chicago Community Program for Clinical Research on AIDS
711 W. North Ave., Suite 201
Chicago, IL 60610
Roberto Luskin/Renslow Sherer, community program for clinical research on AIDS

Chicago Women's AIDS Project
5249 N. Kenmore
Chicago, IL 60640

Chicken Soup Brigade
1002 E. Seneca St.
Seattle, WA 98122
Carol Sterling, Executive Director

Christo AIDS Ministry
1029 E. Turney Ave.
Phoenix, AZ 85014

Christopher House
2820 E. Martin Luther King Blvd.
Austin, TX 78703
Carol Cody

Circle of Care/Stewart B. McKinney Foundation
P.O. Box 338
Fairfield, CT 06430

Citizens' Committee on AIDS/HIV
P.O. Box 93357
Cleveland, OH 44101

Clark County AIDS Task Force
301 S. Fountain Ave.
Springfield, OH 44506
Judy Andrews, Director of Nursing

Clarksville CARES
1300 Madison St.
United Way Building
P.O. Box 336
Clarksville, TN 37041
Jane E. Grimes

Cleveland AIDS Council
3122 Euclid Ave.
Cleveland, OH 44115

Coastal Area Support Team
P.O. Box 2356
2917 A Cypress Mill Rd.
Brunswick, GA 31521
Lauretta M. Sams

Coastal Bend AIDS Foundation
1118 3rd St.
P.O. Box 331416
Corpus Christi, TX 78463
Judy J. Hales

Colorado AIDS Hotline
800-252-2437

Colorado AIDS Project
P.O. Box 18529
Denver, CO 80218

Colorado Health Action Project/ The Denver Buyer's Club
P.O. Box 300339
Denver, CO 80203
Buyer's club

Columbus AIDS Task Force
1500 W. 3rd Ave., Suite 329
Columbus, OH 43212-2843
Gloria Smith, Executive Director

The Common Factor
The Committee of Ten Thousand
c/o The Wellness Center at
Packard Manse
583 Plain St.
Stoughton, MA 02072

Commonwealth of Puerto Rico STD-HIV Prevention Program
P.O. Box 71423
San Juan, PR 00936
Eddie Escudero

Community AIDS Awareness Program
P.O. Box 457
Rumford, ME 04276

Community AIDS Council
506 E. Camelback Rd.
Phoenix, AZ 85012
Robert Aronin, Executive Director

Community AIDS Partnership
P.O. Box 24667
250 Ventura Circle
Nashville, TN 37202
Kelly Kraft

Community AIDS Partnership of Central Alabama
3600 8th Ave. S.
P.O. Box 320189
Birmingham, AL 35232
Harry Brown

The Community AIDS Partnership Project
1400 Hanna Building
Cleveland, OH 44115
Robert Eckardt

Community Consortium
3180 18th St., Suite 201
San Francisco, CA 94110
Donald T. Abrams/Thomas Mitchell, community program for clinical research on AIDS; publishes "Directory of Clinical Trials in the Bay Area"

Community Counseling & Consultation Center, Inc.
Desert AIDS Project
750 S. Vella Rd.
Palm Springs, CA 92264
Irene Anthony

Community Health Center
401 3rd Ave.
North Fargo, ND 58102
Doug Johnson

Community Health Project
208 W. 13th St.
New York, NY 10011
Dean J. LaBate, Executive Director

Community Health Services
405 Castle Creed Rd. #6
Aspen, CO 81611
Kitty Smith

Community Research Initiative of New England
338 Newbury St., 3rd Fl.
Boston, MA 02115
Janine Grant

Community Research Initiative of New England
320 Washington St.
Brookline, MA 02146
Cal Cohen, MD

Community Research Initiative of South Florida
1508 San Ignacio Ave., Suite 200
Coral Gables, FL 33146
Rick Siclari/Paula Sparti, MD

Community Research Initiative on AIDS / CRIA
275 7th Ave., 20th Fl.
New York, NY 10001
Spencer Cox/Joseph Sonnabend

Community Task Force on AIDS Education
P.O. Box 941
Naples, ME 04055

Comprehensive AIDS Alliance of Detroit
Wayne State University School of Medicine
Division of Infectious Diseases/ Detroit Medical Center
4160 John R., Suite 202
Detroit, MI 48201
Lawrence Crane/Constance Rowley, community program for clinical research on AIDS

Computerized AIDS Ministries Network
800-542-5921

Condom Crusaders
706 W. 42nd St., Suite 107
Kansas City, MO 64111
Rhonda Weimer, Program Director

Connecticut AIDS Hotline
800-342-AIDS

The CORE Program
7740 1/2 Santa Monica Blvd.
West Hollywood, CA 90046
Ralph Mayo, Education

Cornell AIDS Action
Gannett Health Center
Cornell University
Ithaca, NY 14853

Crater AIDS Action Program
32 E. Wythe St.
Petersburg, VA 23803
Ron Ellis, Director

Critical Path AIDS Project
2062 Lombard St.
Philadelphia, PA 19146

Cumberland County AIDS Task Force
P.O. Box 1764
Fayetteville, NC 28302

Cure AIDS Now, Inc.
111 S.W. 3rd St., 2nd Fl.
Miami, FL 33130
Dominick Magarelli

The Cutting Edge
P.O. Box 392
Fremont, CA 94537
Cade Fields Newman

Keith Cylar
Housing Works
594 Broadway, 7th Fl.
New York, NY 10012

DAAIR
31 E. 30th St., #2A
New York, NY 10016
Buyer's club

The Damien Center
1350 N. Pennsylvania St.
Indianapolis, IN 46202
David Hudson, Executive Director

Dancers Responding to AIDS
148 W. 23rd St., Suite 7H
New York, NY 10011

Davis Clinic
P.O. Box 425
Hunstville, AL 35804

The Dayton Regional AIDS Partnership
184 Salem Ave.
Dayton, OH 45406
Luigi S. Procopio, II

DBC Alternatives (Dallas)
214-528-4460

DC Women's Council on AIDS/ Sistercare
715 8th St. S.E.
Washington, DC 20003

Deaf AIDS Coalition
2863 N. Clark St.
Chicago, IL 60657

Martin Delaney
Project Inform
1965 Market St., Ste. 220
San Francisco, CA 94103
Founder, Project Inform

Delaware AIDS Hotline
800-422-0429

Delaware AIDS Task Force
561 W. Central Ave.
Delaware, OH 43015

Delaware Community Program for Clinical Research on AIDS
Medical Center of Delaware
501 W. 14th St.
Wilmington, DE 19801
William Holloway/Arlene Bincsik, community program for clinical research on AIDS

Delaware County AIDS Network
907 Chester Pike
Sharon Hill, PA 19026
Dennis M. Murphy

Delaware Lesbian & Gay Health Advocates
601 Delaware Ave. #5
Wilmington, DE 19801
John L. Barnes, Executive Director

Dental Alliance for AIDS/HIV Care
101 Grand Ave., #200
Chicago, IL 60610

Denver AIDS Prevention/Youth in Action
605 Bannock, Rm. 217
Denver, CO 80204-4507

Denver Community Program for Clinical Research on AIDS
605 Bannock St.
Denver, CO 80204-4507
David Cohn, community program for clinical research on AIDS

DIFFA
150 W. 26th St., Suite 602
New York, NY 10001
Rosemary Kuropat

DIFFA / Chicago
885F Merchandise Mart
Chicago, IL 60654
Dennis Krause, Executive Director

DIFFA / Dallas
1400 Turtle Creek, #143
Lock Box 10
Dallas, TX 75027
Greg Cassell and Jody Clarke, Co-chairs

DIFFA / San Diego
3841 4th Ave., Suite 105
San Diego, CA 92103

Dignity National AIDS Project
1500 Massachusetts Ave., N.W.
Washington, DC 20005
Bill Haedrich/Jim Kimpton

Directory of Alabama AIDS Education & Service Programs
c/o Department of Pathology
University of South Alabama
2451 Fillingim St.
Mobile, AL 33617

Documentation of AIDS Issues and Research
(DAIR)
2336 Market St., Suite 33
San Francisco, CA 94114
Michael Flanagan

Douglas County AIDS Council
3035 Laurel Springs Dr.
Roseburg, OR 97470
Jim Hopper

Down East AIDS Network
114 State St.
Ellsworth, ME 04605

Dubuque Regional AIDS Coalition
1300 Main St.
City Hall Annex
Dubuqe, IA 52001
Mary Rose Corrigan, RN

DuPage County AIDS Project
111 N. County Farm Rd.
Wheaton, IL 60187-3988

Early Advocacy and Care for HIV
(EACH)
944 Market St., Suite 210
San Francisco, CA 94102
Carl Yoshimoto, a project of the Gay Men of Color Consortium

East Bay AIDS Center/East Bay AIDS Response Organization
Alta Bates Medical Center Services
3031 Telegraph Ave., Suite 235
Berkeley, CA 94705
Marilyn Barkin

Eastern Maine AIDS Network
P.O. Box 2038
Bangor, ME 04402-2038
Sally-Loo Patterson

Elkhart County AIDS Community Action Group
306 W. High St.
Elkhart, IN 46516
Duane Cook

Erie County AIDS Task Force
P.O. Box 375
420 Superior St.
Sandusky, OH 44870
Debbie Tolue/ Donna Hirsch

Evergreen AIDS Support Services
1229 Cornwall Ave., Suite 313
Bellingham, WA 98225

FACTS-Family AIDS Center for Treatment & Support
18 Parris Ave.
Providence, RI 02907
Paul Fitzgerald, Executive Director

Fairfield County AIDS Task Force
1587 Granville Pike
Lancaster, OH 43130-1038

Families' & Children's AIDS Network
(FCAN)
721 N. LaSalle St. Suite 301
Chicago, IL 60610
Robert P. Robertson, Executive Director

Family Services Woodfield
475 Clinton Ave.
Bridgeport, CT 06605
Evelyn Figueroa

Family Shoulders AIDS Support Group
1229 Cornwall St., Suite 313
Bellingham, WA 98225

Fenway Community Health Center
7 Haviland St.
Boston, MA 02115
Dale Orlando, Executive Director

Flathead Counseling and Testing
723 5th Ave.,
East Kalispell, MI 59901
Wendy Doely

Patsy Fleming
Office of National AIDS Policy
750 17th St. N.W.
Washington, D.C. 20503
AIDS Czar

Florida AIDS Hotline
800-352-2437

Four State Community AIDS Project
726 Illinois, P.O. Box 3476
Joplin, MO 64803
Cheryl Tullis, Director

Fox Valley AIDS Project
120 N. Morrison St., #201
Appleton, WI 54911

Franklin Area AIDS Network
P.O. Box 356
Chambersburg, PA 17201
J. P. Potter

Franklin Community AIDS Project
50 Miles St.
Greenfield, MA 01301
Andre Lemay/Bob DeRusha

Fredericksburg Area AIDS / HIV Support Services, Inc.
415 Elm St.
Fredericksburg, VA 22401
Susan Vaughn, Coordinator

Bill Freeman
National Association of People with AIDS
1413 "K" St., 10th Fl.
Washington, D.C. 20005
Executive Director

Friends for Life HIV Resources
P.O. Box 40389
Memphis, TN 38174
Michael Coleman, Executive Director

Friends For Life Support Group
P.O. Box 946
Newport, NC 28570
Dee Bryson

Fundacion AIDS de Puerto Rico
Box 36-4842
San Juan , PR 00936
Jose Toro, Executive Director

Gay American Indian AIDS Project
135 Buena Vista E., Suite 2
San Francisco, CA 94117
Randy Burns

Gay and Lesbian Adolescent Social Services
(GLASS)
8901 Melrose Ave., Suite 202
West Hollywood, CA 90069

Gay and Lesbian Medical Association
273 Church St.
San Francisco, CA 94114
Dr. Katherine O'Hanlan

Gay Asian Pacific Alliance Community HIV Project
1841 Market St.
San Francisco, CA 94103
Steve Lew

Gay Community AIDS Project
P.O. Box 713
Champaign, IL 61824
Jennifer Lutman

Gay Men's Health Crisis
129 W. 20th St.
New York, NY 10011
Jeff Richardson, Executive Director

Gay Men's Sex Project
3136 N. 3rd Ave.
Phoenix, AZ 85013

Georgia AIDS Therapy Information Network
800-551-2728
404-377-8895
Atlanta, GA
Information

God's Love We Deliver
895 Amsterdam Ave.
New York, NY 10025
Maureen McGovern, Director

David Gold
Gay Men's Health Crisis
129 W. 20th St., 2nd Fl.
New York, NY 10011
Editor, GMHC Treatment News

Good Samaritan Project
3030 Walnut St.
Kansas City, MO 64108
Ina Rose Pope, Director of Education

Grand Rapids AIDS Resource Center
P.O. Box 6603
1414 Robinson Rd., S.E.
Grand Rapids, MI 49516
Jan Koopman, Executive Director

Great Lakes Psychological Services
111 N. Wabash Ave., Suite 1400
Chicago, IL 60602
Dr. Louis Hemmerich

Greater Bridgeport AIDS Project
P.O. Box 6033
Bridgeport, CT 06606
Nida Swilling/ Shane Morrow

Greater Cincinnati AIDS Consortium
P.O. Box 19353
Cincinnati, OH 45219
Meg Harman, Coordinator

Greater Steubenville AIDS Task Force
312 Market St.
Steubenville, OH 43952

GROW, A Community Service Corporation
Box 4535
Wilmington, NC 28457
Leo Teachout

Guilford County Community AIDS Partnership
First Citizens Bank Building
Suite 307, P.O. Box 207
Greensboro, NC 27402
Jean Goodman

Gulf Coast CARES
1007 32nd Ave.
Gulfport, MS 39501
Art James, Al Jeeter

Haitian Coalition on AIDS
50 Court St., Suite 605
Brooklyn, NY 11201
Marie Carmel Pierre-Louis

Haitian Women's Program
c/o Brooklyn AIDS Task Force
465 Dean St.
Brooklyn, NY 11217
Patricia Benoit, Education

Hancock County AIDS Task Force
115 Municipal Building
Findlay, OH 45840

Hand in Hand
1915 Rosina St.
Santa Fe, NM 87501
Kenton Neidel

Harlem AIDS Treatment Group
Harlem Hospital-Infectious Diseases Section
506 Lenox Ave., Rm. 3107
New York, NY 10037
Wafee El-Sadr/Michelle Hardy, community program for clinical research on AIDS

Hartford Gay & Lesbian Health Collective
P.O. Box 2094
Hartford, CT 06145
Linda Estabrook, Executive Director

Harvey Milk AIDS Education Fund
P.O. Box 14135
San Francisco, CA 94114
Maurice Belote

Hawaii AIDS Research Consortium
3675 Kilauea Ave.
Atherton Building, 2nd Fl.
Honolulu, HI 96816
Margo Heath-Chiozzi

Hawaii AIDS Hotline
800-922-1313

HEAL (Health Education AIDS Liaison)
16 E. 16th St.
New York, NY 10003
Michele Fontaine

The Healing Alternatives Foundation
1748 Market St., Suite 204
San Francisco, CA 94102
Buyer's club

Health Crisis Network
5050 Biscayne Blvd.
Miami, FL 33137
Catherine Lynch, Executive Director

Health Issues Taskforce
2250 Euclid Ave.
Cleveland, OH 44115

Health Link
3213 N. Ocean Blvd., Suite 6
Fort Lauderdale, FL 33308
Marie Wansiki, buyer's club

Heartland AIDS Resource Center
600 E. 31st St.
Kansas City, MO 64109
Mike Flores

Heartland of America Community AIDS Partnership
1080 Washington St.
Kansas City, MO 64105
Gina Pulliman

Helping People with AIDS
P.O. Box 4397
Little Rock, AR 72204

HERO, Inc. (Health Education Resource Organization)
101 W. Read, Suite 825
Baltimore, MD 21201
Hotline: 410-945-AIDS
Susan Kromholz, Acting Director

Hill Health Center
400 Columbus Ave.
New Haven, CT 06519
Si-Hoi Lam, community program for clinical research on AIDS

Hispanic AIDS Forum, Inc.
Bronx Service Center
886 Westchester Ave.
Bronx, NY 10459
Miguelina Maldonado, Executive Director

Hispanic AIDS Forum, Inc.
(Main Office)
121 Ave. of the Americas, Suite 505
New York, NY 10013
Miguelina Maldonado

Hispanic AIDS Forum, Inc.
Queens Service Center
74-09 37th Ave., Suite 306
Jackson Heights, NY 11372
Hilda Roman-Nay, Deputy Director

HIV Care
St. Francis Memorial Hospital
900 Hyde St., 9th Fl.
San Francisco, CA 94109
Ellen LaPointe, community program for clinical research on AIDS

HIV - Ethics Project of the Fortune Society
39 W. 19th St.
New York, NY 10011
Tracy Gallagher, Director, HIV education in prisons

HIV Law Project
841 Broadway, Ste. 608
New York, NY 10003
Terry McGovern, Director

HIV Prevention Project
(formerly Prevention Point)
P.O. Box 170028
San Francisco, CA 94117-0028
George Clark, needle exchange

HIV Resource Consortium
4154 S. Harvard, Suite H-1
Tulsa, OK 74135
Sharon Thoele, Director

HIV Resource Library, AIDS Action Committee of Massachusetts
131 Clarendon St.
Boston, MA 02116

HIV Study Group
Central Texas Medical Foundation
4614 North IH-35
Austin, Texas 78751
Earl Matthew, MD, Director

HIV Wellness Center
502B Oakland St.
Austin, TX 78763
Kathryn Holloway

HIV-AIDS Legal Project
Urban County Government Center
810 Barrett Ave., Suite 652
Louisville, KY 40204
Jeffrey A. Been, Attorney-at-Law

HIV / AIDS Resources, Inc.
3477 E. Amazon Dr.
P.O. Box 5513
Eugene, OR 97405

Derek Hodel
Gay Men's Health Crisis
129 W. 20th St.
New York, NY 10011
Director of Federal Affairs

Holistic AIDS Response Program
3916 Normal St.
San Diego, CA 92103
Khrystie Phoenix, Program Coordinator

Home Nursing Agency AIDS Intervention Project
201 Chestnut Ave.,
P.O. Box 352
Altoona, PA 16603
Gary J. Gates, AIP Director

Hope and Help Center of Central Florida, Inc.
369 N. Orange Ave.
Orlando, FL 32801
Chuck Hummer

Hope House
P.O. Box 2161
Sacramento, CA 95812

Horizon House—Care With Dignity
3601 S. Allison St.
Denver, CO 80235

Housing Works
594 Broadway, 7th Fl.
New York, NY 10012
Charles King and Keith Cylar

Houston Clinical Research Network
P.O. Box 66308
Houston, Texas 77266-6308
Ralph Lasher

HRS AIDS Program
1000 N.E. 16th Ave.
Gainesville, FL 32601
Gay Koehler-Sides

Human Rights Commission - Lesbian, Gay and AIDS Unit
25 Van Ness Ave., Suite 800
San Francisco, CA 94102-4908
Advocacy organization

Hyacinth AIDS Foundation
103 Bayard St., 3rd Fl.
New Brunswick, NJ 08901
Dawn Hare, Office Manager

Idaho AIDS Foundation
P.O. Box 421
Boise, ID 83701
Justin Larson, Program Director

Idaho AIDS Hotline
800-345-2277

Illinois AIDS Hotline
800-243-2437

IMPACT-DC
300 "I" St. N.E., Suite 300
Washington, DC 20002
Michelle Wilson

Indian Health Services Phoenix Area
3738 N. 16th St., Suite A
Phoenix, AZ 85016
Dena Transgrud

Indiana Cares
3951 N. Meridian St., Suite 101
Indianapolis, IN 46208
Stevan Briley

Indiana AIDS Hotline
800-848-2437

Indiana Community AIDS Action Network
3951 N. Meridian, Suite 200
Indianapolis, IN 46208
Donna Dodson, Executive Director

Informe-SIDA
P.O. Box 13501
Austin, TX 78711

Iniciativa Communitaria de Investigation
124 F.D. Roosevelt Ave.
P.O. Box 774, Old San Juan Station
Hato Rey , PR 00917
Jose Vergas-Vidot, MD

Inland AIDS Project
17662 San Bernardino Ave.
Fontana, CA 92335
John Salley, Executive Director

Inland AIDS Project/NAMES Project
1240 Palmyrita, Suite E
Riverside, CA 92507
John Salley, Executive Director

Inner City AIDS Network
912 3rd St., N.W.
Washington, DC 20001
Tarina Hunt

Interventions AIDS Research and Education
140 N. Ashland Ave.
Chicago, IL 60607
Patti Baldino

Iowa AIDS Hotline
800-445-AIDS

Iowa Center for AIDS Resources & Education
(ICARE)
P.O. Box 2989
Iowa City, IA 52244
Laura Hill, Executive Director

Iowa Community AIDS Partnership
101 2nd St., SE, Suite 306
Cedar Rapids, IA 52401

Iowa Hispanic AIDS Coalition
1710 23rd St.
Des Moines, IA 50310

Iowa Interfaith HIV/AIDS Network
601 Keo Way
Des Moines, IA 50309

Iris Center
333 Valencia St., Suite 222
San Francisco, CA 94103
Services for women with substance abuse issues

Iris House, A Center for Women Living With HIV
2271 2nd Ave.
New York, NY 10035
Marie St. Cyr, Executive Director

Mike Isbell
Gay Men's Health Crisis
129 W. 20th St.
New York, NY 10011
Director of Public Policy

Japanese American AIDS Project
1596 Post St., 1st Fl.
San Francisco, CA 94109

Jerusalem House
100 Edgewood Ave. N.E.
Suite 1228
Atlanta, GA 30303
Ann Slaughter, Executive Director

Jewish Community AIDS Task Force
300 S. Dahlia
Denver, CO 80222

Johnson County Education Committee on AIDS
429 Burkarth Rd.
Warrensburg, MO 64093
Shirley Burgin

Kalamazoo AIDS Resource / Educational Services
628 Park St.
Kalamazoo, MI 49007
Cyril Colonius

Kansas City AIDS Research Consortium
2411 Holmes
Kansas City, MO 64108
Gary Johnson and
James F. Stanford, MD

Kansas City Free Health Clinic
101 W. 34th St.
Kansas City, KS 64111
Karen Mitchell

Kentuckiana People With AIDS Coalition
AIDS Services Center
810 Barret Ave., Suite 264
Louisville, KY 40204

Kentuckiana People With AIDS Coalition
P.O. Box 126
Kevil, KY 42053

Kentuckiana People With AIDS Coalition
P.O. Box 109
Owensboro, KY 42302

Kentuckiana People With AIDS Coalition
P.O. Box 54411
Lexington, KY 40515-4411

Kentuckiana People With AIDS Coalition
P.O. Box 236
Morton's Gap, KY 42440

Kentucky AIDS Hotline
800-654-2437

Kentucky Minority AIDS Council
233 W. Broadway, Suite 400
Louisville, KY 40202
Dr. Samuel Robinson

Charles King
Housing Works
594 Broadway, 7th Fl.
New York, NY. 10012

Dr. Mathilde Krim
American Foundation for AIDS Research.
5900 Wilshire Blvd.
Los Angeles, CA 90036-5032
Founder and President, AmFAR

Kupona Network
4611 S. Ellis
Chicago, IL 60653
Paula Henderson

La Alternativa / Hispanic AIDS
176 Jersey St.
Buffalo, NY 14201
Zonya Rivera, Education Cooridinator

La Frontera Center, Inc.
502 W. 29th St.
Tucson, AZ 85701
Floyd H. Martinez, Ph. D

La Verna Heights
104 E. Park Ave.
Savannah, MO 64485
Sister Barbara

Lackawanna County AIDS Council
P.O. Box 815
Scranton, PA 18501
Carla J. Warnock, Board President

Lafayette CARES (Concern for AIDS Relief, Education and Support)
P.O. Box 91446
Lafayette, LA 70509-1446
Gene Dolese

Lake County AIDS Advisory Board
105 Main St.
Painesville, OH 44077
Gail Anderson

Lambda Legal Defense & Education
666 Broadway
New York, NY 10012

Lancaster AIDS Project
44 N. Queen St.
Lancaster, PA 17603
Leanne Porterfield, Executive Director

Lansing Area AIDS Network
855 Grove St., Suite 207
Lansing, MI 48823

Latino AIDS Project
Alliance Medical Center
619 Center St.
Heraldsburg, CA 95448
Rachael Escamilla, Executive Director

Latino AIDS Project, Instituto Familiar de la Raza
Latino AIDS Project
2639 24th St.
San Francisco, CA 94110
Marvin Montenegro

The Lavender Project at Presbyterian-St. Luke's Medical Center
1719 E. 19th Ave.
Denver, CO 80218

League Against AIDS, Inc.
2699 Biscayne Blvd., Suite 3
Miami, FL 33940
Mireille Trible

Lee County AIDS Outreach
P.O. Box 1971
Auburn, AL 36831

Lee County AIDS Task Force
2231-A McGregor Blvd.
Fort Meyers, FL 33901
Mark Geisler

Lee County AIDS Task Force
2231-B McGregor Blvd.
Fort Meyers, FL 33908
Earl Givens

Lehigh Valley AIDS Action Volunteer Coordinator
321 Wyandte St.
Bethlehem, PA 18052

Lesbian AIDS Project (GMHC)
129 W. 20th St.
New York , NY 10011
Amber Hollibaugh

Lesbian Health Project of the Community Health Project
208 W. 13th St.
New York, NY 10011
Dana Greene

Lesbian Health Project of the Whitman-Walker Clinic
1407 "S" St. N.W.
Washington, DC 20009
Amelie Zurn

The Lesbian Resource Project
P.O. Box 26031
Tempe, AZ 85285-6031

Lewis and Clark County AIDS Project
631 Helen Ave., P.O. Box 832
Helena, MT 59624
Julie O'Connor, Executive Director

Licking County AIDS Task Force
40 W. Main St.
Newark, OH 43055

LIFE AIDS Lobby
926 "J" St., Suite 522
Sacramento, CA 95814
Laurie McBride, Executive Director

Life Entitlements Corporation
4 World Trade Center, #5270
New York, NY 10048
Viatical agency

Life Force: Women Against AIDS
165 Cadman Plaza E., Rm. 310
Brooklyn, NY 12201

Life Foundation
The AIDS Foundation of Hawaii
P.O. Box 88980
Honolulu, HI 96815
Carol Murry, Executive Director

Lifelink
811 "L" St. S.E.
Washington, DC 20003
Gregory Hutchings, speakers bureau, coordinator of international candelight vigil

The Living Room
1410 W. 29th St.
Cleveland, OH 44113
Paul Whitehurst

Derek Link
Gay Men's Health Crisis
129 W. 20th St,. 2nd Fl.
New York, NY 10011
Treatment Advocate

Local AIDS/HIV Services: The National Directory
U.S. Conference of Mayors
1620 "I" St. N.W., 4th Fl.
Washington, DC 20006

Long Beach AIDS Services / Center for Community Research and Services
1407 E. 4th St.
Long Beach, CA 90802
Barbara Johnson, publishes "Guide to HIV Services in Long Beach"

Long Island Association for AIDS Care, Inc.
P.O. Box 2859 , Huntington Sta.
New York, NY 11746
Douglas Edelson, Executive Assistant

Los Angeles Shanti Foundation
1616 N. La Brea Ave.
Los Angeles, CA 90028
Sue Crumpton

Louisiana AIDS Hotline
800-922-4379

Louisiana Community AIDS Research Program
1430 Tulane Ave.
New Orleans, LA 70112
C. Lynn Besch/Janice Walker, community program for clinical research on AIDS

Love and Action
3 Church St.
Annapolis, MD 21401
Rev. J. Collins, Executive Director

Low Country AIDS Services
P.O. Box 207
Charleston, SC 29402
Joe Hall

Lower East Side Needle Exchange
39 Avenue C
New York, NY 10009

Lyon-Martin Women's Health Services
1748 Market St., #201
San Francisco, CA 94102
Deborah Riggins, Executive Director

Madison AIDS Support Network
303 Lathrop St.
Madison, WI 53705

Madison County AIDS Program
1308-A Niedringhaus
Granite City, IL 62040
Sandra L. Stokka

Mahoning County AIDS Task Force
P.O. Box 1143
Youngstown, OH 44501
Kate Wallace, President

Maine AIDS Partnership
P.O. Box 3820, 233 Oxford St.
Portland, ME 04104
Joanne Crepeau

Maine AIDS Hotline
800-851-2437

Malama Pono Kaui AIDS Project
P.O. Box 1500
Kapaa, HI 96746
Don Gershberg, Executive Director

Manchester Area Network on AIDS
P.O. Box 8080
Manchester, CT 06040
Kathy Tommilo

Manhattan AIDS Program
P.O. Box 1935
Manhattan, KS 66502
Charles Murphy

Mano a Mano Project, Instituto Familiar de la Raza
Latino AIDS Project
2639 24th St.
San Francisco, CA 94110
Concha Saucedo, services to those diagnosed with AIDS

Maricopa County AIDS Task Force
1845 E. Roosevelt
Phoenix, AZ 85006
Michael Nolin

Maricopa County Community AIDS Partnership
2122 E. Highand Ave., Suite 400
Phoenix, AZ 85016
Jan Kenney

Marion Area AIDS Task Force
P.O. Box 6002
Marion, OH 43301-6002

Maryland AIDS Hotline
800-638-6252

Massachusetts AIDS Hotline
800-235-2331

Maui AIDS Foundation
55 Kaahamanu Ave.
P.O. Box 1538
Kahului, HI 96732
Greg Lamb, Executive Director

Terry McGovern
HIV Law Project
841 Broadway, Suite 608
New York, NY 10003
Director

McLean County AIDS Task Force
P.O. Box 304
Bloomington, IL 61702

Memphis Health Center, Inc.
360 E. H. Crump Blvd.
Memphis , TN 38126

Mercer County AIDS Task Force
87 Stambaugh Ave., Suite 1
Sharon, PA 16146
Jean Maliner

Merrymeeting AIDS Support Services
P.O. Box 57
Brunswick, ME 04011-0057
Brian P. Allen, Executive Director

Metro New York / Names Project
398 Wythe Ave.
Brooklyn , NY 11211
Peter L. Ramos

Metro St. Louis NAMES Project
3236 Nebraska
St. Louis, MO 63118

Metrolina AIDS Project
(MAP)
P.O. Box 32662
Charlotte, NC 28232
Michael Averbuch

Michigan AIDS Fund
c/o The Greystone Groups, Inc.
678 Front St. N.W.
Grand Rapids , MI 49504
Earl Schipper

Michigan AIDS Fund
c/o The Kresge Foundation
P.O. Box 3151
Troy, MI 48007
Barbara Getz

Michigan AIDS Hotline
800-872-2437

Mid-Fairfield County AIDS Project
83 East Ave.
Norwalk, CT 06851

Mid-Missouri AIDS Project
811 E. Cherry St.
Columbia , MO 65201
John Hawkins, Director

Mid-Ohio Valley AIDS Task Force
P.O. Box 1274
Parkersburg, WV 26102
Joanne T. Kowalski

Mid-Oregon AIDS / Support Services
P.O. Box 12547
Salem, OR 97309
C.J. Jones, President

Middletown AIDS Task Force
One City Centre Plaza
Middletown, OH 45042

Midwest AIDS Prevention Project
660 Livernois
Ferndale, MI 48220
Steven Wood, Program Director

Midwest Hispanic AIDS Coalition
P.O. Box 470859
Chicago, IL 80647
Jose Arrom, Executive Director

Milwaukee AIDS Project
AIDS Resource Center of Wisconsin, Inc.
P.O. Box 92505
Milwaukee, WI 53202
Kari DiFonzo

Minnesota AIDS Hotline
800-248-AIDS

Minnesota AIDS Project
2025 Nicolet Ave.
Minneapolis, MN 55404
Mary W. Wallace, Region Coordinator

Minnesota AIDS Project
(MAP)
109 S. 5th St.
Marshall, MN 56258

Minnesota Indian AIDS Task Force
1433 E. Franklin Ave.
St. Paul, MN 55103
Sharon Day

Minority AIDS Education Task Force
2300 "O" St.
Lincoln, NE 65810
Joel Gajardo

Minority AIDS Project (A Ministry of Unity Fellowship Church)
5149 W. Jefferson Blvd.
Los Angeles, CA 90016
L. Paul Davis and Bishop Carl Bean, Directors

Minority Education Committee on AIDS
995 E. Broad
Columbus, OH 43205

Minority Task Force on AIDS
505 8th Ave., 16th Fl.
New York, NY 10018

Missionaries of Mercy
346 Riverdale Dr.
Glendale, CA 91204
John Grigg, Coordinator for home cleaning service for PWAs

Mississippi AIDS Hotline
800-537-0851

Mississippi Gay / Lesbian Alliance
P.O. Box 8342
Jackson, MS 39284
Eddie Sandafer

Missoula AIDS Council
P.O. Box 9102
Missoula, MT 59802
Aylette Wright

Missouri AIDS Hotline
800-533-2437

Missouri HIV/AIDS Education Network
4050 Lindell Blvd.
St. Louis, MO 63108
Al Schon

Mobile AIDS Coalition
Box 40051
Mobile, AL 36640
Gwendolyn Darty

Mobile AIDS Support Services
107 N. Ann St.
Mobile, AL 36604
LaDawn Harrison, Director

Mobilization Against AIDS
584-B Castro St.
San Francisco, CA 94114
Mike Shriver, Executive Director

Momentum AIDS Outreach Program
619 Lexington Ave.
New York, NY 10022
Peter Avitabile, Director

The Momentum Project
19 W. 36th St.
New York, NY 10018

Monroe County AIDS Community Action
645 S. Rogers St.
Bloomington, IN 47403
Jill LaFon

Montana AIDS Hotline
800-233-6668

Montana AIDS Program
Prevention Health Services Bureau
1400 Broadway
Helena, MT 59620

Montgomery AIDS Outreach, Inc.
Box 5213
Montgomery, AL 36103

Montgomery County AIDS Consortium
P.O. Box 2045
Morristown, PA 19404
Mary Catherine Lowert, Executive Director

Mothers of AIDS Patients, Inc
P.O. Box 1763
Lomita, CA 90717
Janet McMahon

Mountain State AIDS Network
235 High St., Suite 306
P.O. Box 1221
Morgantown, WV 26505
Christopher Morrison

Mountains AIDS Coalition
P.O. Box 1862
Asheville, NC 28802

Muskegon Area AIDS Resource Services
928 W. Norton, Box 617
Muskegon, MI 49442
Mark Sorenson

NAMES Project AIDS Memorial Quilt
1613 "K" St., N.W.
Washington, DC 20006
Tammy Reynolds

The NAMES Project Foundation
310 Townsend St.
San Francisco, CA 94107-1607
Cleve Jones

NAMES Project Miami
P.O. Box 370711
Miami, FL 33137

Napa Valley AIDS Project
601 Cabot St.
Napa, CA 94559

Nashville CARES
700 Craighead, Suite 200
P.O. Box 25187
Nashville, TN 37202

The National AIDS Bereavement Center
1953 Columbia Pike, #24
Arlington, VA 22204-4569

National AIDS Brigade
1610 W. Highland, Box 77
Chicago, IL 60660

National AIDS Info Center
800-342-AIDS

National AIDS Information Clearinghouse
800-458-5231
Box 6003
Rockville, MD 20849-6003

National AIDS Minority Information & Education
Howard University, Suite 3B
2139 Georgia Ave., N.W.
Washington, DC 20001
Dr. Peggy Valentine

National Association of People With AIDS
1413 "K" St. N.W., 8th Fl.
Washington, D.C. 20005
Hotline: 800-338-2437
William Freeman, Executive Director

National AIDS Fund
1400 "I" St., Suite 1220
Washington, DC 20005-2208
202-408-4848
Paula Vanness, Executive Director

National Episcopal AIDS Coalition
2025 Pennsylvania Ave., N.W.
Suite 509
Washington, DC 20006
Rev. Ted Carr

National Gay / Lesbian Health Foundation
P.O. Box 65472
Washington, DC 20035
Bill Scott

National Institute of Allergic and Infectious Diseases
9000 Rockville Pike
Bethesda, MD 29892
Dr. Anthony Fauci, Director

National Institutes of Health
9000 Rockville Pike
Bethesda, MD 20892
Harold Varmus, Director

National Lawyers Guild AIDS Network
558 Capp St.
San Francisco, CA 94110
Eileen Hansen

National Minority AIDS Council
300 "I" St., N.E., Suite #400
Washington, DC 20002-4389
Paul Kawata and Moises Agosto

National Native American AIDS Prevention Center
3515 Grand Ave., Suite 100
Oakland, CA 94610
800-283-2437
Andrea Green Rush

National Resource Center on Women and AIDS
2000 "P" St. N.W., Suite 508
Washington, DC 20036
Edna Viruell, Director

National Task Force on AIDS Prevention
631 O'Farrell St.
San Francisco, CA 94109
Reggie Williams

National Women & HIV / AIDS Project
P.O. Box 53141
Washington, DC 20009

Nebraska AIDS Hotline
800-782-AIDS

Nebraska AIDS Project
3624 Leavenworth St.
Omaha, NE 68105
Marcy Singhaus, Office Manager

Nevada AIDS Foundation
1225 Westfield Ave., Suite 3
P.O. Box 478
Reno, NV 89504
Jane Fox

Nevada AIDS Hotline
800-842-2437

New Day Wellness Coalition of Southern Maryland
3030 Brightseat Rd., Suite 202
Glenarden, MD 20706
A. Eileen Horan

New England AIDS Education & Training
Beth Israel Hospital
330 Brookline Ave.
Boston, MA 02215
Donna Gallagher, Contact

New Hampshire AIDS Hotline
800-872-8909

New Jersey AIDS Hotline
800-624-2377

New Jersey AIDS Partnership
Knox Hill Rd., P.O. Box 317
Morristown, NJ 07963
Helena Hansen

New Jersey Buddies
1182 Teaneck Rd., P.O. Box 413
Teaneck, NJ 07666
Tracey Boecherer, Office Manager

New Jersey Community Research Initiative
393 Central Ave., Suite 301
Newark, NJ 07107
George Perez/Bill Orr, community program for clinical research on AIDS

New Jersey Women and AIDS Network
5 Elm Row, Suite 112
New Brunswick, NJ 08901
Marion Banzhof, Executive Director

New London AIDS Educational Counseling and Testing
120 Broad St.
New London, CT 06320
Lizabeth Love Ryan

New Mexico AIDS Hotline
800-545-2437

New Mexico AIDS Services
4200 Silver Ave., S.E., Suite D
Albuquerque, NM 87108
Maria Bavista-Lopez

New Mexico Association of People Living With AIDS
111 Mont Claire, S.E.
Albuquerque, NM 87108
Dennis Dunnum, Executive Director

New Mexico Community AIDS Partnership
227 Otero St.
Santa Fe, NM 87501
Sue Rundstrom

New Orleans AIDS Task Force
1407 Decatur St.
New Orleans, LA 70116
Doug Weiss

New River Valley AIDS Coalition
c/o New River Alliance
Drawer 1127
Dublin, VA 24084
Peggy Eaton, Chairperson

New York AIDS Hotlines
800-541-2437
800-MEDS-4-AIDS

The New York City AIDS Fund
2 Park Ave., 24th Fl.
New York, NY 10016

North Carolina AIDS Hotline
800-342-AIDS

North Carolina Lesbian and Gay Health Project
P.O. Box 9203
Durham, NC 27715
Stan Holt

North Florida AIDS Network
P.O. Box 5755
Gainesville, FL 32602
Abby Goldsmith

North Idaho AIDS Coalition
Panhandle Health District
2195 Ironwood Ct.
Coeur d'Alene, ID 83814

North Iowa AIDS Project
232 2nd St. N.E.
Mason City, IA

North Jersey Community Research Initiative
393 Central Ave., Suite 301
Newark, NJ 07103
Bill Orr

Northeast Ohio Task Force on AIDS
655 N. Main St.
Akron, OH 44310
R. Sue Henderson / John Kennedy

Northern AIDS Task Force
Box 2616
New Orleans, LA 70176
Jeff Campbell, Executive Director

Northern Colorado AIDS Project
Northern Colorado Health Network, Inc.
P.O. Box 182
Fort Collins, CO 80522

Northern Illinois AIDS Project
(NIAP)
P.O. Box 364
McHenry, IL 60051

Northern Lights Alternatives
601 W. 50th St., Suite 503
New York, NY 10019
Amy Amabile, Executive Director

Northern Virginia HIV Consortium
7535 Little River Tpke., Suite 100
Annandale, VA 22003
Callie Gass

Northlake AIDS Network
P.O. Box 2397
Slidell, LA 70459

Northwest AIDS Foundation
127 Broadway E., Suite 200
Seattle, WA 98102-5786
Terry Stone

Northwest Lousiana AIDS Task Force
P.O. Box 832
Shreveport, LA 71162-0832

Northwest Oklahoma AIDS Support Project
P.O. Box 3073
Enid, OK 73702-3073

Northwest Wisconsin AIDS Project
AIDS Resource Center of Wisconsin, Inc.
P.O. Box 11
Eau Claire, WI 54702-0011

Northwestern Connecticut AIDS Project
100 Migeon Ave.
Torrington, CT 06790
Nancy Heaton

Notes From the Underground
PWA Health Group
150 W. 26th St., Suite 201
New York, NY 10001

Oasis Foundation
P.O. Box 57754
Oklahoma, OK 73157
Bob Yowell, Director

Office of AIDS Ministry of Catholic Social Services
Old St. Joseph's Rectory
321 Willings Alley
Philadelphia, PA

Office of AIDS Research
9000 Rockville Pike
Bethesda, MD 29892
William Paul, Director

Office of National AIDS Policy
750 17th St. N.W.
Washington, D.C. 20503
Patsy Fleming

Dr. Katherine O'Hanlan
Gay and Lesbian Medical Association
273 Church St.
San Francisco, CA 941143

Ohio AIDS Coalition
P.O. Box 10034
Columbus, OH 43201

Ohio AIDS Hotline
800-332-2437

Ohio State University AIDS Clinic
Ohio State University, Rm. 4725
Columbus, OH 43210

Oklahoma AIDS Hotline
800-535-2437

Open Door Clinic
164 Division St., Suite 607
Elgin, IL 60120
Hugh Epping

Open Hand Chicago
909 W. Balmont, Suite 100
Chicago , IL 60657
Matthew Hamilton

Operation Bridge
701 N. 114th St.
Omaha, NE 68154
Toby Taubenhelm, CEO

Oregon AIDS Hotline
800-777-2437
620 S.W. 5th St., Suite 300
Portland, OR 97204
Tom Richardson

Oregon AIDS Task Force
The Research and Education Group
2701 N.W. Vaughn St., Suite 770
Portland, OR 97210
James Sampson, MD/Rob Forrest, community program for clinical research on AIDS

Oregon Minority AIDS Coalition
408 S.W. 2nd St., Suite 428
Portland, OR 97204
D'Norgia Price, Program Director

Outreach, Inc.
3030 Campbellton Rd. S.W.
Atlanta, GA 30311
Sedrick Gardner, Director

Oxford Hills Community AIDS Network
P.O. Box 113
Paris, ME 04271-0113

PAACNOTES
Physicians Assocation for AIDS Care Publishing
101 W. Grand Ave., Suite 200
Chicago, IL 60601

PACT For Life Buyers Club
801 W. Congress
Tucson, AZ 85745
Dan Munoz, buyer's club

Palmetto AIDS Services
Life Support of South Carolina
P.O. Box 12124
Columbia, SC 29211

Panhandle AIDS Support Organization
604 W. 8th St.
Amarillo, TX 79101
Stuart Shuman

Panos Institute
1717 Massachusetts Ave. N.W. #301
Washington, DC 20036-3001
International AIDS issues

William Paul
Office of AIDS Research
9000 Rockville Pike
Bethesda, MD 29892
Director, Office of AIDS Research, NIAID/NIH

Peer to Peer, Inc. K.C. Youth AIDS Project
706 W. 42nd St., Suite 106
Kansas City, MO 64111
J.R. Gourley

Peninsula AIDS Foundation
326 Main St.
Newport News, VA 23601
Wendi Burke, Education Coordinator

Pennsylvania AIDS Hotline
800-662-6080

People of Color Against AIDS Network
1200 S. Jackson, Suite 25
Seattle, WA 98144
P. Catlin Fullwood, Director

People of Color AIDS Coalition, Inc.
Education and Support, Inc.
P.O. Box 14365
Tallahassee, FL 32317
Virginia Robson, Executive Director

People of Color in Crisis
462 Bergen St.
Brooklyn, NY 11217
Sharon Gray

People With AIDS Coalition of Arizona
801 W. Congress
Tucson, AZ 85745
Jerome Beillard

People With AIDS Coalition of Baltimore, Inc
101 W. Read St., Suite 808
Baltimore, MD 21201
John Stuban, Chairperson

People With AIDS Coalition of Broward County
2294 Wilton Dr.
Fort Lauderdale, FL 33305
Michael McCord

People With AIDS Coalition of Colorado
P.O. Box 300339
Denver, CO 80203
Earl Thomas

People With AIDS Coalition of Houston
1475 W. Gray, Suite 163
Houston, TX 77019
Ingrid Saenger, Executive Director

People With AIDS Coalition of Jacksonville
1628 San Marco Blvd., Suite 5
Jacksonville, FL 32207
Roy Blighton

People With AIDS Coalition of Key West
709 Olivia St.
Key West, FL 33040
George Gugleotti

People With AIDS Coalition of Long Island, Inc.
1170 Route 109
Lindenhurst, NY 11757
Sue C. Farino

People With AIDS Coalition of Maine
377 Cumberland Ave.
Portland, ME 04101
Roxanne Hurtubise

People With AIDS Coalition of Miami
3890 Biscayne Blvd.
Miami, FL 33137
Gene Suarez

People With AIDS Coalition of New Jersey
1576 Palisades Ave.
Ft. Lee, NJ 07024
Joci Tuckerser

People With AIDS Coalition of New Orleans
704 N. Rampart
New Orleans, LA 70116

People With AIDS Coalition of New York
50 W. 17th St., 8th Fl.
New York, NY 10011
John Hatchett, Executive Director

People With AIDS Coalition of Utah
1406 South 1100 East, Suite 107
Salt Lake City, UT 84105-2435

People With AIDS Coalition of West Palm Beach
2580 Metrocentre Blvd.
West Palm Beach, FL 33407
Tom Damheller

The Personal Liberty Fund
P.O. Box 1431
New Brunswick, NJ 08903
Norman Clevey

Pet Owners With AIDS / ARC Resource Services
Box 1116
New York, NY 10159
Steve Kohn, Executive Director

Pets Are Wonderful Support
(PAWS)
539 Castro St.
San Francisco, CA 94114
Steven Crider, Director

Philadelphia FIGHT
201 N. Broad St., 6th Fl.
Philadelphia, PA 19107
Jane Shull, Executive Program Director

Philadelphia Lesbian / Gay Task Force
1616 Walnut St., Suite 105
Philadelphia, PA 19103
Rita Adessa, Executive Director

The Phoenix Shanti Group
1314 E. McDowell Rd.
Phoenix, AZ 85006
Randall Gorbette, President & CEO

Physicians Association for AIDS Care
101 W. Grand Ave., Suite 200
Chicago, IL 60610

PI Perspective and The Briefing Paper
Project Inform
1965 Market St., Suite 200
San Francisco, CA 94103

Pierce County AIDS Foundation
625 Commerce St., Suite 370
Tacoma, WA 98406
Jeannie Darnielle, Executive Director

Pierce County Community AIDS Partnership
734 Broadway, P.O. Box 2215
Tacoma, WA 98401
Emery M. Ivery

Pitt County AIDS Service Organization
P.O. Box 8685
Greenville, NC 27835

Pittsburgh AIDS Task Force
P.O. Box 7256
Pittsburgh, PA 15213
Cynthia Klemanski

Point Defiance AIDS Project
535 E. Dock St., Suite 112
Tacoma, WA 98402

Portage County AIDS Task Force
6847 N. Chestnut
Ravenna, OH 44266

Positive A.C.T.I.O.N.S.
1418 N. Main St.
Findlay, OH 45840
Browning Payne

Positive Directions
140 Clarendon St., Suite 805
Boston, MA 02116

Positive News
P.O. Box 426182
San Francisco, CA 94142-6182

Positively Aware
Test Positive Area Network
1340 W. Irving Park, Box 259
Chicago, IL 60613

POZ Magazine
Box 1279, Old Chelsea Station
New York, NY 10113-1279

Prison Pen Pal Project of the People With AIDS Coalition of New York
(PWAC-NY)
50 W. 17th St., 8th Fl.
New York, NY 10011

Proceed, Inc.
815 Elizabeth Ave.
Elizabeth, NJ 07201
Hiberto Soto

Project AIDS Lafayette, Inc.
810 North St.
P.O. Box 5375
Lafayette, IN 47903
Barry Reynolds, Care Coordinator

Project Aries
800-999-7511
Counseling program for gay and bi men at risk of HIV through unsafe sexual contact

Project AWARE (Association for Women's AIDS Research and Education) / UCSF
3180 18th St. #205
San Francisco, CA 94110
Judith Cohen

Project C.A.R.E. AIDS Advocacy Center
P.O. Box 2097
New Bedford, MA 02741
Paul Cassidy, Program Director

Project H.E.L.P.
P.O. Box 11434
Birmingham, AL 35202
Thomas Ellison

Project Inform
Hotline (National) 800-822-7422
Hotline (CA) 800-344-7422
1965 Market St., Suite 220
San Francisco, CA 94103
Martin Delaney and Annette Brands, Founding Director and Executive Director

Project Lazarus
P.O. Box 3906
New Orleans, LA 70177
Hugh J. McCabe, Executive Director

Project Open Hand
2720 17th St.
San Francisco, CA 94110
Meals and groceries

Prototypes / Pomona Women's Center
845 E. Arrow Hwy.
Pomona, CA 91767

Prototypes / Women & AIDS Risk Network
5601 Santa Monica Blvd.
West Hollywood, CA 90230

Prototypes / Women's Link Program
4410 Sepulveda Blvd.
Culver City, CA 90230

Provincetown AIDS Support Group
96-98 Bradford St., P.O. Box 1522
Provincetown, MA 02657
Alice Foley, Executive Director

Provincetown Positive / People with AIDS Coalition
406 Commercial St., P.O. Box 1465
Provincetown, MA 02657
Sean Current, Office Manager

Proyecto Contra SIDA Por VIDA
3690 18th St.
San Francisco, CA 94110

Proyectos Comunitarios Arizona
Sonora, Inc.
801 W. Congress
Tucson, AZ 85745
Richard Martinez

Puerto Rico AIDS Hotline
800-765-1010

PWA Health Group
150 W. 26th St., Suite 201
New York, NY 10001
Buyer's club

PWA Newsline
PWA Coalition of New York, Inc.
31 W. 26th St., 5th Fl.
New York, NY 10010

Quad City AIDS Coalition, Inc.
605 Main St., Suite 6A
Davenport, IA 52803-5245
Jaan Sturgis, Executive Director

Quan Yin Healing Arts Center
1748 Market St.
San Francisco, CA 94188
Misha Cohen

The Queens Medical Center
AIDS Community Care Team
1301 Punchbowl St.
Honolulu, HI 96744
Sue McCourt

Rainbow Wellness Center
P.O. Box 1158, Suite 300
1718 Reynolds St.
Waycross, GA 31502
Ann Knowlton

Rapids AIDS Project
c/o Grant Wood Area Red Cross
3601 42nd St. N.E.
Cedar Rapids, IA 52402
David Packard

Regional AIDS Interfaith Network
1000 Howard Ave.
New Orleans, LA 70113
Ron Unger

Regional HIV Treatment Center
1216 Trotwood Ave.
Columbia, TN 38401
Mary H. Coble

The Reimer Foundation
3023 N. Clark
Chicago, IL 60657
Del Barrett, Chairman

Rhode Island AIDS Hotline
800-726-3010

Rhode Island Project / AIDS
95 Chestnut St., 3rd Fl.
Providence, RI 02903
Philip Kane

Richmond AIDS Consortium
Box 49, MCV Station
Richmond, VA 23298
Thomas Kerkering

River Valley AIDS Project
120 Maple St.
Springfield, MA 01103
Francis Lopomo, Director

Roanoke AIDS Project
P.O. Box 4367
Roanoke, VA 24015
Lee Radecke, Chairperson

Rochester Area Task Force on AIDS
1350 University Ave., Suite C
Rochester, NY 14607

Rocky Mountain OIC AIDS Project
P.O. Box 2723
402 E. Virginia St.
Rocky Mount, NC 27802
Pat Oxendine-Hunter

Rumford Area AIDS Support Group / Phoneline
Mexico Congregational Church
43 Main St.
Mexico, ME 04257
207-364-8603

Rural AIDS Information Network (RAIN) Arkansas
509 S. Scott St.
Little Rock, AR 72202

Sacramento AIDS Foundation
920 20th St., 2nd Fl.
Sacramento, CA 95814-3133

Saline County Nursing Service
700 E. Slayter St., P.O. Box 218
Marshall, MO 65340
Billie Vardiman, RN

Salk Institute for Biological Studies
P.O. Box 858000
San Diego, CA 92138
Jonas Salk

Salud
2701 Ontario Rd. N.W., #2
Washington, DC 20009
Alex Compagnet

Samuel Rodgers Community Health Center
825 Euclid Ave.
Kansas City, MO 64124
Samuel Reynolds

San Angelo AIDS Foundation, Inc.
3017 Knickerbocker, Suite 201
P.O. Box 62474
San Angelo, TX 76906
Teri Scott Gilwanger

San Antonio AIDS Foundation
818 E. Grayson St.
San Antonio, TX 78208
Sharen L. Rupp, Executive Director

San Antonio PWA Coalition
1215 Jones Maltsberger, #210
San Antonio, TX 78247
Peter Peterson

San Diego Community Research Group
3800 Ray St.
San Diego, CA 92104
John Connolly/Daniel Pearce

San Diego County Regional Advisory Board on AIDS
P.O. Box 85524
San Diego, CA 92186
Binnie Callander

San Francisco AIDS Foundation
25 Van Ness Ave., Suite 660
San Francisco, CA 94102
Pat Christen, Executive Director

San Francisco Black Coalition on AIDS
1042 Divisadero
San Francisco, CA 94115
Gerald Lenoir, Executive Director

San Francisco City Clinic Study
25 Van Ness Ave., Suite 500
San Francisco, CA 94102
Paul O'Malley, long-term natural history of HIV in men

San Francisco Department of Public Health AIDS Office
25 Van Ness Ave., Suite 500
San Francisco, CA 94102
Mitchell Katz

Sandusky County AIDS Task Force
Sandusky Department of Public Health
2000 Countryside Dr.
Fremont, OH 43402
Kenneth W. Kerik

Santa Cruz AIDS Project/Proyecto SIDA Santa Cruz
911A Center St.
Santa Cruz, CA 95060
Michael Tossy

Sapphex Learn
14002 Clubhouse Circle #206
Tampa , FL 33624

Sarasota AIDS Support, Inc.
3002 North Tamiami Trail, #4
Sarasota, FL 34234

Ben Schatz
American Association of Physicians for Human Rights
273 Church St.
San Francisco, CA 941143
Executive Director

Schloemer & Associates—Host Agency for AIDS Anonymous
204 Executive Park
Louisville, KY 40207
Ida Lee, Office Manager

Seacoast AIDS Response
10 Vaughn Mall, # 3
Portsmouth, NH 03801
Ed Shannon

SEARCHLIGHT
SEARCH Alliance
7461 Beverly Blvd., #304
Los Angeles, CA 90036

Seattle AIDS Information Bulletin Board Service
1202 E. Pike, #658
Seattle, WA 98122-3934
modem 206-323-4420

Seattle Treatment Education Project
127 Broadway East, Suite 200
Seattle, WA 98102
Laury McKean

Seneca County AIDS Task Force
c/o Seneca County General Health District
3140 South State Route 100
Tiffin, OH 44883-9709
Martin J. Tremmel

Shanti Foundation
602 North 4th Ave.
Tucson, AZ 85705
Ann Maley

Shanti of Juneau
P.O. Box 22655
Juneau, AK 99802
Client Services Director

Shanti Project
525 Howard St.
San Francisco, CA 94105
Gloria Sandoval

Shanti-Seattle
P.O. Box 20698
Seattle, WA 98102
Robert Lux/Tina Karp

SHE (Sexual Health Enlightenment)
14002 Clubhouse Circle, #206
Tampa , FL 33624
Publication

The Sheridan Group
1775 "T" St. N.W.
Washington, DC 20009
Tom Sheridan

SIDAhora
PWA Coalition of New York, Inc.
50 W. 17th St., 8th Fl.
New York, NY 10011

Siouxland AIDS Coalition
1512 Pierce St.
Sioux City, IA 51105

Sister Love
1432 Donnelly Ave.
Atlanta, GA 30310
Dazon Dixon, Executive Director

Solano AIDS Task Force
P.O. Box 749
Fairfield, CA 94533

South Arkansas Fights AIDS
1616 W. Block
El Dorado, AR 71730

South Carolina AIDS Hotline
800-322-2437

South Carolina AIDS Education Network, Inc.
2798 Decker Blvd., Suite 98
Columbia, SC 29206
DiAna DiAna

South Central AIDS Assistance Network
2A Kline Village, Suite A
Harrisburg, PA 17104
Peg Dierkers, Executive Director

South Dakota AIDS Education and Training Center
University of South Dakota
1000 W. 4th St.
Yankten, SD 57078
Lori Pflanz, RN

South Dakota AIDS Hotline
800-592-1861

South Florida AIDS Network
Jackson Memorial Hospital
1611 N.W. 12th Ave., Old M.E.
Miami, FL 33136
Bill Lowrance

South Florida Community AIDS Partnership
200 S. Biscayne Blvd., Suite 2780
Miami, FL 33131
JoAnne Bander, Vice President

South Jersey AIDS Alliance
1301 Atlantic Ave.
Atlantic City, NJ 08401
Michele Wilson

South Mississippi AIDS Task Force
478 Caillavet
Biloxi, MS 35530
J. R. Harrington

South Plains AIDS Resource Center
4204 B 50th St., P.O. Box 6949
Lubbock, TX 79493
David L. Crader, Executive Director

Southeast Wisconsin AIDS Project
AIDS Resource Center of Wisconsin, Inc.
P.O. Box 0173
Kenosha, WI 53141-0173
William Houtz, Director

Southeastern Connecticut AIDS Project
38 Granite St
New London, CT 06320-5931

Southern Colorado AIDS Project
P.O. Box 311
Colorado Springs, CO 80901
Beth Bowman

Southern Nevada NAMES Project
1111 Desert Ln.
Las Vegas, NV 89102

Southern Ohio AIDS Task Force
602 Chillicothe
Portsmouth, OH 45662

Southern Tier AIDS Program, Inc.
122 Baldwin St.
Johnson City, NY 13790
Diane L. Brown, Executive Director

Southern Tier NAMES Project
122 Baldwin St.
Binghampton, NY 13905
Sandra Crandall

Southwest AIDS Committee
1505 Mescalero
El Paso, TX 79925
Terry D. Call, Executive Director

Southwest Community Based AIDS Treatment Group
1800 N. Highland, Suite 610
Los Angeles, CA 90028
Bisher Akil / Jill Glassbrenner

Southwest Louisiana AIDS Council
435 10th St.
Lake Charles, LA 70601
Marilyn S. Dunn, Executive Director

The Spellman Center for HIV-Related Disease
St. Clares Hospital
415 W. 51st St.
New York, NY 10019
Thomas Dougherty, Administrator

Spokane AIDS Network
1613 W. Gardner
Spokane, WA 99201

St. John Valley AIDS Task Force
c/o NMMC
143 East Main St.
Fort Kent, ME 04743

St. Louis Effort for AIDS, Inc
5622 Delmar Blvd., Suite 104E
St. Louis, MO 63112
Mary E. Hizer, Executive Director

St. Louis Metropolitan AIDS Program
634 N. Grant
St. Louis, MO 63103
Don Connor, Clinical Manager

Peter Staley
Treatment Action Group
147 2nd Ave., Suite 601
New York, NY 10003

Stamp Out AIDS
240 W. 44th St.
New York, NY 10036
John Glines

Stark County AIDS Task Force
420 N. Market Ave.
Canton, OH 44702-1544
Thomas Wingert

STEP Perspective
127 Broadway E., Suite 200
Seattle, WA 98102
Publication of Seattle Treatment Education Project

Steps
280 Sutter St.
San Francisco, CA 94108
Alternative treatment program

Stop AIDS Chicago
909 W. Belmont
Chicago, IL 60657
Jim Harvey, Director

Stop AIDS Chicago—African-American Program
2154 East 71st St.
Chicago, IL 60649

Stop AIDS Chicago—Latino/a-American Office
1352 N. Western Ave.
Chicago, IL 60622

STOP AIDS Project
201 Sanchez St.
San Francisco, CA 94114
Frederic Sonenberg, outreach to gay and bisexual men via bars, etc.

The Stop AIDS Project Boston
40 Plympton St.
Boston, MA 02118
Sue Hyde

Stop AIDSLA
c/o Gay & Lesbian Community Services Center
1625 N. Hudson Ave.
Los Angeles, CA 90028-6250

Stopping AIDS Is My Mission
2074 Abington Rd.
Cleveland, OH 44106

Summit AIDS Housing Corporation
333 S. Main
Akron, OH 44308
William DiTirro

Sussex County AIDS Committee
Delaware Lesbian and Gay Health Advocates
P.O. Box 712
Rehoboth Beach, DE 19971

Tampa AIDS Network
11215 N. Nebraska, Suite B-3
Tampa, FL 33612
Melissa Perry

Tarrant County Community AIDS Partnership
P.O. Box 202574
Arlington, TX 76006
Sue Grossman

Teens Teaching AIDS Prevention
800-234-TEEN

Tenderloin AIDS Resource Center
187 Golden Gate Ave.
San Francisco, CA 94102
Len Chavez-Smith

Tennessee AIDS Hotline
800-525-2437

Test Positive Aware
1340 W. Irving Park, Box 259
Chicago, IL 60613
Michael Thurnherr, Interim Executive Director; Michael Pleasants, Board President

Texarkana AIDS Project
P.O. Box 3243
Texarkana, AR 75504

Texas AIDS Hotline
800-299-2437

Texas AIDS Network
P.O. Box 2395
Austin, Texas 78768
Paul Clover

Three Rivers AIDS Coalition, Inc.
369-A Highway 604
Kinsale, VA 22488
Lawrence Wilson

Topeka AIDS Project
1915 S.W. 6th St
Topeka, KS 66606
Ray Bell

Treatment Action Group
147 2nd Ave., Suite. 601
New York, NY 10003

Treatment Issues
Gay Men's Health Crisis
129 W. 20th St.
New York, NY 10011
Publication

Tri County AIDS Task Force
Jersey County Health Department
208 S. Lafayette
Jerseyville, IL 62052
Karen Schroeder, RN

Tri-Cities AIDS Project
Box 231
Johnson City, TN 37605
Mary Kay Bearden

Triangle AIDS Network
2544 Broadway, P.O. Box 12279
Beaumont, TX 77702
Sherridan Tutt

Triangle AIDS Services Project
P.O. Box 3203
Durham, NC 27715

Trumbull County Area AIDS Task Force
P.O. Box 1638
Warren, OH 44482-1638

Tucson AIDS Project, Inc.
151 S. Tucson Blvd., #252
Tucson, AZ 85716
Craig Snow, Executive Director

Tucson HIV / AIDS Care Consortium
6601 E. Grant Rd., Suite 111
Tucson, AZ 85715
Roger Harlen

Tulsa Community AIDS Partnership
1430 S. Boulder
Tulsa, Oklahoma 74119
Janice Nicklas

Tyler AIDS Services, Inc.
P.O. Box 131293
Tyler, TX 75713
Dotti Fitchett

Unique Community Women's Clubs, Inc.
102 Kelly Ave., P.O. Box 364
Soperton, GA 30457
Eloise Dixon Phillips

United Service for AIDS Foundation
704 N. Rampart St.
New Orleans, LA 70116
Larry Sanders, Executive Director

United Spirit for AIDS, Inc.
2103 Farlow St., Suite 102
Myrtle Beach, SC 29577-3168

University Hospital Hospice
2021 Perdido St.
New Orleans, LA 70112

University of Chicago Medical Center HIV Support Group
Department of Psychiatry MC 3077
University of Chicago Medical Center
5841 S. Maryland
Chicago, IL 60637
For gay and bisexual men

Upper Manhattan Task Force on AIDS
55 W. 125th St., Suite 1103
New York, NY 10027
Mary Ida Gardner

Utah AIDS Foundation
1408 South 1100 East
Salt Lake City, UT 84105
LaDonna Moore, Executive Director

Utah AIDS Hotline
800-366-2437

Valley AIDS Council
2220 Haine Dr., Suite 33
Harlingen, TX 78550
Celia P. Garrity

Valley AIDS Network
P.O. #6
Harrisonburg, VA 22801

Vanderbilt AIDS Project
Department of Psychiatry
A-2215 Medical Center North
Nashville, TN 37232
Dr. A. Gene Copello, Director

Harold Varmus
National Institutes of Health
9000 Rockville Pike
Bethesda , MD 20892
Director of NIH

Vermont AIDS Hotline
800-882-2437

Vermont CARES
P.O. Box 5248
30 Elmwood Ave.
Burlington, VT 05402
Sylvia Racca, Coordinator

Village AIDS Day Treatment Program
133 W. 20th St.
New York, NY 10011
Patricia Rineon, Director

Virginia AIDS Hotline
800-533-4138

Virx Medical Group, Inc.
655 Sutter St., Suite 600
San Francisco, CA 94102

Visiting Nurse Association AIDS Project
2025 Gateway Pl., Suite 205
San José, CA 95110

Visual AID: Artists for AIDS Relief
530 Bush St., Suite 405
San Francisco, CA 94108
Wayne Salazar, vouchers for art supplies to professional artists with life-threatening illnesses

Visual AIDS
131 W. 24th St.
New York, NY 10011
Artists collective; organizes Day Without Art

Waldo-Knox AIDS Coalition
P.O. Box 956
Belfast, ME 04915

Walter Reed Medical Center
Henry M. Jackson Foundation
6825 16th St. N.W.
Washington, DC 20307

Washington AIDS Hotline
800-272-2437

Washington Community AIDS Program
VA Medical Center
Department of Infectious Disease
50 Irving St., N.W., Rm. 4B102
Washington, DC 20422
Fred Gordin/John Scott, community program for clinical research on AIDS

Washington County AIDS Task Force
P.O. Box 4224
Fayetteville, AR 72702
Angela Peace

Waterbury AIDS Program
402 E. Main St.
Waterbury, CT 06702
Laura Minor

West Alabama AIDS Outreach
P.O. Box 031947
Tuscaloosa, AL 35403
Deborah LeBron

West Virginia AIDS Hotline
800-642-8244

Western Colorado AIDS Project
812 Rood Ave.
Grand Junction, CO 81501
Shelly Nielsen

Western New York AIDS Program
121 W. Tupper St.
Buffalo, NY 14201-2142
Kate Gallivan

Western North Carolina AIDS Project
P.O. Box 2411
Asheville, NC 28802-2411
Jim Taylor

Western NY Regional HIV / AIDS Educational/Training Center
1050 Maryvale Dr.
Cheektowaga, NY 14225
Jane Ogilvia

Whitman Walker Clinic
1407 "S" St., N.W.
Washington, DC 20009
Peter Hawley, MD, community based clinical trials

Wichita Community Clinical AIDS Program
317 W. 11th Ave.
Wichita, KS 67203
Datrona Harnson, RN

Williamsburg AIDS Network
P.O. Box 1066
Williamsburg, VA 23187

Phill Wilson
APLA
1313 N. Vine St.
Los Angeles, CA 90028
Policy Director, AIDS Project Los Angeles

Windsor Village AIDS Ministry
6000 Heatherbrook Dr.
Houston, TX 77085
Brenda Smith

Wisconsin AIDS Hotline
800-334-AIDS

Wisconsin Community-Based Research Consortium
c/o Milwaukee AIDS Project
315 W. Court St.
Milwaukee, WI 53212
Ian Gilson

Women and AIDS Resource Network
30 3rd Ave. #212
Brooklyn, NY 11217
Yvonne Chambers, Deputy Director

Women At Risk
252 7th Ave., 11th Fl.
New York, NY 10001
June Scarlett, services for HIV positive women and those at risk, also child care and therapy

Women Being Alive
3626 Sunset Blvd.
Los Angeles, CA 90026

Women Organized to Respond to Life Threatening Diseases
P.O. Box 11535
Oakland, CA 94611

Women's AIDS Network
c/o San Francisco AIDS Foundation
P.O. Box 426182
San Francisco, CA 94101-6182

Women's AIDS Project
8240 Santa Monica Blvd.
West Hollywood, CA 90046

Women's AIDS Video Enterprise
(WAVE)
Brooklyn AIDS Task Force
465 Dean St.
Brooklyn, NY 11217-2114
Media

Women's Program of the Cascade AIDS Project
620 S.W. 5th Ave.
Portland, OR 97204

The Women's Project
2224 S. Main St.
Little Rock, AR 72206
Janet Perkins, Director

Women's Services Program of AIDS Health Project
P.O. Box 0884
San Francisco, CA 94143

Wood County AIDS Task Force
541 W. Wooster Ave.
Bowling Green, OH 43402
Janet DeLong

Wyandott County AIDS Task Force
127-A S. Sandusky Ave.
Upper Sandusky, OH 43351

Wyoming AIDS Hotline
800-327-3577

Wyoming AIDS Project
Box 9353
Casper, WY 82609
Gene Ferris, President

Yellowstone AIDS Project
3308 2nd Ave., N.
P.O. Box 1748
Billings, MT 59601
Bill Geelan, President

YHESSI
101 E. Market St.
York, PA 17401
Charlie Horns/Catherine Perez

Youth Advocates—Teen HIV Program
555 Cole St., Suite 6
San Francisco, CA 94117
Danny Keenan

Youth and AIDS Project
428 Oak Grove St.
Minneapolis, MN 55403
Youth Service Provider

YWCA AIDS Minority Community Outreach Program
YWCA Allendale Branch
700 Pierre Ave.
Shreveport, LA 71103

Athletes, Artists & Entertainers

Pedro Almodovar
El Deseo Ltd.
Calle Ruiz Perello 15
Bajo Centro
28028 Madrid, Spain
Filmmaker

Gregg Araki
Strand Productions
225 Santa Monica Blvd., Suite 810
Santa Monica, CA 90401
Independent filmmaker

Alexis Arquette
Three Arts Entertainment
7920 Sunset Blvd., Suite350
Los Angeles, CA 90046
Actor

Ron Athey
c/o L.A. Weekly
6715 Sunset Blvd.
Los Angeles, CA 90028
Performance artist

Kevyn Aucoin
c/o HarperCollins
10 E. 53th St.
New York, NY 10022
Makeup artist/Author

The B-52s
P.O. Box 506
New York, NY 10013
Recording artists

Amanda Bearse
Bragman, Nyman & Capparelli
9171 Wilshire Blvd.
Penthouse Suite
Beverly Hills, CA 90210
Actress, Married With Children

Sadie Benning
c/o Video Data Bank
112 S. Michigan Ave.
Chicago, IL 90069
Independent filmmaker

Sandra Bernhard
Levine Schneider Publicity
8730 Sunset Blvd., 6th Fl.
Los Angeles, CA 90069
Actor

Adele Bertei
1157 N. Highlands, 1st Fl.
Los Angeles, CA 90038
Recording artist

Ross Bleckner
77 White St.
New York, NY 10013
Artist

Cee Scott Brown
Art Matters Inc.
131 W. 24th St.
New York, NY 10011
Executive Vice-President

Charles Busch
114 5th Ave.
New York, NY 10011
Actor

Simon Callow
Writers & Artists Agency
924 Westwood Blvd., Suite 900
Los Angeles, CA 90024

Kate Clinton
P.O. Box 103
Provincetown, MA 02657
Comic

Wilson Cruz
c/o ABC
77 W. 66th St., 9th Fl.
New York, NY 10023
Actor

Lea Delaria
c/o Stace Nelson
820 North Genessee
Los Angeles, CA 90046
Comic

David Drake
c/o Bauman Hiller Associates
Suite 2223
New York, NY 10107

Echobelly
c/o Girly Action
270 Lafayette, Suite 1201
New York, NY 10012
Recording artists

Rob Epstein & Jeffrey Freidman
347 Delores St., #307
San Francisco, CA 94110
Documentary filmmakers

Erasure
75 Rockefeller Plaza
New York, NY 10019
Recording artists

Anneliese Estrada
DIFFA
150 W. 26th St., Suite 602
New York, NY 10010
Creative Director, DIFFA

Melissa Etheridge
400 Lafayette St.
New York, NY 10003
Recording artist

Rupert Everett
c/o Samuel Goldwyn
888 7th Ave., Ste. 2907
New York, NY 10106

Lynne Fernie and Aerlan Weissman
c/o Women Make Movies
462 Broadway, 5th Fl.
New York, NY 10013
Filmmakers, Forbidden Love

Harvey Fierstein
Greene -Siegel Promotions
8730 Sunset Blvd.
Los Angeles, CA 90069
Actor/Playwright

Fifth Column
3 Warwick Ave, Apt #1
Toronto, Ontario, M6C 1T5
Canada
Rock band

The Flirtations
c/o Christopher Malarkey
316 33rd Ave.
Seattle, WA 98122
Vocal Group

Diamanda Galas
140 W. 22nd St., Suite 10-A
New York, NY 10011
Rock opera singer

Spencer Gates
Matador Records
676 Broadway
New York, NY 10012
CEO, *Matador Records*

Gay & Lesbian Association of Choruses
4016 S.W. 57th Ave.
Portland, OR 97221
Plans annual conferences for directors

David Geffen
9130 Sunset Blvd.
Los Angeles, CA 90069
Geffen Records, CEO

Garrett Glaser
KNBC TV
3000 W. Alameda Ave.
Burbank, CA 91523
Entertainment reporter

Richard Glatzer
Strand Productions
225 Santa Monica Blvd. Suite 810
Santa Monica, CA 90401
Director, Grief

Robert Gober
c/o Distributed Art Publishers
636 Broadway, 12th Floor
New York, NY 10012
Artist

God Is My Co-Pilot
P.O. Box 490, Cooper Station
New York, NY 10276
Recording artists

Nan Goldin
334 Bowery, #3R
New York, NY 10012
Photographer

Marga Gomez
P.O. Box 460368
San Francisco, CA 94146

Fred Hersch
c/o Hellenn Greece
107 St. John's Pl.
Brooklyn, NY 11217
Jazz musician

Holly Hughes
151 1st Ave., Suite 218
New York, NY 10003
Performance artist

Indigo Girls (Amy Ray and Emily Saliers)
c/o Russell Carter Artist
Managament
315 W. Ponce de Leon Ave.
Suite 755
Decatur, GA 30030
Musicians

Bob and Rod Jackson-Paris
c/o Kenny Rahtz
Greater Talent Network
150 5th Ave., 9th Fl.
New York, NY 10011
Authors

Elton John
c/o Sarah McMullan
345 N. Maple Dr., Suite 235
Beverly Hills, CA 90210
Musician

Bill T. Jones
Bill T. Jones Arnie Zane Dance Co.
853 Broadway, Suite 1706
New York, NY 10003
Dancer/Choreographer

Isaac Julien
18 Richmond Ave.
Islington, London
England N10NF
Filmmaker

Tom Kalin
Apparatus
525 Broadway
New York, NY 10012
Filmmaker

John Kelly
425 W. 23rd St., #1E
New York, NY 10011
Choreographer/Performance artist

Tony Kushner
c/o Joyce Ketay Agency
1501 Broadway, Suite 1910
New York, NY 10036
Playwright

L7
c/o Barbara Mitchell
Slash
7381 Beverly Blvd.
Los Angeles, CA 90036
Rock band

Lady Bunny
102 Greenwich Ave., #8
New York, NY 10011
Organizer, Wigstock

k.d. lang
41 Britain St., Suite 200
Toronto, Ontario M5A 1R7
Canada
Recording artist

Lavender Light Black and People of All Colors Lesbian and Gay Gospel Choir
70A Greenwich Ave.
New York, NY 10011

Lesbian and Gay Bands of America
(LGBA)
PO Box 300788
Houston, TX 77230-0788

Doug Litwin
1519 Mission St.
San Francisco, CA 94103-2512
President, Lesbian and Gay Bands of America

Liberace Museum
1775 E. Tropicana
Las Vegas, NV 89119

Greg Louganis
c/o Jed Mattes
200 W. 72nd St., #50
New York, NY 10023
Swimmer; Author, Breaking the Surface

Terrence McNally
Manhattan Theater Club
453 W. 16th St.
New York, NY 10011
Playwright

Tyson Meade
630 Chautauqua, #2
Norman, OK 73069
Lead singer, Chainsaw Kittens

Steven Meisel
Art & Commerce
46 Wooster St., 4th Fl.
New York, NY 10012
Photographer

Meredith Monk
1540 Broadway
New York, NY 10036-4098
Composer, Atlas

Morrissey
3300 Warner Blvd.
Burbank, CA 91505
Recording Artist

Martina Navratilova
c/o Linda Dozoretz
8033 Sunset Blvd, Suite 626
Los Angeles, CA 90046
Tennis player; Author, The Total Zone

Me'shell NdegeOcello
c/o Carol Hawkes
Warner Records
75 Rockefeller Plaza
New York, NY 10019
Recording artist

Todd Oldham
120 Wooster, 3rd Fl.
New York, NY 10012
Fashion designer

Pansy Division
Jon Ginoli
P.O. Box 460885
San Francisco, CA 94146
Recording artists

Pratibha Parmar
c/o Women Make Movies
462 Broadway, 5th Fl.
New York, NY 10013
Filmmaker

Phranc
1141 26th St., Apt.B
Santa Monica, CA 90403
Singer

Pomo Afro Homos
c/o Creative Management Services
316 33rd Ave.
Seattle, WA 98122
Performance art trio

Reno
Codicow, Carroll, & Regis
680 5th Ave.
New York, NY 10019
Comedian

Herb Ritts
8748 Holloway Dr.
West Hollywood, CA 90069
Photographer

David Rousseve
280 Broadway, Suite 412
New York, NY 10007-1896
Choreographer

RuPaul
World of Wonder
1157 N. Highlands, 1st Floor
Los Angeles, CA 90038
Recording artist

San Francisco Band Foundation Inc.
Jon Sims Center for the Performing Arts
1519 Mission St.
San Francisco, CA 94103-2512

Kate Schellenbach
110 W. 14th St., #7
New York, NY 10011
Member, Luscious Jackson

Patty Schemel
c/o Gold Mountain
120 W. 44th St., Suite 704
New York, NY 10036
Drummer, Hole

John Schlesinger
1896 Rising Glenn Rd.
Los Angeles, CA 90069
Filmmaker

Jenny Shimizu
c/o Women Model Management
107 Greene St.
New York, NY 10012
Model

Ingrid Sischy
Interview
575 Broadway, 5th Floor
New York, NY 10012
Editor, Interview

Bob Smith
Bob Reid Management
4542 Gloria Ave.
Encino, CA 91436
Comedian, writer, publisher

Stephen Joshua Sondheim
65 E. 55th St., #702
New York, NY 10022
Composer

Stephen Spinella
c/o Bob Fennell
Boneau, Bryan-Brown
165 W. 46th St., Suite 600
New York, NY 10036
Actor

Michael Stipe
75 Rockefeller Plaza
New York, NY 10019
Lead singer, R.E.M.

Scott Thompson
c/o Broadway Video
25 St. Nicholas St., 4th Fl.
Toronto, Ontario M4Y 1W5
Canada
Actor, Kids in the Hall

Lily Tomlin
P.O. Box 27700
Los Angeles, CA 90027
Actress

Rose Troche & Guinevere Turner
c/o Apparatus
525 Broadway
New York, NY 10012
Filmmakers

Christine Vachon
c/o Apparatus
525 Broadway
New York, NY 10012
Film producer

Gus Van Sant
c/o Cottrell & Lindeman
7223 Beverly Blvd., Suite 203
Los Angeles, CA 90036
Filmmaker

John Waters
c/o Bill Block
ICM
8899 Beverly Blvd.
Los Angeles, CA 90048
Filmmaker

Suzanne Westenhoffer
Glenn Schwartz Management
101 W. 57th St., #6H
New York, NY 10019
Comedian

Josephine Wiggs
c/o Gold Mountain
120 W. 44th St., Suite 704
New York, NY 10036
Bassist, The Breeders

Karen Williams
26151 Lake Shore Blvd., # 2112
Euclid, OH 44132
Comic

George C. Wolfe
Joe Papp Public Theater
425 Lafayette St.
New York, NY 10003
Producer

Thalia Zedek
c/o Tim Johnston Management
123 Newburry St., 4th Fl.
Boston, MA 02116
Lead singer, Come

Bookstores

Lodestar Books
2029 11th Ave. S.
Birmingham, AL 35205

Opening Books
403 Pratt Ave., NE
Huntsville, AL 35801

Alaska Women's Bookstore
2440 E. Tudor Rd., #304
Anchorage, AK 99507-1129

Aradia Books
116 W. Cottage
Flagstaff, AZ 86002

Changing Hands Bookstore
414 S. Mill Ave.
Tempe, AZ 85281

Antigone Books
600 N. 4th Ave.
Tucson, AZ 85705

Women's Project
2224 Main St.
Little Rock, AR 72206

Wild Iris Bookstore
143A Harvard Ave.
Claremont, CA 91711

Fig Garden Bookstore
5148 N. Palm Ave.
Fresno, CA 93704

Valley Women Books & Gifts
1118 N. Fulton
Fresno, CA 93728

Boadecia's Books
398 Colusa Ave.
Kensington, CA 94707

A Different Drummer Bookshop
1027 N. Coast Hwy., #A
Laguna Beach, CA 92651

Pearls Booksellers
224 Redondo Ave.
Long Beach, CA 90803

Circus of Books
4001 Sunset Blvd.
Los Angeles, CA 90029

Lavender Books
1213 N. Highland Ave.
Los Angeles, CA 90038

Sisterhood Bookstore
1351 Westwood Blvd.
Los Angeles, CA 90024

Mama Bears
6536 Telegraph Ave.
Oakland, CA 94609

Stepping Stones
The Artifactory
226 Hamilton Ave.
Palo Alto, CA 94301

Page One: Books By & For Women
1196 E. Walnut St.
Pasadena, CA 91106

Lioness Books
2224 "J" St.
Sacramento, CA 95816

Obelisk: The Bookstore
1029 University Ave.
San Diego, CA 92103

Paradigm Women's Bookstore
3343 Adams Ave.
San Diego, CA 92116

A Different Light
489 Castro St.
San Francisco, CA 94114

Feminist Bookstore News
2358 Market St.
San Francisco, CA 94114
Newsletter

Old Wives' Tales
1009 Valencia St. at 21st St.
San Francisco, CA 94110

Sisterspirit Bookstore / Coffeehouse
175 Stockton Ave.
San José, CA 95126-2760

Choices Books & Music
901 N. De La Vina St.
Santa Barbara, CA 93101-3220

St. Maur—Bookseller
820 N. Madison
Stockton, CA 95202

A Different Light
8853 Santa Monica Blvd.
West Hollywood, CA 90069

Circus of Books
8230 Santa Monica Blvd.
West Hollywood, CA 90046

Unicorn Bookstore
8940 Santa Monica Blvd.
West Hollywood, CA 90069

Abaton Books
2525 W. Pikes Peak, Unit C
Colorado Springs, CO 80904

Book Garden
2625 E. 12th Ave.
Denver, CO 80206

Category Six Books
1029 E. 11th Ave.
Denver, CO 80218

BOOKSTORES

Inland Book Company
P.O. Box 120261
East Haven, CT 06512
Distributor

Lambda Rising Bookstore
1625 Connecticut Ave. N.W.
Washington, DC 20009-1013

Lammas Women's Books & More
1426 21st St. N.W.
Washington, DC 20036

Lambda Rising Bookstore
39 Baltimore Ave.
Rehoboth Beach, DE 19978

Outbooks
1239 E. Lasolas Blvd.
Ft. Lauderdale, FL 33301

Iris Books
802 W. University Ave.
Gainesville, FL 32601

A Bookstore Named Desire
420 Applerouth Lane
Key West, FL 33040

Lambda Passages
7545 Biscayne Blvd.
Miami, FL 33138

GW Miami Beach
718 Lincoln Road Mall
Miami Beach, FL 33139

Out & About Books
930 N. Mills Ave.
Orlando, FL 32803

Lifestyle Books
3150 5th Ave. N.
St. Petersburg, FL 33713

Rubyfruit Books
666-4 W. Tennessee St.
Tallahassee, FL 32304

Tomes & Treasures
202 S. Howard Ave.
Tampa, FL 33606

Charis Books & More
1189 Euclid Ave. N.E.
Atlanta, GA 30307

Outwrite Bookstore & Coffeehouse
931 Monroe Dr., #108
Atlanta, GA 30308

Roads Less Travelled Enterprises
3017 W. State St.
Boise, ID 83704

People Like Us Books
3321 N. Clark St.
Chicago, IL 60657

Women & Children First
5233 N. Clark St.
Chicago, IL 60640

BOOKSTORES

Pride Agenda Bookstore
1109 Westgate
Oak Park, IL 60301

Aquarius Books
116 N. Grant St.
Bloomington, IN 47408

Dreams & Swords
6503 Ferguson St.
Indianapolis, IN 46220-1148

Visions & Dreams
3143 W. Maple
Wichita, KS 67213

Hibiscus Bookstore
635 Main St.
Baton Rouge, LA 70802

Lambda Rising Bookstore
241 W. Chase St.
Baltimore, MD 21201

Thirty-First St. Bookstore Co-op
425 E. 31st St.
Baltimore, MD 21218

Food for Thought Books
106 N. Pleasant St.
Amherst, MA 01002

Glad Day Bookshop
673 Boylston St, 2nd Fl.
Boston, MA 02116

New Words
186 Hampshire St.
Cambridge, MA 02139

Radzukina's Gifts, Books & Music for Womyn
714 N. Broadway
Haverhill, MA 01832

Crones Harvest
761 Centre St.
Jamaica Plain, MA 02130

Lunaria Feminist Bookstore
90 King St.
Northhampton, MA 01060

Now Voyager
357 Commercial St.
Provincetown, MA 02657

Womencrafts
376 Commercial St.
Provincetown, MA 02657

Common Language Bookstore
215 S. 4th Ave.
Ann Arbor, MI 48104

Sons and Daughters
962 Cherry St. S.E.
Grand Rapids, MI 49506

Pandora Books for Open Minds
226 W. Lovell
Kalamazoo, MI 49007

The Real World Emporium
P.O. Box 13125
Lansing, MI 48901-3125

Chosen Books of Michigan
120 W. 4th St.
Royal Oak, MI 48067

A Brothers Touch
2327 Hennepin Ave.
Minneapolis, MN 55405

Amazon Bookstore Inc.
1612 Harmon Pl.
Minneapolis, MN 55403

Quatrefoil Library
1619 Dayton Ave.
St. Paul, MN 55104

Our World Too
11 S. Vandeventer
Saint Louis, MO 63108

Arbor Moon Alternative Bookstore
2017 "O" St.
Lincoln, NE 68502

New Realities
Old Market Passageway
1026 Howard
Omaha, NE 68102

Bright Pink Literature
P.O. Box 19360
Las Vegas, NV 89132-0360

Get Booked
4643 Paradise Rd.
Las Vegas, NV 89109

Grapevine Books
1450 S. Wells Ave.
Reno, NV 89502

Women's Words Books
902B Upper Straw Rd.
Hopkinton, NH 03229

Lady Iris
10 Ladd St.
Portsmouth, NH 03801-4010

Perrin & Treggett Booksellers
3130 Route 10 W.
Denville, NJ 07834

Pandora Book Peddlers
885 Belmont Ave.
North Haledon, NJ 07508

Tapestry Books
P.O. Box 359
Ringoes, NJ 08551-0359

Full Circle Books
2205 Silver Ave. S.E.
Albuquerque, NM 87106

Sisters' and Brothers' Bookstore
4011 Silver Ave. S.E.
Albuquerque, NM 87108-2633

Lifestyle Books
37 Central Ave.
Albany, NY 12210

A Room of Our Own
444 9th St.
Brooklyn, NY 11215

Lavender Jade's
P.O. Box 3308
Glens Falls, NY 12801

Womankind Books
5 Kivy St.
Huntington Station, NY 11746

Smedley's Bookshop
307 W. State St.
Ithaca, NY 14850

A Different Light Bookstore
151 W. 19 St.
New York, NY 10011

Judith's Room
681 Washington St.
New York, NY 10014

Oscar Wilde Bookstore
15 Christopher St.
New York, NY 10014

Wild Seeds Bookstore & Cafe
162 Crosman Terrace
Rochester, NY 14620-1830

My Sisters' Words
304 N. McBride St.
Syracuse, NY 13203

American Booksellers Association
828 S. Broadway
Tarrytown, NY 10591

Rising Moon Books & Beyond
316 East Blvd.
Charlotte, NC 28203

White Rabbit/Charlotte
314 Rensselear Ave.
Charlotte, NC 28203

Southern Sisters
411 Morris St.
Durham, NC 27701

White Rabbit Books
1833 Spring Garden St.
Greensboro, NC 27403

Crazy Ladies Bookstore
4039 Hamilton Ave.
Cincinnati, OH 45223

Pink Pyramid
36A W. Court St.
Cincinnati, OH 45202

Body Language
3291 W. 115th St.
Cleveland, OH 44111

Fan the Flames Feminist Bookstore
3387 N. High St.
Columbus, OH 43202

Rainbow Bookstore
772 N. High St.
Columbus, OH 43215

Mother Kali's Books
2001 Franklin Blvd. #5
Eugene, OR 97403

Widdershins Books
1996 SE Ladd Ave.
Portland, OR 97214

Her Story: A Women's Bookstore
2 W. Market St.
Hellam, PA 17406

Book Gallery
19 W. Mechanic St.
New Hope, PA 18938

Giovanni's Room
345 S. 12th St.
Philadelphia, PA 19107

Gertrude Stein Memorial Bookshop
1003 E. Carson
Pittsburgh, PA 15203

Visions & Voices
255 Harris Ave.
Providence, RI 02909

Meristem
930 S. Cooper
Memphis, TN 38104

Book Woman
324 E. 6th St.
Austin, TX 78701

Liberty Books
1014B N. Lamar Blvd.
Austin, TX 78703

Lobo Book Store
3204A Guadalupe
Austin, TX 78705

Crossroads Market & Bookstore
3930 Cedar Springs Rd.
Dallas, TX 75219

Lobo After Dark
4008C Cedar Springs Rd.
Dallas, TX 75219

Sources of Hope Bookstore
P.O. Box 35466
5910 Cedar Springs Rd.
Dallas, TX 75235

Inklings: An Alternative Bookshop
1846 Richmond Ave.
Houston, TX 77098

Lobo Book Store
1424C Westheimer St.
Houston, TX 77006

Ellie's Garden
2812 34th St.
Lubbock, TX 79410

Textures
5309 McCullough
San Antonio, TX 78212

Heartland Books
P.O. Box 1105 H
East Corinth, VT 05040

The Purple Moon
810 Caroline St.
Fredericksburg, VA 22401

Max Images
808 Spotswood Ave.
Norfolk, VA 23512

Pride Bookstore
P.O. Box 1026
Norfolk, VA 23501-1026

Phoenix Rising
19 N. Belmont Ave.
Richmond, VA 23221

Outright Books/Rainbow Cafe
485 S. Independence Blvd., #111
Virginia Beach, VA 23452

Beyond the Closet Bookstore
1501 Belmont Ave.
Seattle, WA 98122

Imprints Bookstore
917 1/2 N. 2nd St.
Tacoma, WA 98403

A Room of One's Own
317 W. Johnson St.
Madison, WI 53703

Afterwords
2710 N. Murray
Milwaukee, WI 53211

Business

Above and Beyond Travel
3568 Sacramento St.
San Francisco, CA 94118
Kevin Kailey

Addington, Eubank and Associates
IDS Financial Services
14800 Landmark Blvd., Suite 800
Dallas, TX 75240
S. Kreg Bartley

Alamo Business Council
P.O. Box 15481
San Antonio, TX 78212

Alternate Professionals Together
10308 Metcalf Ave., Suite 128
Overland Park, KS 66212

Angle Media
2200 N. Lamar, Suite 208
Dallas, TX 75202
Todd Cunningham

Architectural Services
1133 Connecticut Ave. N.W.
Suite 800
Washington, DC 20036
David Schwarz, Architect

Atlantis Events, Inc.
8335 Sunset Blvd.
West Hollywood, CA 90069
Thom Kennedy and Rich Campbell

Castwood Insurance Agency, Ltd.
250 Hempstead Ave.
Malverne, NY 11565
Jeffrey Wodicka and Neil Castro

Christopher St. Financial
80 Wall St., #1214
New York, NY 10005
Robert Costellano

Colorado Business Council
P.O. Box 480794
Denver, CO 80248-0794

Community Spirit
c/o Overlooked Opinions
3162 Broadway
Chicago, IL 60657
Jeffrey Vitale, long distance company

Cream City Business Association
7200 W. Center St.
Milwaukee, WI 53210

Desert Business Association
P.O. Box 773
Palm Springs, CA 92263

Detour Publications, Inc.
1016 3rd Ave.
Sacramento, CA 95818
Jon Nicholson

Dominion Ventures
84 State St., 10th Fl.
Boston, MA 02109
Geoff "Chester" Woolley, Founder & CEO

Don't Panic
98 Christopher St.
New York, NY 10014
Business, paraphernalia

Don't Panic
11264 Playa Court
Culver City, CA 90230

EIDolon
156 5th Ave.
New York, NY 10010
Dennis Lonergan and John Graves

Equidex, Inc.
19 Sutter St.
San Francisco, CA 94104
Jim Hormel

Gallin Morey Associates
8730 Sunset Blvd., PH West
Los Angeles, CA 90069
Sandy Gallin

Gay Entertainment Television
7 E. 17th St.
New York , NY 10003
Marvin Schwam, Founder

Gay & Lesbian Business & Professional Association
940 Royal St., Box 350
New Orleans, LA 70116

Gay & Lesbian Business & Professionals Guild
P.O. Box 8392
White Plains, NY 10602-8392

GBLA Productions
912 S. Croft Ave., #104
Los Angeles, CA 90069
Sandy Sachs

David Geffen
9230 W. Sunset Blvd.
Los Angeles, CA 90069

Golden Gate Business Association
1550 California St., #L1
San Francisco, CA 94107

Greater Boston Business Council
P.O. Box 1059
Boston, MA 02117-1059

Greater San Diego Business Association
P.O. Box 33848
San Diego, CA 92163-3848

Greater Seattle Business Association
2033 6th Ave., #804
Seattle, WA 98121-2526

Impressions Unlimited
612 Fleming St.
Key West, FL 33040
Bill Hawkins

Indianapolis Business Outreach Association
P.O. Box 501915
Indianapolis, IN 46250

International Gay Travel Association
P.O. Box 4974
Key West, FL 33041
Kevin Kailey

Islander's Club
183 W. 10th St.
New York, NY 10014
Shelley Schusterhoff

Kennedy Travel
267-10 Hillside Ave.
Floral Park, NY 11004
Fred Kohn

Key West Business Guild
P.O. Box 1208
Key West, FL 33041

Krost Chapin Management
9911 W. Pico Blvd., PH#1
Los Angeles, CA 90035
Barry Krost

Men on Vacation
1111 Ft. Stockton, Suite E
San Diego, CA 92103
Michael Acker

Metropolitan Business Association
P.O. Box 150364
Altamonte Springs, FL

Motor Home Dealers of America
300 Orchard City Dr., Suite 234
Campbell, CA 95008
G. Lee Fitzgerald, CEO

Mulryan / Nash
161 Ave. of the Americas
New York, NY 10013

Multi-Travel & Tours Inc.
855 Washington Ave.
Miami Beach, FL 33139
Francisco Angulo

Odyssey Travel
P.O. Box 8209
Rancho Santa Fe, CA 92067
Bill Green

Olivia Women's Cruises & Resorts
4400 Market St.
Oakland, CA 94608
Judy Dlugacz, travel company

Olympus Vacations
8424 Santa Monica Blvd., #721
West Hollywood, CA 90069
Michael Reilly

Our Family Abroad
40 W. 57th., Suite 430
New York, NY 10019
Peter Schulze

Overlooked Opinions
3162 Broadway
Chicago, IL 60657
Jeffrey Vitale

Palm Springs Gay Tourism Council
P.O. Box 2885
Palm Springs, CA 92263

PointOne Management Company
6350 Pennsylvania Ave. S.E.
Washington, DC 20003
John Unger

Portland Area Business Association
P.O. Box 4724
Portland, OR 97208

Pride Network
c/o TransNational
133 Federal St., Suite 1R
Boston, MA 02199-0001
Michele M. Frost

Prime Access
18 W. 27th St., 8th Fl.
New York, NY 10001
Howard Buford, Founder

Provincetown Business Guild
P.O. Box 421
Provincetown, MA 02657

Quark, Inc.
1800 Grant St.
Denver, CO 80203
Tim Gill, Founder, Quark, Inc.

Robin Tyler's Women's Tours Cruises Events
15842 Chase St.
North Hills, CA 91343
Robin Tyler

Ron / Owen & Partners
345 Hudson St.
New York, NY 10014
Ron Antman and Owen Frager

RSVP Travel Productions
2800 University Ave. SE
Minneapolis, MN 55414-4697
Kevin Mossier

Shocking Gray
1216 E. Euclid
San Antonio, TX 78212
Cindy Cesnalis, Founder

South Beach Business Guild
718 Lincoln Rd.
Miami Beach, FL 33139

South Carolina Gay & Lesbian Business Guild
SCGLBG
P.O. Box 7913
Columbia, SC 29202-7913

St. Louis Business Guild
P.O. Box 16822
St. Louis, MO 63105

Steve Berman Productions
3231B Buford Hwy.
Atlanta, GA 30329
Steve Berman

Strubco
349 W. 12th St.
New York, NY 10014
Sean Strub, Founder

Tampa Bay Business Guild
1222 S. Dale Mabry, #656
Tampa, FL 33629

Ulysses Press
3286 Adeline St., #1
Berkeley, CA 94703

Wall St. Project
217 E. 85th St., #162
New York, NY 10028

Winmark Concepts
1711 Connecticut Ave. N.W.
Washington, DC 20009
Andrew Isen

Working Assets Capital Management
1 Harbour Pl., Suite 525
Portsmouth, NH 03801
Sofia Collier

Community Centers

Vancouver Gay and Lesbian Center
1170 Bute St.
Vancouver, BC V6E 1Z6
Canada

Association of Lesbians, Gays and Bisexuals of Ottawa Centre
P.O. Box 2919, Station D
Ottawa, ON K1P 5W9 Canada

Pink Triangle Services
P.O. Box 3043, Station D
Ottawa, ON K1P 6H6 Canada

Lambda Resource Center
205 32nd St. S.
Birmingham, AL 35255

Lesbian and Gay Community Center
3136 N. 3rd Ave.
Phoenix, AZ 85013
Bonnie Demeth

Lesbian and Gay Community Switchboard
P.O. Box 16423
Phoenix, AZ 85011
Bonnie Demeth

Wingspan: Tucson's Lesbian, Gay & Bisexual Community Center
422 N. 4th Ave.
Tucson, AZ 85705
Ken Godat, president

Pacific Center for Human Growth
2712 Telegraph Ave.
Berkeley, CA 94705
Akaya Windwood

Gay & Lesbian Resource Center of Ventura County
363 Mobil Ave.
Camarillo, CA 93011
Claire Connelly

Stonewall Alliance of Chico
P.O. Box 8855
Chico, CA 95927

Gay and Lesbian Center of Orange County
12832 Garden Grove Blvd., Suite A
Garden Grove, CA 92643
Dan Wooldridge

The Center (Long Beach)
2017 E. 4th St.
Long Beach, CA 90814
Rich Morrissey

Los Angeles Gay and Lesbian Community Services Center
1625 N. Hudson Ave.
Los Angeles, CA 90028-9998
Lorri Jean

Pomona / San Gabriel Valley Gay & Lesbian Coalition
281 S. Thomas, Suite 505
Pomona, CA 91766-1704

South Bay Center: The Lesbian, Gay and Bi Community Organization
P.O. Box 2777
2009 Artesia Blvd., Suite A
Redondo Beach, CA 90278
Mary Parrish

Lambda Community Center
1931 "L" St.
Sacramento, CA 95816
Joanna Cassese

Spectrum, Center for Lesbian, Gay and Bisexual Concerns
1000 Sir Francis Drake Blvd., #10
San Anselmo, CA 94960
John Graykoski, Interim Executive Director

Gay and Lesbian Community Services Center
P.O. Box 6333
San Bernardino, CA 94212-6333

The Lesbian & Gay Men's Community Center
3916 Normal St.
San Diego, CA 92103
Karen Marshall

Deaf Gay & Lesbian Center
25 Taylor St.
San Francisco, CA 94102

San Francisco Community Center Project
3543 18th St., Box 21
San Francisco, CA 94110
Ken Bukowski

Women's Building
3543 18th St.
San Francisco, CA 94110
Shoshana Rosenberg

Billy DeFrank Lesbian & Gay Community Center
175 Stockton Ave.
San José, CA 95126
Dr. Kurtis Lile

The Gay & Lesbian Resource Center
126 E. Haley St., Suite A-17
Santa Barbara, CA 93101
Derek Gordon

Lesbian, Gay, Bisexual & Transgendered Community Center
1338 Commerce Lane
Santa Cruz, CA 95060
Kwai Lam, Co-chair

Aspen Gay and Lesbian Community Center
P.O. Box 3143
Aspen, CO 81612-3143

Pikes Peak Gay & Lesbian Community Center
P.O. Box 607
Colorado Springs, CO 80901-0607

Gay & Lesbian Association
550 Palmer St., Suite 103
Delta, CO 81416
Terry Salisbury

Gay, Lesbian and Bisexual Community Services Center of Colorado
1245 E. Colfax, Suite 125
Denver, CO 80218
Cheryl Schwartz

Lambda Community Center
155 N. College Ave., #219
Fort Collins, CO 80524

Triangle Community Center, Inc.
25 Van Zant St.
E. Norwalk, CT 06855
Michael Pavlicin

Gay, Lesbian & Bisexual Community Center
1841 Broad St.
Hartford, CT 06114-1780

Griffin Community Center
214 Market St.
Wilmington, DE 19801

The Center of Florida
P.O. Box 2820
Belleview, FL 34421

Gay and Lesbian Community Center
P.O. Box 4567
Ft. Lauderdale, FL 33304
Alan Shubert

Gainesville Gay Switchboard
P.O. Box 12002
Gainesville, FL 32604
Doug Dinkle

Lesbian Gay Community Association
P.O. Box 27061
Jacksonville, FL 32205
Alyn Wambeke, President

Lesbian, Gay & Bisexual Community Center
1335 Alton Rd.
Miami Beach, FL 33139-3811
Mitchell Haymes

Gay and Lesbian Community Services
714 E. Colonial Dr.
Orlando, Fl 32853-3446
Bart Zarcone

Gay Hotline, Inc.
1222 S. Dale Mabry, #608
Tampa, FL 33629

The Center / Compass Incorporated
2677 Forest Hill Blvd., #106
West Palm Beach, FL
33405-5941
Lisa McWhorter

Atlanta Gay and Lesbian Community Center
63 12th St. N.E.
Atlanta, GA 30309
Ken Lillich

Atlanta Lambda Community Center
P.O. Box 15180
Atlanta, GA 30333
Sandye Locke, David Herman

Gay & Lesbian Community Services Center
1820 University Ave., 2nd Fl.
Honolulu, HI 96822
Dan McInerney, Reinette Cooper

The Community Center
P.O. Box 323
Boise, ID 83701

Horizons Community Services, Inc.
961 W. Montana
Chicago, IL 60614
Thomas Buchanan, Executive Director

Midwest Men's Center
P.O. Box 2547
Chicago, IL 60690
Earl Welther, Mark Johnson

The Les-Bi-Gay Community Center of Chicago
3023 N. Clark St., Suite 747
Chicago, IL 60657
Dale Muehler

Oak Park Lesbian & Gay Association
P.O. Box 0784
Oak Park, IL 60303

Up the Stairs Community Center
3426 Broadway
Fort Wayne, IN 46807

Gay and Lesbian Resource Center
P.O. Box 1643
Cedar Rapids, IA 52406-1643
Kate Saller, Bill Arensborf

Gay and Lesbian Resource Center
4211 Grand Ave.
Des Moines, IA 50312

Women's Resource & Action Center
130 N. Madison
Iowa City, IA 52242
Monique DiCarlo, Coordinator

The Center
P.O. Box 1357
Wichita, KS 67201

Lesbian & Gay Community Center of New Orleans
816 N. Rampart St.
New Orleans, LA 70116
Renee Parke, Clarke Broel, Co-chairs

St. Louis Community Center
1022 Barracks St.
New Orleans, LA 70116
Ellen McNair, Director

Northern Lambda Nord
P.O. Box 990
Caribou, ME 04736

Bisexual Resource Center
95 Berkeley St., Suite 613
Boston, MA 02116
Wayne Bryant

Gay & Lesbian Community Center of Baltimore
241 W. Chase St.
Baltimore, MD 21201
Gilbert L. Morrisette, President

Affirmations Lesbian & Gay Community Center
195 W. Nine Mile Rd., Suite 106
Ferndale, MI 48220
Jan Stevenson, Executive Director

Lesbian & Gay Community Network of Western Michigan
909 Cherry St. S.E.
Grand Rapids, MI 49506-1403

Kalamazoo Gay & Lesbian Resource Center
P.O. Box 1532
Kalamazoo, MI 49005-1532

Aurora: A Northland Lesbian Center
The Building for Women
32 E. 1st St., #104
Duluth, MN 55802
Laura Stolle, Coordinator

Northland Gay Men's Center
Temple Opera Block, #309
8 N. 2nd Ave. E.
Duluth, MN 55802

Brian Coyle Community Center
420 15th Ave. S.
Minneapolis, MN 55454
Bob Farwley, Director

District 202
2524 Nicollet Ave. S.
Minneapolis, MN 55404
Michael Kaplan, Executive Director

G.L. Friendly, Inc. Community Center
311 Caillavet St.
Biloxi, MS 39530
April Richards/Todd Emerson

Greater St. Louis Lesbian, Gay, Bisexual and Transgender Community Center Project
P.O. Box 4589
St. Louis, MO 63108
Mark Moloney, Office Coordinator

Gay & Lesbian Community Center of Las Vegas
P.O. Box 60301
Las Vegas, NV 89160

Gay & Lesbian Community Center of Northern Nevada
Reno, NV
Christine Viconti

Gay & Lesbian Community Center of New Jersey
515 Cookman Ave.
Asbury Park, NJ 07712
Richard Norve, President

Rainbow Place of South Jersey
1103 N. Broad St.
Woodbury, NJ 08096
Allen Reese

Common Bond, Inc.
4013 Silver Ave. S.E.
Albuquerque, NM 87108
P.J. Sadillo

Capital District Gay and Lesbian Community Center
332 Hudson Ave.
Albany, NY 12201-0131
Bill Pape, President of the Board

The Women's Building
79 Central Ave.
Albany, NY 12206-3001
Deanne Grimaldi, Executive Director

The S.P.A.C.E.
213 State St.
Binghamton, NY 13901

Shades of Lavender
295 9th St.
Brooklyn, NY 11215
Amanda Lichtenberg

The Long Island Center
Unitarian Universalist Church
223 Stewart St.
Garden City, NY 11530

Lesbian and Gay Community Services Center
208 W. 13th St.
New York, NY 10011-7799
Richard Burns, Executive Director

Gay Alliance of the Genesee Valley
179 Atlantic Ave.
Rochester, NY 14607-1255
Tanya Smolinsky, Director

The Loft: The Lesbian and Gay Community Services Center, Inc.
P.O. Box 1513
White Plains, NY 10602-1513
Lester Goldstein, Co-director

The Women's Center
210 Henderson
Chapel Hill, NC 27514

Our Own Place
P.O. Box 11732
Durham, NC 27703

Greater Cincinnati Gay / Lesbian Center
P.O. Box 19158
Cincinnati, OH 45219

Lesbian and Gay Community Service Center
P.O. Box 6177
Cleveland, OH 44101

Stonewall Community Center
P.O. Box 10814
Columbus, OH 43201-7814
Phyllis Gorman

Lorain Lesbian / Gay Center
P.O. Box 167
Lorain, OH 44052

Mentor Center
P.O. Box 253
Mentor, OH 44061-0251

Herland Sister Resources
2312 N.W. 39th
Oklahoma City, OK 73112

Oasis Gay & Lesbian Community Resource Center
2135 N.W. 39th St.
Oklahoma City, OK 73112
Bruce DeVault, Director

Lesbian Community Project
P.O. Box 5931
Portland, OR 97228
LaVerne Lewis

Oregon Gay & Lesbian Cultural Resource Center Task Force
P.O. Box 6012
Portland, OR 97228
Carla "KC" Hanson

Phoenix Rising
620 S.W. 5th Ave., #710
Portland, OR 97204-1422

Penguin Place: Gay / Lesbian Community Center of Philadelphia
201 S. Camac St.
Philadelphia, PA 19107

Voyage House, Inc.
1431 Lombard St.
Philadelphia, PA 19146-1650

Gay & Lesbian Community Center
P.O. Box 5441
Pittsburgh, PA 15206

Coalicion Puertorriquena de Lesbianas y Homosexuales
Apartado 1003
Estacion Viejo San Juan
San Juan, PR 00902-1003

South Carolina Gay & Lesbian Community Center
1108 Woodrow St.
Columbia, SC 29205
Matt Tischler

Memphis Gay & Lesbian Community Center
P.O. Box 41074
Memphis, TN 38174-1074
Charles Butler

The Center for Lesbian & Gay Community Services
703 Berry Rd.
Nashville, TN 37204-2803

Gay and Lesbian Community Center
2701 Reagan St.
Dallas, TX 75219
John Thomas

Lambda Services
P.O. Box 31321
El Paso, TX 79931-0321

Community Outreach Center
P.O. Box 64746
Lubbock, TX 79464-4746

The Resource Center
121 W. Woodlawn
San Antonio, TX 78212

Utah Stonewall Center
770 South 300 West
Salt Lake City, UT 84101

Triangle Services Center
P.O. Box 11471
Norfolk, VA 23517

Lesbian Resource Center
1808 Bellevue Ave., Suite 204
Seattle, WA 98122-1932
Valerie Reuther, Executive Director

The United
14 W. Mifflin St., Suite 103
Madison, WI 53703
Jane Vanderbosch, Administrative Coordinator

Fashion

Victor Alfaro
130 Barrow St., Suite 105
New York, NY 10014

James Arpad-Original Pave Inc.
54 W. 39th St.
New York, NY 10018

Mark Badgley
Badgley Mischka
525 7th Ave., 14th Fl.
New York, NY 10018

Jeffrey Banks
15 E. 26th St. #1811
New York, NY 10010

John Bartlett
48 W. 21th St.
New York, NY 10010

Bradley Bayou
2400 W. 35th St., Suite 501
New York, NY 10001

Ron Chereskin
18 E. 48th St.
New York, NY 10017

David Cohen
David, Inc.
65 W. 36th St., 6th Fl.
New York, NY 10019

Victor Costa
7600 Ambassador Row
Dallas, TX 75247

Louis Dell'Olio
300 E. 33rd St.
New York, NY 10016

Stephen DiGeronimo
202 W. 40th St.
New York, NY 10018

Raymond Dragon
126 7th Ave.
New York, NY 10011

Mr. Fabrice
24 W. 57th St.
New York, NY 10019

Jean Paul Gaultier
30 Rue Du Faubourg
Saint Antoine
Paris, France 75012

Stan Herman
Stan Herman Studio
80 W. 40th St.
New York, NY 10018

Marc Jacobs
113 Spring St., 3rd Fl.
New York, NY 10012

Michael Katz
Michael Katz, Ltd.
13 E. 17th St., 7th Fl.
New York, NY 10003

Michael Kors
550 7th Ave., 7th Fl.
New York, NY 10018

Byron Lars
202 W. 40th St., 9th Fl.
New York, NY 10018

Bob Mackie
431 S. Fairfax
Los Angeles, CA 90069
Designer

Gene Meyer
625 Broadway, #11F
New York, NY 10012

James Mischka
Badgley Mischka
525 7th Ave., 14th Fl.
New York, NY 10018

Isaac Mizrahi
104 Wooster St.
New York, NY 10012

Thierry Mugler
4 W. 58th St., 9th Fl.
New York, NY 10019

Todd Oldham
120 Wooster St., 3rd Fl.
New York, NY 10012
Fashion designer

Susan Peterson
530 7 Ave., 25 Fl.
New York, NY 10018
Designer, Kenar

Fernando Sanchez
5 W. 19th St.
New York, NY 10011

Ingrid Sischy
Interview
575 Broadway, 5th Fl.
New York, NY 10012
Fashion Writer / Editor

Eric Smith
World Love Prod.
224 W. 29th St.
New York, NY 10001

Koos Van Den Akker
Koos & De Wilde Ltd.
550 7th Ave.
New York, NY 10018

Fundraising/ Philanthropy

A Territory Resource
Carol Pencke
603 Stewart St., #221
Seattle, WA 08101
Funder of gay, lesbian, and AIDS issues

Aaron Diamond Foundation
Vincent McGee
1270 Ave. of the Americas
Suite 2624
New York, NY 10020
Funder of gay/lesbian issues

AIDS Foundation of Chicago
Karen Fishman,
Executive Director
1332 N. Halsted St., Suite 303
Chicago, Illinois 60622-9904
Funder concerned about AIDS

American Foundation for AIDS Research (AmFAR)
Dr. Ellen Cooper, Director of Clinical Research and Information
6000 Executive Blvd., Suite 606
Rockville, MD 20852
Funder concerned about AIDS

American Foundation for AIDS Research (AmFAR)
733 3rd Ave., 12th Fl.
New York, NY 10017
Ardis Cheng, Program Manager, Basic Research; Jerome Radwin, Senior Vice President; Rev. Margaret Reinfeld, Director of Social and Behavioral Research and Information, Funder concerned about AIDS

An Uncommon Legacy Foundation
Vivian Shapiro
147 W. 79th St., Suite 4A
New York, NY 10024
Funder of gay/lesbian issues

Appalachian Community Fund
Wendy Johnson
517 Union Ave., #206
Knoxville, TN 37902
Funder of gay/lesbian issues

Arkansas Community Foundation
Karen Moore
Central Arkansas Community AIDS Partnership
700 S. Rock St.
Little Rock, AR 72201-3257
Funder concerned about AIDS

Astraea National Lesbian Action Fund
Katherine Acey
666 Broadway, Suite 520
New York, NY 10012
Funder of gay/lesbian issues

Babcock Foundation
Mary Reynolds
Sandra Mikush
102 Reynolda Village
Winston-Salem, NC 27106-5123
Funder of gay/lesbian issues

Beatty Trust
Helen Groome
Patricia Kling
P.O. Box 7899
Philadelphia, PA 19101-7899

Ben & Jerry's Foundation
Ellen Furnari
P.O. Box 299
Waterbury, VT 05676-0299
Funder of gay/lesbian issues

Boston Foundation
Anna Faith Jones
1 Boston Pl., 24th Fl.
Boston, MA 02108
Funder of gay/lesbian issues

Boston Women's Fund
Hayat Iman
31 James Ave., # 902
Boston, MA 02116
Funder of gay/lesbian issues

Bread and Roses Community Fund
Judy Claude
924 Cherry St., 2nd Fl.
Philadelphia. PA 19107
Funder of gay/lesbian issues

Bremer Foundation
Otto Lynda Miner
445 Minnesota St., Suite 2000
St. Paul, MN 55101-2107
Funder of gay/lesbian issues

Broadway Cares / Equity Fights AIDS
Zach Manna
Executive Director
56 W. 57th St., 4th Fl.
New York, NY 10019
Funder concerned about AIDS

Brother Help Thyself
Bruce Forchheimer
P.O. Box 23499
Washington, D.C. 20020
Funder of gay/lesbian issues

Broward Community Foundation
Jan Crocker, Executive Director
Broward AIDS Partnership
2601 Oakland Park Blvd., Suite 202
Ft Lauderdale, FL 33306
Funder concerned about AIDS

California Community Foundation
Jack Shakely
606 S. Olive St., #2400
Los Angeles, CA 90014
Funder of gay/lesbian issues

Catalyst Project
Tim Gibbs
P.O. Box 30050
Wilmington, DE 19805
Funder of gay/lesbian issues

Chase Manhattan Bank
Steve Gelston
1 Chase Manhattan Plaza, 9th Fl.
New York, NY 10081
Funder of gay/lesbian issues

Chicago Community Trust
Sandy Cheers
222 N. LaSalle St., Suite #1400
Chicago, IL 60601
Funder of gay/lesbian issues

Chicago Foundation for Women
Marianne Philbin
230 W. Superior, #400
Chicago, IL 60610-3536
Funder of gay/lesbian issues

Chicago Resource Center
Mary Ann Snyder
104 S. Michigan, Suite 1220
Chicago, IL 60603
Funder of gay/lesbian issues

Chinook Fund
Laura Goldin
2412 W. 32nd Ave.
Denver, CO 80211
Funder of gay/lesbian issues

Citicorp
Paul M. Ostergard
850 3rd Ave., 13th Fl., Zone 10
New York, NY 10043
Funder of gay/lesbian issues

Classical Action
Charles Hamlen,
Executive Director
165 W. 46th St., Suite 1309
New York, NY 10036
Funder concerned about AIDS

Cleveland Foundation
Steven A. Minter
1400 Hanna Building
Cleveland, OH 44115-2001
Funder of gay/lesbian issues

Colin Higgins Foundation
Ellen Friedman
1388 Sutter St., Suite 1010
San Francisco, CA 94109
Funder of gay/lesbian issues

The Community Foundation for the Capital Region
Judith Lyons, Executive Director
P.O. Box 3198
Albany, NY 12203-0198
Funder concerned about AIDS

Community Foundation of New Jersey
Helena Hansen, Program Officer
New Jersey AIDS Partnership
P.O. Box 317, Knox Hill Rd.
Morristown, NJ 07963-0317
Funder concerned about AIDS

The Community Foundation Serving Richmond & Central Virginia
Darcy Oman, Executive Director
Richmond AIDS Partnership Fund
9211 Forest Hill Ave., Suite 109
Richmond, VA 23235
Funder concerned about AIDS

Community Service Council of Greater Tulsa
Janice Nicklas, Senior Planner
Tulsa Community AIDS Partnership
1430 S. Boulder
Tulsa, OK 74119
Funder concerned about AIDS

Community Shares of Wisconsin / Liesel Blockstein Community Grants
Denise Matyka
14 W. Mifflin St., Suite 314
Madison, WI 53703
Funder of gay/lesbian issues

Corestates Corporate Giving Program
John Whealin
Community Development Dept,
P.O. Box 7618/1-9-2-52
Philadelphia, PA 19101
Funder of gay/lesbian issues

Council of Fashion Directors of America
Fern Mallis, Executive Director
1412 Broadway, Suite 1714
New York, NY 10018
Funder concerned about AIDS

Cream City Foundation, Inc.
William Frank
P.O. Box 204
Milwaukee, WI 53201
Funder of gay/lesbian issues

Crossroads Fund
Alice Cottingham
3411 W. Diversey, #20
Chicago, IL 60647
Funder of gay/lesbian issues

Dade Community Foundation
Ruth Shack, President
200 S. Biscayne Blvd., Suite 2780
Miami, FL 33123-2343
Funder concerned about AIDS

David Geffen Foundation
Andy Spahn
9130 Sunset Blvd.
Los Angeles, CA 90069
Funder of gay/lesbian and AIDS issues

Dayton Hudson Foundation
Vivian Stuck
777 Nicollet Mall
Minneapolis, MN 55402-2055
Funder of gay/lesbian issues

Design Industries Foundation Fighting AIDS (DIFFA)
Rosemary Kuropat
Executive Director
150 W. 26th St., Suite 602
New York, NY 10001

Dietrich Foundation
William Dietrich
1811 Chestnut St. #304
Philadelphia, PA 19103
Funder of gay/lesbian issues

Digital Equipment Corporation
Jane Hamel
111 Powder Mill Rd.
MSO1-1/b14
Maynard, MA 01754
Funder of gay/lesbian issues

The Diller Foundation
Eva Montfort
10345 W. Olympic Blvd.
Los Angeles, CA 90064
Funder of gay/lesbian issues

Dolfinger-McMahon Foundation
Marlene Valcich
1 Liberty Pl.
Philadelphia, PA 19103-7396
Funder of gay/lesbian issues

El Paso Community Foundation
Dolores Gutierrez Gross
Program Officer
1616 Texas Commerce Bank Bldgs.
El Paso, TX 79901
Funder concerned about AIDS

Elton John AIDS Foundation
John Scott
Executive Director & President
1249 Stillwood Dr.
Atlanta, GA 30306
Funder concerned about AIDS

Escheated Estates Fund - D.C.
Kathy Arnold
Office of the Secretary
1 Judiciary Sq.
441 4th St. N.W., Suite 1130
Washington, D.C. 20001
Funder of gay/lesbian issues

Family AIDS Network
Mary Fisher, Founder
1707 L St., N.W., Suite 1010
Washington, DC 20036
Funder concerned about AIDS

Fels Fund
Samuel S. Helen Cunningham
1616 Walnut St., Suite 800
Philadelphia, PA 19103
Funder of gay/lesbian issues

Flower Foundation
P.O. Box 602
Northampton, MA 01061
Funder of gay/lesbian issues

Foundation for the Carolinas
William L. Spencer
President and CFO
P.O. Box 34769
Charlotte, NC 28234-4769
Funder concerned about AIDS

Foundation of the Carolinas
Donna Arrington
The Regional HIV/AIDS Consortium
301 S. Brevard St.
Charlotte, NC 28202
Funder concerned about AIDS

The Foundation of Greater Greensboro
Jean Goodman, Grants & Projects Manager
Guilford Community AIDS Partnership
100 Elm St., Suite 307
Greensboro, NC 27401-2638
Funder concerned about AIDS

Fund for Southern Communities
Joan Garner
552 Hill St. S.E.
Atlanta, GA 30312
Funder of gay/lesbian issues

Fund of the Four Directions
Gary Schwartz
8 W. 40th St., 10th Fl.
New York, NY 10018
Funder of gay/lesbian issues

Funders Concerned About AIDS
Michael Seltzer
310 Madison Ave., Suite 1630
New York, NY 10017

Global Fund for Women
Virginia Wright
2480 Sand Hill Rd. #100
Menlo Park, CA 94025-6941
Funder of gay/lesbian issues

Gramercy Park Foundation
Norman Motechin
Zemlock, Levy, Bick & Karnbad
225 Broadway
New York, NY 10007
Funder of gay/lesbian issues

The Greater Cedar Rapids Foundation
Martha Bentley, Program Officer
Iowa Community AIDS Partnership
101 2nd St. S.E., Suite 306
Cedar Rapids, IA 52401
Funder concerned about AIDS

The Greater Harrisburg Foundation
Sandy Pepinsky, Program Officer
The AIDS Alliance for Greater Harrisburg - Communities in Partnership
121 State St.
Harrisburg, PA 17108-0678

Greater Houston Women's Foundation
Linda May
3040 Post Oak Blvd., #350
Houston, TX 77056
Funder of gay/lesbian issues

Greater Richmond Community Fund
Darcy Oman
9211 Forst Hill Ave., #109
Richmond, VA 23235
Funder of gay/lesbian issues

Greater Seattle Business Associations Scholarship Fund
2033 6th Ave., Suite 804
Seattle, WA 98121
Funder of gay/lesbian issues

Greater Wichita Community Foundation
James D. Moore, Executive Director
151 N. Main St., Suite 860
Wichita, KS 67202
Funder concerned about AIDS

Green Mountain Fund for Popular Struggle
Ann Lipsitt
RR1, Box 295
Westford, VT 05494
Funder of gay/lesbian issues

Gund Foundation
Judith Simpson
1845 Guildhall Bldg.
45 Prospect Ave.
West Cleveland, OH 44115
Funder of gay/lesbian issues

Harmony Women's Fund
Joan Drury
P.O. Box 300105
Minneapolis, MN 55403
Funder of gay/lesbian issues

Hartford Foundation for Public Giving
85 Gillett St.
Hartford, CT 06105
Michael R. Bangser, Executive Director; Beverly Boyle, Coordinator Greater Hartford AIDS Consortium, Funder concerned about AIDS

Haymarket People's Fund
Tommie Harris
42 Seaverns Ave.
Boston, MA 02130
Funder of gay/lesbian issues

Headwaters Fund
Steve Newcom
122 W. Franklin Ave.
Minneapolis, MN 55404
Funder of gay/lesbian issues

The Health Foundation of Greater Indianapolis
Betty Wilson, Executive Director
401 Marott Center
342 Massachusetts Ave.
Indianapolis, IN 46204
Funder concerned about AIDS

Heart of America United Way
Gina Pulliam, Group Vice President
Integrated Community-Wide Relations
Heart of America Community AIDS Partnership
1080 Washington St.
Kansas City, MO 64105
Funder concerned about AIDS

Hilles Fund
Judith Bardes
P.O. Box 8777
Philadelphia, PA 19101-8777
Funder of gay/lesbian issues

Holding Our Own
Naomi Jaffe
79 Central Ave.
Albany, NY 12206
Funder of gay/lesbian issues

Hollywood Supports
Richard Jennings
Executive Director
8455 Beverly Blvd., Suite 305
Los Angeles, CA 90048
Funder concerned about AIDS

Horizons Foundation
Doug Braley
870 Market St., #718
San Francisco, CA 94102
Funder of gay/lesbian issues

Indiana State Department of Health, Operational Services Commission
Dennis L. Stover
1330 W. Michigan St.
Indianapolis, IN 46202
Funder concerned about AIDS

Jerome Foundation
Cindy Gehrig
W1050 First National
Bank Building
332 Minnesota St.
St. Paul, MN 55101-1312
Funder of gay/lesbian issues

Jules and Doris Stein Foundation
Linda Valliant
P.O. Box 30
Beverly Hills, CA 90213
Funder of gay/lesbian issues

Kent Atwater
Hope Annan
101 Springer Building
3411 Silverside Rd.
Wilmington, DE 19810
Funder of gay/lesbian issues

Kongsgaard-Goldman Foundation
Martha Kongsgaard
4408 Beech Drive, S.W.
Seattle, WA 98116
Funder of gay/lesbian issues

Kresge Foundation
Alfred Taylor
3215 W. Bix Beaver Rd.
Troy, MI 48007
Funder of gay/lesbian issues

Levi Strauss Foundation
Deborah Wallace
1155 Battery St.
San Francisco, CA 94120
Funder of gay/lesbian issues

Liberty Hill
Margarita Ramirez
1316 3rd St.
Promenade, Rm. B-4
Santa Monica, CA 90401
Funder of gay/lesbian issues

Lifebeat
Tim Rosta
810 7th Ave., 8th Fl.
New York, NY 10019
Funder concerned about AIDS

Long Island Community Foundation
Suzy Sonenberg
1740 Old Jericho Turnpike
Jericho, NY 11753
Funder of gay/lesbian issues

Los Angeles Community AIDS Partnership
California Community Foundation
Judy Spiegel, Project Director
606 S. Olive St., Suite 2400
Los Angeles, CA 90014-1526
Funder concerned about AIDS

Maine Community Foundation
P.O. Box 148
210 Main St.
Ellsworth, ME 04605
Funder concerned about AIDS

Maine Women's Fund
JoAnne Peterson
P.O. Box 5135
Portland, ME 04101
Funder of gay/lesbian issues

Maricopa County Community AIDS Partnership
Wayne Tormala
Executive Director
2211 E. Highland Ave., Suite 115
Phoenix, AZ 85016
Funder concerned about AIDS

Marin Community Foundation
17 E. Sir Francis Drake Blvd.
Suite 200
Larkspur, CA 94939
Funder of gay/lesbian issues

Mary's Pence
Maureen Gallagher
P.O. Box 29078
Chicago, IL 60629-9078
Funder of gay/lesbian issues

McKenzie River Gathering Fund
Linda Reymers
454 Williamette
Eugene, OR 97401
Funder of gay/lesbian issues

Mellon Foundation
Richard King, George Taber
525 William Penn Pl.
Pittsburgh, PA 15219
Funder of gay/lesbian issues

Joyce Mertz-Gilmore Foundation
Robert Crane
218 E. 18th St.
New York, NY 10003
Funder of gay/lesbian issues

Michigan AIDS Fund
Barbara Getz, Chair
c/o Kresge Foundation
P.O. Box 3151
Troy MI 48007-3151
Funder concerned about AIDS

Michigan AIDS Fund
Earl Schipper
c/o The Greystone Group, Inc.
678 Front St., N.W.
Grand Rapids, MI 49504
Funder concerned about AIDS

Minneapolis Foundation
Brian Malloy
A200 Foshay Tower
821 Marquette Ave.
Minneapolis, MN 55402
Funder of gay/lesbian issues

Minnesota Women's Fund
Nancy Fakhreddine
A200 Foshay Tower
821 Marquette Ave.
Minneapolis, MN 55402
Funder of gay/lesbian issues

Model Foundation
Allen Model
310 Juniper St.
Philadelphia, PA 19107
Funder of gay/lesbian issues

Ms. Foundation for Women
Tani Takagi
120 Wall St.
New York, NY 10005
Funder of gay/lesbian issues

National AIDS Fund
Paula van Ness, Executive Director
1140 Connecticut Ave., N.W.
Washington, DC 20036
Funder concerned about AIDS

National Leadership Coalition on AIDS
B.J. Stiles, President
1730 "M" St., N.W., Suite 905
Washington, DC 20036
Funder concerned about AIDS

National Lesbian and Gay Community Funding Partnership
Carrolle Fair Perry, Director
666 Broadway, Suite 520
New York, NY 10012

National Scholarship Fund for Gay and Lesbian Studies
P.O. Box 341331
Los Angeles, CA 90034
Scholarship fund

Needmor Fund
Lynn Gisi
1730 15th St.
Boulder, CO 80302
Funder of gay/lesbian issues

New Harvest Foundation
P.O. Box 1786
Madison, WI 53701
Funder of gay/lesbian issues

The New Mexico Community AIDS Partnership
Janet Voorhees, Project Manager
c/o The New Mexico Community Foundation
P.O. Box 149
Santa Fe, NM 87504
Funder concerned about AIDS

New Mexico Women's Foundation
Diane Wood
5200 Cooper N.E.
Albuquerque, NM 87108
Funder of gay/lesbian issues

New York Community Trust
2 Park Ave., 24th Fl.
New York, NY 10016
Joyce M. Bove, Vice President,
Lorie Slutsky; Len McNally, Senior Program Officer,
Funder concerned about AIDS

New York Foundation
Madeleine Lee
350 5th Ave., No. 2901
New York, NY 10118
Funder of gay/lesbian issues

New York Life Foundation
51 Madison Ave.
New York, NY 10010
Funder concerned about AIDS

Norman Foundation
Michele Lord
147 E. 48th St.
New York, NY 10017
Funder of gay/lesbian issues

North Shore Unitarian Universalist Veatch Program
Marjorie Fine
48 Shelter Rock Rd.
Manhasset, NY 11030
Funder of gay/lesbian issues

North Star Fund
Betty Kapentanakis
666 Broadway, #500
New York, NY 10012
Funder of gay/lesbian issues

Northern California Grantmakers
AIDS Task Force
Wendy Everett
116 New Montgomery St., Suite 742
San Francisco, CA 94105
Funder concerned about AIDS

Northern Virginia HIV Consortium
Goli Mojdehi
Northern Virginia Planning District Commission
7535 Little River Tpke., Suite 100
Annandale, VA 22003
Funder concerned about AIDS

Open Meadows
Nancy Dean
P.O. Box 197
Bronx, NY 10464
Funder of gay/lesbian issues

Out Fund for Lesbian & Gay Liberation / Funding Exchange
Jan Strout
666 Broadway, Suite 500
New York, NY 10012
Funder of gay/lesbian issues

Out of the Closet Thrift Shop & Foundation
Edward Maloney
P.O. Box 20084, Cherokee Station
New York, NY 10028
Funder of gay/lesbian issues

Penn Foundation
Bernard Watson
1630 Locust St.
Philadelphia, PA 19103-6305
Funder of gay/lesbian issues

People's Fund
Rick Rothschiller
1325 Nuuanu Ave.
Honolulu, HI 96814
Funder of gay/lesbian issues

Philadelphia Foundation
Greg Goldman
1234 Market St., Suite 1900
Philadelphia, PA 19107
Funder of gay/lesbian issues

Philanthrofund Foundation
Tom Borrup
1619 Dayton Ave.
St. Paul, MN 55104
Funder of gay/lesbian issues

Philip Morris Companies
Mark Bodden, Manager
Corporate Contributions
120 Park Ave.
New York, NY 10017
Funder concerned about AIDS

Pittsburgh Foundation
Alfred Wishart, Jr.
30 CNG Tower
625 Liberty Ave.
Pittsburgh, PA 15222-3115
Funder of gay/lesbian issues

Planning / Agency Relations
Director, Harry Brown
United Way of Central Alabama
Community AIDS Partnership
of Central Alabama
3600 8th Ave. S.
P.O. Box 320189
Birmingham, AL 35232-0189
Funder concerned about AIDS

Playboy Foundation
Cleo Wilson
919 N. Michigan Ave.
Chicago, IL 60611
Funder of gay/lesbian issues

Polaroid Foundation
Donna Furlong
750 Main St., 2nd fl.
Cambridge, MA 02139
Funder of gay/lesbian issues

Pride Foundation
Ted Lord
2820 E. Madison
Seattle, WA 98112-4841
Funder of gay/lesbian issues

Pride in Scholarship Fund
167 Milk St., Apt. 154
Boston, MA 02109
Scholarship fund

Public Welfare Foundation
Larry Kressley
2600 Virginia Ave., N.W., #505
Washington, DC 20037-1977
Funder of gay/lesbian issues

Puerto Rico Community Foundation
Ethel Rios de Betancourt President
Royal Bank Center
255 Ponce de Leon Ave.
Suite 1417
Hato Rey, PR 00917
Funder concerned about AIDS

Rapoport Foundation
Jane Schwartz
220 E. 60th St., Suite 14K
New York, NY 10022
Funder of gay/lesbian issues

Resist
Nancy Moniz
1 Summer St.
Somerville, MA 02143
Funder of gay/lesbian issues

Reynolds Foundation
Z. Smith
Thomas Lambeth
101 Reynolda Village
Winston-Salem, NC 27106-5199
Funder of gay/lesbian issues

Rockefeller Family Fund
Donald Ross
1290 Ave. of the Americas
Suite 3450
New York, NY 10104
Funder of gay/lesbian issues

Rockefeller Foundation
Lynda Mullen
1133 Ave. of the Americas
New York, NY 10036
Funder of gay/lesbian issues

Rudin Foundation
Susan Rapaport
345 Park Ave.
New York, NY 10154
Funder of gay/lesbian issues

San Diego Community Foundation
Jill Houska, Program Officer
San Diego Grantmakers AIDS Collaboration
101 Broadway, Suite 1120
San Diego, CA 92101
Funder concerned about AIDS

San Francisco Foundation
685 Market St., Suite 910
San Francisco, CA 94105
Funder of gay/lesbian issues

Sister Fund
Kimberly Otis
1255 5th Ave.
New York, NY 10029
Funder of gay/lesbian issues

Christopher D. Smithers Foundation, Inc.
Adele Smithers
P.O. Box 67, Oyster Bay Rd.
Mill Neck, NY 11765
Funder of gay/lesbian issues

Stamp Out AIDS
240 W. 44th St.
New York, NY 10036
Funder concerned about AIDS; sells stamps to benefit Broadway Cares

Stonewall Community Foundation
Fred Hochberg
825 3rd Ave., Suite 3315
New York, NY 10022
Funder of gay/lesbian issues

Streisand Foundation
Margery Tabankin
3679 Motor Ave.
Los Angeles, CA 90034
Funder of gay/lesbian issues

Tarrant County Community AIDS Partnership
Sue Grossman
Project Coordinator
P.O. Box 202574
Arlington, TX 76006
Funder concerned about AIDS

Threshold Foundation
Drummond Pike
1388 Sutter St., 10th Fl.
San Francisco, CA 94109
Funder of gay/lesbian issues

Tucson Community Foundation
Jane Conklin
Tucson HIV/AIDS Care Consortium
6601 E. Grant Rd., Suite 111
Tucson, AZ 85715
Funder concerned about AIDS

Tulsa Area United Way
Kathleen Coan, President
1430 S. Boulder
Tulsa, OK 74119
Funder concerned about AIDS

The United States Conference of Mayors
Richard Johnson, Director
Health Program AIDS/HIV Program and AIDS Information Exchange
1620 "I" St. N.W.
Washington, DC 20006
Information resource

United Way of Greater Portland
Meg Baxter, Executive Director
P.O. Box 3820, 233 Oxford St.
Portland, ME 04104-3820
Funder concerned about AIDS

United Way of Metropolitan Atlanta, Inc.
Ken Town, Director
Atlanta AIDS Fund
P.O. Box 2692
Atlanta, GA 30371-4601
Funder concerned about AIDS

United Way of Middle Tennessee
Mary Speiden
Community AIDS Partnership
P.O. Box 24667
250 Venture Circle
Nashville, TN 37202-4667
Funder concerned about AIDS

United Way of Pierce County
Emery M. Ivery, Vice President
Planning, Allocations and
Community Services
Tacoma/Pierce County
Community AIDS Partnership
734 Broadway, P.O. Box 2215
Tacoma, WA 98401-2215
Funder concerned about AIDS

United Way of Pulaski County
Central Arkansas Community
AIDS Partnership
Sally Michael, Project Coordinator
615 W. Markham, P.O. Box 3257
Little Rock, AR 72201-3257
Funder concerned about AIDS

United Way of the Greater Dayton Area
Luigi S. Procopio II,
Community Building Associate
The Dayton Regional AIDS
Partnership
184 Salem Ave.
Dayton, OH 45406
Funder concerned about AIDS

United Way Sacramento Area
Peter Simpson
Regional AIDS Planning &
Coordinating Committee
8912 Volunteer Lane, Suite 200
Sacramento, CA 95826-3221
Funder concerned about AIDS

Valentine Foundation
Alexandra Walling
900 Old Gulph Rd.
Bryn Mawr, PA 19010
Funder of gay/lesbian issues

Van Ameringen Foundation
Harry van Ameringen
509 Madison Ave.
New York, NY 10022-5501
Funder of gay/lesbian issues

Vanguard Public Foundation
Hari Dillon
383 Rhode Island St., Suite 301
San Francisco, CA 94103
Funder of gay/lesbian issues

Ventura County Community Founcation
Kristina Brook, Program Officer
1355 del Norte Rd.
Camarillo, CA 93010
Funder concerned about AIDS

Walt Disney Company Foundation
Doris Smith
500 S. Buena Vista St.
Burbank, CA 91521-0968
Funder of gay/lesbian issues

Washington AIDS Partnership
J. Channing Wickham, Director
1400 16th St. N.W., Suite 430
Washington, DC 20036
Funder concerned about AIDS

Whitman-Brooks Foundation
Lesbian and Gay Scholarship Fund
P.O. Box 48320
Los Angeles, CA 90048
Scholarship fund

William Caspar Graustein Memorial Fund
David M. Nee, Executive Director
205 Church St., 3rd Fl.
New Haven, CT 06510
Funder concerned about AIDS

Wisconsin Community Fund
Steve Starkey
122 State St., #508
Madison, WI 53703
Funder of gay/lesbian issues

Women's Community Foundation
Emily Ford
12200 Fairhill Rd., #E008
Cleveland, OH 44120
Funder of gay/lesbian issues

Women's Foundation
Paula Ross
3543 18th St., #9
San Francisco, CA 94110
Funder of gay/lesbian issues

Women's Foundation of Oregon
Mary Heffernan
921 S.W. Morrison, #422
Portland, OR 97205
Funder of gay/lesbian issues

Women's Foundation of Texas
Susan Wendel
P.O. Box 5861
Austin, TX 78763
Funder of gay/lesbian issues

Women's Fund - Santa Clara County
Corinne Gutierrez
1691 The Alameda, #235
San José, CA 95126
Funder of gay/lesbian issues

Women's Sports Foundation
Donna Lopiano
Eisenhower Park
E. Meadow, NY 11554
Funder of gay/lesbian issues

Women's Way
Corinne Sylvia
1233 Locust St., #300
Philadelphia, PA 19107
Funder of gay/lesbian issues

The Xerox Foundation
Robert Gudger, Vice President
P.O. Box 1600
Stamford, CT 06904
Funder concerned about AIDS

Libraries

AID Atlanta
1438 W. Peachtree St.
Atlanta, GA 30309
Lola Halpin

AIDS Archives
Gay Men's Health Crisis
129 W. 20th St.
New York, NY 10011

AIDS Education and General Information System (AEGIS)
Mary.Elizabeth@AEGIS.hivnet.org
Sister Mary Elizabeth

AIDS Information Network
32 N. 3rd St.
Philadelphia, PA 19106
Lauren Ferguson

AIDSLINE: National Library of Medicine
8600 Rockville Pike
Bethesda, MD 20894

The AIDS Patent Database
http://patents.
cnidr.org/welcome.html

Alternative Press Center
1443 Gorsuch Ave.
Baltimore, MD 21218

Alternative Press Collection
Special Collections Department
University of Connecticut Library
Storrs, CT 06268

American Library Association Gay and Lesbian Task Force
c/o ALA
50 E. Huron St.
Chicago, IL 60611

American Library Association Gay / Lesbian / Bisexual Task Force
1576 McLendon Ave.
Atlanta, GA 30307
The library information clearinghouse

American Radical History Collection
Special Collections Division
Michigan State University Libraries
East Lansing, MI 48824

Archives for the Protection of Gay History & Literature
P.O. Box 6368, Station A
St. John, New Brunswick
E2L 4R8 Canada

Archives Gaes du Quebec
CP 395 succ
Place du Parc
Montreal, Quebec
H2W 2N9 Canada

Archivos Gay de Occidente
A. Postal 36-218
44760 Guadalajara, Mexico

Baker Archives
350 S. Center St., #350
Reno, NV 89501

Black Gay Archives
P.O. Box 30004
Philadelphia, PA 19103

Blanche Baker Memorial Library & Archives
(One, Inc.)
3340 Country Club Dr.
Los Angeles, CA 90019
Jim Morrow

Boston Lesbian and Gay History Project
285 Harvard St. , Apt. 202
Cambridge MA 02139

Brooklyn Historical Society
128 Pierpont
Brooklyn, NY 11201
David Kahn, Executive Director

Buffalo Women's Oral History Project
255 Parkside Ave.
Buffalo, NY 14214

CAIN: Computerized AIDS Info Network
Los Angeles Gay and Lesbian Community Services Center
1213 N. Highland Ave.
Los Angeles, CA 90038
Russ Toth

California Lesbian Archives
107 659th St.
Oakland, CA 94608

California State University, Northridge
Special Collections Library
Oviatt and South Libraries
1811 Nordhoff St.
Northridge, CA 91330

Canadian Women's Movement Archives
P.O. Box 128, Station P
Toronto, Ontario
M5S 2S7 Canada

The Center for Medical Consumers
237 Thompson St.
New York, NY 10012
Jessica Cooperman, Resource Coordinator

Center for Research and Education in Sexuality
San Francisco State Library
1600 Holloway Ave.
San Francisco CA 94132
John DeCecco

Chicago Gay / Lesbian History Project
P.O. Box 60046
Chicago, IL 60660

Cincinnati Gay / Lesbian Archives
408 Ludlow, #56
Cincinnati, OH 45220

Collection on Human Sexuality
Department of Manuscripts and University Archives
John M. Olin Library
Cornell University
Ithaca, NY 14853

Connecticut Women's Archives
Hartford Women's Center
350 Farmington Ave.
Hartford, CT 16105

Constance Barber Collection on Lesbian History
Women's Resource Center Library
250 Golden Bear Center
University of California, Berkeley
Berkeley, CA 94720

Contemporary Culture Collection
Howard-Tilton Memorial Library
Tulane University
7001 Freret St.
New Orleans, LA 70188

Contemporary Culture Collection
Samuel Paley Library
Temple University
Berks and 13th Sts.
Philadelphia, PA 19122

Cornell University Library
Human Sexuality Collection
Carl A. Kroch Library
Ithaca, NY 14853-5302
Brenda Marston

Dallas Gay / Lesbian Historic Archives
P.O. Box 190869
Dallas, TX 75219
Phil Johnson, Curator

The Dawn D. Rasmussen Memorial Library
c/o Center For Anti-Violence Education
421 5th Ave.
Brooklyn, NY 11215

Delaware Lesbian & Gay Archives
P.O. Box 974
Wilmington, DE 19899

Dissent and Social Change Collection
California State University Library, Sacramento
2000 Jed Smith Dr.
Sacramento, CA 95819

Division of Special Collections
New York Public Library
5th Ave. and 42nd St.
New York, NY 10018

Documentation of AIDS Issues and Research
2336 Market St., #33
San Francisco, CA 94114
Michael Flanagan, by phone only at 415-673-0862

Douglas County Gay Archives
P.O.Box 942
Dillard, OR 97432-0942
Billy Russo, Director

The Feminist Library
c/o Y.W.C.A.
809 Rector St.
Durham, NC 27707

Florida Collection of Lesbian Herstory
P.O. Box 5605
Jacksonville, FL

Gay Alliance of the Genesee Valley Library
713 Monro Ave.
Rochester, NY 14607

Gay and Lesbian Archives of Philadelphia
Penguin Place
P.O. Box 12814
Philadelphia, PA 19108

Gay and Lesbian Archives of Texas
P.O. Box 16401
Houston, TX 77222

Gay and Lesbian Archives of Washington D.C.
P.O. Box 4218
Falls Church, VA 22044

Gay and Lesbian Collection Eureka Valley / Harvey Milk Memorial Branch Library
San Francisco Public Library
3555 16th St.
San Francisco, CA 94114

Gay and Lesbian Historical Society Archives of Utah
341 N. Center St., #2
Salt Lake City, UT 84103

Gay and Lesbian Historical Society of Northern California
P.O. Box 424280
San Francisco, CA 94142
Ruth Mahaney, Board Chair

Gay & Lesbian Resource Center
Resource Room and Archives
P.O. Box 11152
Fort Wayne, IN 46856

Gay Archives Collective
P.O. Box 3130, MPO
Vancouver, British Columbia
U6B 3XS Canada

Gay Community News Library
62 Berkeley St.
Boston, MA 02116

Gay History Film Project
P.O. Box 77043
San Francisco, CA 94107

Gay History Project
P.O. Box 7508, Station Main
Saskatoon, Saskatchewan
S7K 4L4 Canada

Gay & Lesbian on Stamps Club
P.O. Box 3940
Hartford, CT 06103

Gay Men's Health Crisis
129 W. 20th St., 2nd Fl.
New York, NY 10011
Timothy McCarron

Gerber / Hart Gay & Lesbian Library / Archives
3352 N. Paulina St.
Chicago, IL 60657

Hamilton-Wentworth Gay Archives
P.O. Box 44, Station B
Hamilton, Ontario
L8L 7T5 Canada

Happy Foundation
c/o Gene Elder
411 Bonham St.
San Antonio, TX 78205

Harvey Milk Archives
3930 17th St.
San Francisco, CA 94114
Scott Smith

Healing Alternatives Foundation Library
1748 Market St., Suite 204
San Francisco, CA 94102
Judy Berkowitz

Henry Gerber / Pearl M. Hart Library and Archives
Midwest Lesbian/Gay
Resource Center
3352 N. Paulina St.
Chicago, IL 60657

Herizon Archives
P.O. Box 1082
Binghampton, NY 13902

Heyman Memorial Library
c/o Dignity/Maine
P.O. Box 7021
Lewistown, ME 04240

History Department Oakland Museum
1000 Oak St.
Oakland, CA 94607

HIV Fight Back Library
3626 Sunset Blvd.
Los Angeles, CA 90026

HIV Resource Library
AIDS Action Committee
131 Clarendon St.
Boston, MA 02116
Jonathan Pozner

Homophile Association of London, Ontario
(HALO Library)
649 Colbourne St.
London, Ontario
N6A 3Z2 Canada

Homophile Research Library
Church of the Beloved Disciple
132 W. 24th St.
New York, NY 10011

Homosexual Information Center
115 Monroe St.
Bossier City, LA 71111-4539
Bill Glover, Vice-President

Humanical Library
New College of California
777 Valencia
San Francisco, CA 94110

Humanities Research Center
University of Texas at Austin
2114 Harry Ransom Center
Austin, TX 78713

Institute for Advanced Study of Human Sexuality
Research Library
1523 Franklin St.
San Francisco, CA 94109

Institute of Social Ethics
1 Gold St., #22-ABC
Hartford, CT 06103

International Gay and Lesbian Archives
P.O. Box 38100
Los Angeles CA 90038-0100
Jim Kepner, Curator

International Gay History Archive
P.O. Box 2, Village Station
New York, NY 10014

International Gay Information Center Archives
The New York Public Library
5th Ave. at 42nd St.
New York, NY 10018
Mary Bowling, Curator of Manuscripts

International Gay Information Center Archives (and Special Collections)
Rare Books Division
New York Public Library
5th Ave. and 42nd St.
New York, NY 10018

James Fraser Library
Canadian Gay Archives
56 Temperance St., Suite 201
P.O. Box 639, Station A
Toronto, Ontario
M5W 1G2 Canada

Joan Ruth Rose Library
P.O. Box 509
Yellow Springs, OH 45387

Jon Greenberg Library of Alternative Therapies for HIV / AIDS
APLA
1313 N. Vine St.
Los Angeles, CA 90028

June L. Mazer Lesbian Collection
626 N. Robertson Blvd.
West Hollywood, CA 90069
Degania Golove, Coordinator

Kentucky Collection of Lesbian Herstory
P.O. Box 1701
Louisville, KY 40201

Kentucky Gay & Lesbian Archives & Library
Williams-Nichols Institute
P.O. Box 4264
Louisville, KY 40204
David Williams

Kinsey Institute for Research in Sex, Gender, and Reproduction
Indiana University
Room 313, Morrison Hall
Bloomington, IN 47405

Labadie Collection
Department of Rare Books and Special Collections
University of Michigan
711 Hatcher Library
Ann Arbor, MI 48109

Lambda, Inc. Barnes Library
516 S. 27th St.
Birmingham, AL 35355

Lambda Services-Queer Archive Project
P.O. Box 31321
El Paso, TX 79931-0321
Rob Knight

Lambda United Library
P.O. Box 6024
Bismark, ND 58502

Latina Lesbian History Project
P.O. Box 627, Stuyvesant Station
New York, NY 10009

Lavender Archives
P.O. Box 28977
Santa Anna, CA 92799

Leather Archives & Museum
5015 N. Clark St.
Chicago, IL 60640
Charles Renslow, President

Lesbian and Gay Archives of Naiad Press
P.O. Box 10543
Tallahassee, FL 32302

Lesbian and Gay Heritage Alliance of the Pacific Northwest
1425 E. Prospect St.
Seattle, WA 98112

Lesbian and Gay History Group of Toronto
P.O. Box 639, Station A
Toronto, Ontario
M5W 1G2 Canada

Lesbian / Gay Archives of San Diego
P.O. Box 40389
San Diego, CA 92164

Lesbian Herstory Archives
Lesbian Herstory Educational Foundation, Inc.
P.O.Box 1258
New York, NY 10116
Joan Nestle, historical society

Lesbian Resource Center Library
P.O. Box 180446
Dallas, TX 75218

Librarie Lesbienne, Feministe, Gaie
3636 Blvd.
St. Laurent, Montreal, Quebec
H2G 3C9 Canada

Library and Archives
Gay and Lesbian Community Center of Pittsburgh
P.O. Box 5441
Pittsburgh, PA 15206

Library of Social Alternatives
Salem State College
Salem, MA 01970

Library Office of Lesbian / Gay / Bisexual Life
Dobbs University Center, Rm. 246
Emory University, P.O. Box 24075
Atlanta, GA 30322

Library / Information Center
Capital City Community Center
227 Congress Ave., Suite 390
Austin, TX 78701

Los Angeles Library
California School of Professional Psychology
100 S. Fremont Ave.
Alhambra, CA 91803

Matrices
Women's Studies Department
492 Ford Hall
University of Minnesota
Minneapolis, MN 55455
Jacqueline Zita

Medic Aware
3109 21st Ave. S.
Minneapolis, MN 55407
Tom Holte

Metropolitan Community Church Library
1919 Decateur St.
Houston, TX 77007

Milwaukee Lesbian Archives
c/o MLA /Mary Frank
3363 N. Richard St.
Milwaukee, WI 53212

Mina Ross Library
Center for Lesbian and Gay Studies
Graduate Center
City University of New York
33 W. 42nd St.
New York, NY 10036

National AIDS Clearinghouse ONLINE
Centers for Disease Control and Prevention
800-458-5231
John Watson

National Ecumenical Coalition Library
4300 Old Dominion Dr., Suite 803
Arlington, VA 22207

National Museum of Lesbian and Gay History
208 W. 13th St.
New York, NY 10001

Nevada Women's Herstorical Society
1298 S. Christy Ln.
Las Vegas, NV 89122

New Alexandria Lesbian Library
P.O. Box 402, Florence Station
Northhampton, MA 01060

New Jersey Gay & Lesbian Archives
123 Livingston Ave.
New Brunswick, NJ 08901
M. Kafka, Curator

New York Academy of Medicine
1216 5th Ave.
New York, NY 10029
Len Valenzuela

Northwest Ohio Lesbian / Gay Archives
Western Reserve Historical Society
10825 E. Blvd.
Cleveland, OH 44106

Northwestern University
Special Collections Department
1937 Sheridan Rd.
Evanston, IL 60201

Ohio Lesbian Archives
4039 Hamilton Ave.
Cincinnati, Ohio 45223
Phebe Beiser, President

Opening Books
403 Pratt Ave.
Huntsville, AL

Out in Montana Resource Center
P.O. Box 7223
Missoula, MT 59807

Out on the Shelves
1170 Bute St.
Vancouver, BC V6E 1Z6 Canada

Pat Parker / Vito Russo Library
Lesbian & Gay Community
Services Center
208 W. 13th St.
New York, NY 10011

Popular Culture Collection
William T. Gerome Library
Bowling Green State University
Bowling Green, OH 43403

Project Inform
1965 Market St., Suite 220
San Francisco, CA 94103
Ben Collins, by phone only at
800-822-7422

Quatrefoil Library
1619 Dayton Ave., Suites 105-107
St. Paul, MN 55104

Queer Resources Directory
AIDS folder
QRDstaff@vector.casti.com

Richard G. Katzoff Collection
Department of Special Collections
John Hay Library
Brown University
Providence, RI 02912

Ron Shipton HIV Information Center
715 N. San Vicente
West Hollywood, CA 90069
Nancy Mattoon

San Francisco Public Library
The Gay and Lesbian Center
Civic Center
San Francisco, CA 94102
Jim van Buskirk

Saving Our Stories
P.O. Box 402063
Austin, TX 78704

Schlesinger Library
Radcliffe College
10 Garden St.
Cambridge, MA 02138

Seattle Treatment Education Project
127 Broadway E., Suite 200
Seattle, WA 98102-5786
John Arnaldo

Social Protest Project
Bancroft Library
University of California, Berkeley
Berkeley, CA 94720

Southeastern Lesbian Archives
Atlanta Lesbian Feminist Alliance
Library
P.O. Box 5502
Atlanta, GA 30307

Stanford Special Collections
Green Library
Stanford University
Stanford, CA 94305-6004
Allen Ginsberg, papers

State Historical Society of Wisconsin Library
816 State St.
Madison, WI 53706

Stonewall Library
Holy Spirit Metropolitan Community Church
330 S.W. 27th St.
Ft. Lauderdale, FL 33315

T.S. Library
2425 Indiana, P.O. Box 1144
Topeka, KS 66601

Tennessee Lesbian Archives (TLA)
c/o Hornsby
303 Kennon Rd.
Knoxville, TN 37909

Terry Mangan Memorial Library
Gay and Lesbian Community Center of Colorado
1245 E. Colfax Ave., #319
P.O. Drawer E
Denver, CO 80218

Test Positive Aware Network
1340 W. Irving Park, Box 259
Chicago IL 60613
Timothy Gates

Traces / Archives Lesbiennes
CP 244 succ Beaubien
Montreal, Quebec
H2G 3C9 Canada

Treatment Resource Library
AIDS Survival Project
44 12th St. N.E.
Atlanta, GA 30309
Dawn Averitt-Doherty

Triangle Institute
P.O. Box 2296
Washington, DC 20013

UCLA Department of Special Collections
University Research Library
UCLA
Los Angeles, CA 90024-1575
Dan Luckenbill, contains papers of Paul Monette

University of Southern California Reference Center
Doheny Memorial Library
University of Southern California
Los Angeles, CA 90089-0182
John Waiblinger, gay and lesbian bibliographer

Utah Gay and Lesbian Historical Archives
Utah Stonewall Center
450 South 900 E., Suite 140
Salt Lake City, UT 84102

West Coast Lesbian Collection
P.O. Box 25753
Oakland, CA 94623

What She Wants
Feminist Library
P.O. Box 18465
Cleveland, OH 44118

Williams-Nichols Institute
P.O. Box 4264
Louisville, KY 40204

Winnipeg Gay / Lesbian Resource Center
P.O. Box 1661
Winnipeg, Manitoba
R3C 2Z6 Canada

Womansline Books
711 Richmond St.
London, Ontario
N6A 3H1 Canada

Women's Center Library
Boston University
775 Commonwealth Ave.
North Tower
Boston, MA 02215

Women's Movement Archives and Library
46 Pleasant St.
Cambridge, MA 02139

Womens' Library
17 1/2 N. Block Ave.
Fayetteville, AR 72701

World Congress of Gay & Lesbian Jewish Organizations
Resource Library
P.O. Box 18961
Washington, DC 20036

Yale University, Beinecke Rare Books and Manuscripts Library
P.O. Box 208240
New Haven, CA 06520-8240
Patricia Willis, Curator, American Literature (including the papers of Violet Quill)

Media

10+ Inc./A-TV
50 Lexington Ave., Suite27C
New York, NY 10010
Barry Z, news magazine and variety talk show

Activision
6443 Colby St.
Oakland, CA 94618

After Hours
KPFT 90.1 FM
419 Lovett
Houston, TX 77006-4018

AIDS Call-in Live
TV 21—Chicago Access Corporation
322 S. Greene
Chicago, IL 60607
Evelyn D. Holmes, Producer

AIDS Community Television
12 Wooster St.
New York, NY 10013
James Wentzy

Alternating Currents
P.O. Box 6126
WAIF-FM 88.3FM
Cincinnati, OH 45206

Amazon Country
WXPN-FM 88.5
3905 Spruce St.
Philadelphia, PA 19104

Aware: HIV Talk Radio
444 N. Michigan Ave., Suite 1600
Chicago, IL 60611
Chris DeChant, Producer

Because We're Here
KRCL Radio Station
208 West 800 South
Salt Lake City, UT 84101

Bread & Roses Show
KBOO Radio
20 S.E. 8th
Portland, OR 97214

The Closet Case Show
P.O. Box 790
New York, NY 10108

Concerning Gays and Lesbians
KRCL-FM 91
208 West 800 South
Salt Lake City, UT 84101
Becky Moss, Producer

Deep Dish Television
339 Lafayette St.
New York, NY 10012

Dish Production Inc.
P.O. Box 9164
West Hollywood, CA
91609-0164
Steven J. McCarthy
a.k.a. Madame Dish, Host

Dyke TV
Sang-Froid
P.O. Box 55
Prince St. Station
New York, NY 10012
Mary Patierno/Ana Simo, Producers

Electric City
133 Collingwood
San Francisco, CA 94114

Fem TV (Feminist Television)
P.O. Box 66604
Houston, TX 77266-6604

Frameline
346 9th St.
San Francisco, CA 94103

Fresh Fruit
KFAI 90.3 FM
1808 Riverside Ave.
Minneapolis, MN 55454-1035

Fruitpunch
KPFA Radio
2207 Shattuck Ave.
Berkeley, CA 94704

Gay Alternative
P.O. Box 41773
WEVL-FM 90
Memphis, TN 38104-1773

Gay and Lesbian Independent Broadcasters
c/o WBAI
P.O. Box 18
New York, NY 10018

Gay and Lesbian Media Coalition
8828 Sunset Blvd., #308
West Hollywood, CA 90046

Gay Broadcasting System / "Out in the Nineties"
178 7th Ave., #A3
New York, NY 10011

Gay Cable Nashville
703 Berry Rd.
Nashville, TN 37204-2803

Gay Cable Network
150 W. 26th St., Suite 703
New York, NY 10001
Lou Maletta

Gay Cable Network
P.O. Box 6399
Pittsburgh, PA 15212-0399

Gay Entertainment Television
7 E. 17th St., 3rd Fl.
New York, NY 10003
Marvin Schwam

Gay Fairfax
P.O. Box 2322
Springfield, VA 22152

Gay Spirit
WRSU-FM 88.7
126 College Ave.
New Brunswick, NJ 08903

The Gaydar Show
KOPN Radio 89.5 FM
915 E. Broadway
Columbia, MO 65201

Gaydreams Radio
WXPN-FM 88.5
3905 Spruce St.
Philadelphia, PA 19104

GayNet
P.O. Box 25524
Albuquerque, NM 87125-0524
News service

Steve Gendel
NBC
30 Rockefeller Plaza
New York, NY 10112
CNBC Reporter

Green and Yellow TV
P.O. Box 40
Eagle Lake, MN 56024

HIV Update
PAAC
101 W. Grand Ave., #200
Chicago, IL 60610

Homovisión Producciones
P.O. Box 1995
New York, NY 10009
Candido Negron/Gamalier de Jesus

IMRU: "What's New?"
KPFK-FM Radio
3729 Cahuenga Blvd. W.
North Hollywood, CA 91604
Cindy Friedman, Producer

In the Life Media Inc.
30 W. 26th St., 7th Fl.
New York, NY 10010
John Scagliotti

Inside / Ouside the Beltway
IOB Productions
P.O. Box 13
Springfield, VA 22150-0013
Dennis Brooks, Producer

Just for the Record
Box 35373
Dallas, TX 75235-0373

The Lambda Report
P.O. Box 9742
Denver, CO 80209

Lambda Reports
KRJY Radio Station
8081 Manchester Rd.
St. Louis, MO 63144
Charles Koehler, Producer

Lambda Weekly Radio
P.O. Box 35031
Dallas, TX 75235

Latinos en Acción
c/o Project Achieve
853 Broadway
New York, NY 10003
Carlos Cordero

Lavender Lounge
2300 Market St., Suite 29
San Francisco, CA 94114
Mark Klein, variety show

Lavender Wimmin Radio Show
WUSB 90.1FM
SUNY Stonybrook
Stonybrook, NY 11794

Lesbian & Gay Voices
KPFT 90.1 FM
419 Lovett
Houston, TX 77006-4018

Lesbian Sisters
Overnight Productions
c/o KPFK
3729 Cahuenga Blvd. W.
North Hollywood, CA 91604

Lesbigay Radio
c/o WCBR FM 92.7
120 W. University Dr.
Arlington Hts., IL 60004

Los Angeles International Gay & Lesbian Film Festival
8228 Sunset Blvd., #308
West Hollywood, CA 90046

Lovie TV
c/o Manhattan's Neighborhood Network
110 E. 23rd St., 10th Fl.
New York, NY 10010
Lovie

Milwaukee Gay / Lesbian Cable Network
TriCable Tonight
Yellow on Thursday
P.O. Box 204
Milwaukee, WI 53201

Network Q
884 Monroe
Atlanta, GA 30308
David Surber

The New Festival
462 Broadway #510
New York, NY 10013-2618

Night Scene
13 N.W. 13th Ave.
Portland, OR 97209

Nothing to Hide Productions
4701 Judy Lane
Madison, WI 53704

One in Ten People
KABS
1501 Arch St.
Little Rock, AR 72202

Our World Television
3976 Park Blvd.
San Diego, CA 92103

Out & About TV
Alliance for Equal Rights
P.O. Box 240423
Honolulu, HI 96824

Outfront: Gay & Lesbian TV
5710 Winton Rd., Suite 111-B
Cincinatti, OH 45232

Outlook: Gay & Lesbian VideoMagazine
950 N. Rengstorff Ave.
Mountain View, CA 94043
Phillip Moss, Executive Producer

Outpunk
PO Box 170501
San Francisco, CA 94117
Matt Wobensmith

Outtakes
Gays and Lesbians in Public Radio
P.O. Box 50993
Washington, DC 20091

Positive Image
PO Box 4087
North Hollywood, CA
91617-0087

Ready For Radio
KOOP
P.O. Box 49340
Austin, TX 78765

"The Queer Program"
P.O. Box 93951
Milwaukee, WI 53203

Queer Talk
WFTL Radio
P.O. Box 100819
Fort Lauderdale, FL

The Red Hot Organization
73 Spring St., Suite 602
New York, NY 10012
Publisher/Production Company

Southern Gay Dreams
P.O. Box 5332
c/o WFRG
Atlanta, GA 30307

Stonewall Union Lesbian / Gay Pride Report
Box 10814
Columbus, OH 43201-7814

Straight from the Heart
3145 Geary Blvd., Box 421
San Francisco, CA 94118

Testing the Limits
39 W. 14th St.
Room 402
New York, NY 10011
David Meieran, Executive Director

This Way Out
P.O. Box 38327
Los Angeles, CA 90038
Greg Gordon, Producer

Tinseltown's Queer
7985 Santa Monica Blvd.
Suite 450
West Hollywood, CA 90046

To Tell the Truth Television
Cathedral of Hope MCC
P.O. Box 35466
Dallas, TX 75235

Triangle Express Productions
P.O. Box 90711
Oakland, CA 90809-0711

TriAngle Video Productions
550 Westcott, Suite 400
Houston, TX 77007

Tricks
7985 Santa Monica Blvd.
Suite 109-448
West Hollywood, CA 90046
David van Cheney, Executive Producer

Women Make Movies
462 Broadway, 5th Fl.
New York, NY 10013
Deborah Zimmerman

Women's Educational Media
2017 Mission St., 2nd Fl.
San Francisco, CA 94110

Womenergy
KOPN Radio 89.5 FM
915 E. Broadway
Columbia, MO 65201

Parents

Mothers' AIDS Support Group Hotline
800-828-3280

Auburn PFLAG Representative
230 E. Samford, Suite 107
Auburn, AL 36830

Mobile PFLAG Representative
957 Church St.
Mobile, AL 36604

Gay and Lesbian Parents Coalition International—Gulf Coast Chapter
P.O. Box 1990
Semmes, AL 36575-1990

Anchorage Lesbian Moms' Group
Alaska Women's Center
2440 E. Tudor, Box 304
Anchorage, AK 99507

Southcentral Alaska PFLAG Chapter
P.O. Box 203231
Anchorage, AK 99520-3231

Fairbanks PFLAG Chapter
3135 Forrest Dr.
Fairbanks, AK 99709-5742

Palmer PFLAG Representative
P.O. Box 2888
Palmer, AK 99645

Kingman PFLAG Representative
805 Country Club
Kingman, AZ 86401

Gay and Lesbian Support Network
P.O. Box 66823
Phoenix, AZ 85082-6823

Valley of the Sun PFLAG Chapter
P.O. Box 37525
Phoenix, AZ 85069

Prescott PFLAG Chapter
920 E. Goodwin St., Suite A
Prescott, AZ 86303

Tucson PFLAG Chapter
P.O. Box 36264
Tucson, AZ 85740-6264

Northwest Arkansas PFLAG Chapter
P.O. Box 2897
Fayetteville, AR 72702

Fort Smith PFLAG Representative
600 N. 6th, Suite 8
Fort Smith, AR 72901

Little Rock PFLAG Chapter
P.O. Box 251191
Little Rock, AR 72225

Bakersfield Parent's Group
2002 19th St.
Bakersfield, CA 93311

Bakersfield PFLAG Representative
2012 "E" St.
Bakersfield, CA 93311

Chain of Life
P.O. Box 8081
Berkeley, CA 94707
Newsletter concerning adoption

Chico PFLAG Chapter
555 Vallombrossa, Suite 73
Chico, CA 95926

Claremont / Pomona Valley Area PFLAG Chapter
607 Leyden Ln.
Claremont, CA 91711-4236

Concord Area PFLAG Representative
P.O. Box 21
Concord, CA 94522

Gay / Lesbian Parents
P.O. Box 1332
El Toro, CA 92630

Fresno PFLAG Chapter
P.O. Box 27382
Fresno, CA 93729-7382

Hayward PFLAG Chapter
P.O. Box 3493
Hayward, CA 94544

Sonoma County PFLAG Chapter
P.O. Box 1266
Healdsburg, CA 95448

Idyllwild PFLAG Chapter
P.O. Box 485
Idyllwild, CA 92549

Lesbian Mother's Group
1401 E. 4th St., Suite C
Long Beach, CA 90802

Long Beach PFLAG Chapter
P.O. Box 8221
Long Beach, CA 90808

Gay and Lesbian Parents
c/o Gay & Lesbian Community Services Center
1625 N. Hudson Ave.
Los Angeles, CA 90028-9998
Support services

Los Angeles PFLAG Chapter
P.O. Box 24565
Los Angeles, CA 90024

Eureka PFLAG Chapter
5755 Dow's Prairie Rd.
McKinleyville, CA 95521

Marin County PFLAG Chapter
P.O. Box 1626
Mill Valley, CA 94941

Modesto PFLAG Chapter
P.O. Box 4311
Modesto, CA 95353

Monterey County PFLAG Chapter
P.O. Box 9052
Monterey, CA 93942

Palm Springs PFLAG Chapter
244 Pinyon Crest
Mt. Center, CA 92561

Oakland PFLAG Chapter
100 Monte Cresta Ave., Suite 209
Oakland, CA 94611-4802

Pasadena PFLAG Chapter
300 Cherry
Pasadena, CA 91105

Pleasanton / Dublin / Livermore PFLAG Chapter
1452 Parkview Ct.
Pleasanton, CA 94566

Redlands PFLAG Chapter
1 E. Olive Ave.
Redlands, CA 92373

Riverside PFLAG Chapter
3891 Ridge Rd.
Riverside, CA 92506

Sacramento PFLAG Chapter
P.O. Box 661855
Sacramento, CA 95866

San Diego PFLAG Chapter
P.O. Box 82762
San Diego, CA 92138

Lesbian & Gay Parenting Program
1784 Market St.
San Francisco, CA 94102
Support services

Lesbians Considering Parenthood
Lyon-Martin Women's Health Services
1748 Market St., Suite 201
San Francisco, CA 94102

National Center for Lesbian Rights
870 Market St., #570
San Francisco, CA 94102

San Francisco PFLAG Chapter
P.O. Box 640223
San Francisco, CA 94164-0223

Baylands Family Circle
Billy de Frank Community Center
175 Stockton Ave.
San José, CA 95126

Central Coast PFLAG Chapter
P.O. Box 3313
San Luis Obispo, CA 93403

Danville / San Ramon PFLAG Chapter
P.O. Box 3315
San Ramon, CA 94583

Orange County / Santa Ana PFLAG Chapter
P.O. Box 28662
Santa Ana, CA 92799-8662

Santa Barbara PFLAG Chapter
P.O. Box 41152
Santa Barbara, CA 93140-1152

Santa Cruz County PFLAG Chapter
849 Almar, Suite C-222
Santa Cruz, CA 95060-5856

Mid-Peninsula PFLAG
P.O.Box 8265
Stanford, CA 94305

Stockton PFLAG Chapter
P.O. Box 77725
Stockton, CA 95267

Peninsula PFLAG Chapter
P.O. Box 2718
Sunnyvale, CA 94087

Ventura County PFLAG Chapter
P.O. Box 5401
Ventura, CA 93005

Walnut Creek PFLAG Chapter
P.O. Box 94
Walnut Creek, CA 94597

Gay / Lesbian Parents of Los Angeles
7985 Santa Monica Blvd.
#109-346
West Hollywood, CA 90046

Yolo County PFLAG (Woodland-Davis-Winters)
17801 County Rd. 97
Woodland, CA 95695

Yreka PFLAG Chapter
420 Jackson St.
Yreka, CA 96097

San Luis Valley PFLAG Chapter
P.O. Box 1581
Alamosa, CO 81101

Boulder PFLAG Chapter
P.O. Box 19696
Boulder, CO 80308-2696

GLPCI of Denver
P. O. Drawer E
Denver, CO 80203

Colorado Springs PFLAG Chapter
P.O. Box 10076
Colorado Springs, CO 80917

Denver PFLAG Chapter
P.O. Box 18901
Denver, CO 80218

Summit County PFLAG Chapter
P.O. Box 1350
Dillon, CO 80435-1350

Durango PFLAG Chapter
203 W. 22nd St.
Durango, CO 81301-4617

Estes Park PFLAG Representative
P.O. Box 1349
Estes Park, CO 80517-1349

Evergreen / Mountain Area PFLAG Chapter
P.O. Box 265
Evergreen, CO 80439

Western Colorado PFLAG Chapter
P.O. Box 4904
Grand Junction, CO 81502

Collegiate Peaks PFLAG Chapter
P.O. Box 516
Hartsell, CO 80449

Longmont PFLAG Chapter
P.O. Box 611
Longmont, CO 80502

Fort Collins PFLAG Chapter
2607 Gilpin Ave.
Loveland, CO 80538

Pueblo PFLAG Chapter
P.O. Box 4484
Pueblo, CO 81006

Coventry PFLAG Representative
P.O. Box 752
Coventry, CT 06238-3200

Madison / Shoreline PFLAG Chapter
66 Bower Rd.
Madison, CT 06443

Gay Fathers of Greater New Haven
P.O. Box 7321
New Haven, CT 06519

New Haven PFLAG Representative
600 Prospect St., H 8
New Haven, CT 06511

Norwich Area PFLAG Chapter
Norwich, CT 06365-8604

Tri-State PFLAG Chapter
P.O. Box 278
Salisbury, CT 06068-0278

Hartford PFLAG Chapter
49 Beechwood Ln.
South Glastonbury, CT 06073-2201

Fairfield County PFLAG Chapter
P.O. Box 16703
Stamford, CT 06905-8703

Gay and Lesbian Parents Coalition International
(GLPCI)
P.O. Box 50360
Washington, DC 20091
Support services

Gay Fathers Coalition
P.O. Box 19891
Washington, DC 20036

Lesbians Choosing Children / Children of Sexual Minority Parents
Whitman-Walker Clinic
1407 "S" St. N.W.
Washington, DC 20009

Parents and Friends of Lesbians and Gays, National Office
(PFLAG)
1012 14th St. N.W., Suite 700
Washington, DC 20005

PFLAG Newsletter
1012 14th St. N.W., Suite 700
Washington, DC 20005
Media - Newsletter

Washington DC Metro Area PFLAG Chapter
P.O. Box 28009
Washington, DC 20038

National Association of Women for Understanding
P.O. Box 404
Montchanin, DE 19710

Parents Support Group
P.O. Box 404
Montchanin, DE 19710

PFLAG of Northern Delaware
P.O. Box 26049
Wilmington, DE 19899

Tri-County PFLAG Chapter
P.O. Box 12267
Brooksville, FL 34614

Fort Lauderdale PFLAG Chapter
8747 S.W. 52nd St.
Cooper City, FL 33328

South Florida PFLAG Chapter
7652 Mansfield Hollow
Delray Beach, FL 33446

North Miami Beach PFLAG Representative
16530 Lake Tree Dr.
Ft. Lauderdale, FL 33326

Ft. Myers PFLAG Chapter
5100-318 S. Cleveland Ave.
Suite 219
Ft. Myers, FL 33907

Gainesville / Ocala PFLAG Chapter
P.O. Box 140176
Gainesville, FL 32606

Jacksonville PFLAG Chapter
3820 La Vista Circle, #116
Jacksonville, FL 32217

Lakeland PFLAG Chapter
519 Cresap St.
Lakeland, FL 33801-4709

Miami PFLAG Representative
305-666-0770

Women's Preservation Society
4300 S.W. 73rd Ave.
Miami, FL 33155
Lesbian mothers' group

Daytona Beach PFLAG Chapter
199 N. Timberland Dr.
New Smyrna Beach, FL 32168

GLPCI-Central Florida Chapter
P.O. Box 561504
Orlando, FL 32856-1504

Pensacola PFLAG Representative
P.O. Box 34479
Pensacola, FL 32507-4479

Sanibel PFLAG Representative
1932 Woodring Rd.
Sanibel, FL 33957

Sarasota PFLAG Chapter, Inc.
P.O. Box 7382
Sarasota, FL 34278-7382

Tampa PFLAG Chapter
16301 Sonsoles Dr.
Tampa, FL 33613

Venice PFLAG Representative
P.O. Box 327
Venice, FL 34284-0327

Vero Beach PFLAG Representative
181 Springline Dr.
Vero Beach, FL 32963

Atlanta PFLAG Chapter, Inc.
P.O. Box 8482
Atlanta, GA 31106-0482

Lesbian & Gay Parents
P.O. Box 2107
Decatur, GA 30031

Macon PFLAG Representative
P.O. Box 7304
Macon, GA 31209-7304

Gay Parents & Partners
The Center
114 Jefferson
Savannah, GA 31401

Hawaii Lesbian Network
c/o University YWCA
P.O. Box 911
Honolulu, HI 96808

Oahu PFLAG Representative
2085 Ala Wai Blvd.
Twin Towers, Suite 16-3
Honolulu, HI 96815

Kailua-Kona PFLAG Representative
74-5615 Luhia St., D-2
Kailua-Kona, HI 96740

Treasure Valley PFLAG Chapter
3773 Cayuga Pl.
Boise, ID 83709

Caldwell PFLAG Representative
1415 Filmore
Caldwell, ID 83605

Eastern Idaho PFLAG Chapter
P.O. Box 50191
Idaho Falls, ID 83405-0191

Mountain Home PFLAG Representative
Route 2, Box 488
Mountain Home, ID 83647

Twin Falls PFLAG Chapter
1434 Pole Line Rd. E.
Twin Falls, ID 83301

PFLAG of Southern Illinois
505 Orchard Dr.
Carbondale, IL 62901

Chicago PFLAG Chapter
P.O. Box 11023
Chicago, IL 60611-0023

Family Circle
4156 W. School St.
Chicago, IL 60641

St. Louis PFLAG Chapter
114 Westridge
Collinsville, IL 62234

Northern Illinois PFLAG Chapter
112 E. Taylor St.
De Kalb, IL 60115

Downer's Grove / Suburban PFLAG Chapter
P.O. Box 105
Downer's Grove, IL 60516

Evansville Gay & Lesbian Parents Coalition
P.O. Box 2479
Evansville, IN 47728
Support services

Evansville Tri-State PFLAG Chapter
P.O. Box 113
Evansville, IN 47701

Fort Wayne PFLAG Representative
5042 Stellhorn
Fort Wayne, IN 46815

GLPCI of Indianapolis
P.O. Box 831
Indianapolis, IN 46206

Indianapolis PFLAG Chapter
P.O. Box 441633
Indianapolis, IN 46244-1633

Mothers & Others
1434 State Run Rd., #66
New Albany, IN 47150

Seymour PFLAG Representative
110 Windhorst Ct.
Seymour, IN 47274

South Bend PFLAG Chapter
P.O. Box 4195
South Bend, IN 46634

Terre Haute PFLAG Chapter
135 Aikman Pl.
Terre Haute, IN 47803

Ames PFLAG Representative
1216 Scott Ave.
Ames, IA 50010

Cedar Valley PFLAG Chapter
514 W. 4th St.
Cedar Falls, IA 50613-2804

Lesbian Parents Group
Gay & Lesbian Resource Center
4211 Grand Ave.
Des Moine, IA 50312

NE Iowa Area PFLAG Representative
P.O. Box 136
Garnavillo, IA 52049

Lesbian Mothers
Women's Resource & Action Center
130 N. Madison
Iowa City, IA 52240

Shenandoah PFLAG Representative
1002 S. Elm St.
Shenandoah, IA 51601

Waterloo PFLAG Chapter
317 Hartman Ave.
Waterloo, IA 50701

Waterville PFLAG Representative
1730 Elon Dr.
Waterville, IA 52170-9733

Central Iowa PFLAG Chapter
804 15th St.
W. Des Moines, IA 50265-3425

Hays PFLAG Chapter
2910 Country Ln.
Hays, KS 67601-1710

Lindsborg PFLAG Representative
P.O. Box 364
Lindsborg, KS 67456

Lesbian Moms / Gay Dads
Wichita Lesbians and Gay Community Center
111 Spruce
Wichita, KS 67214

Wichita PFLAG Chapter
P.O. Box 686
Wichita, KS 67201-0686

Bowling Green PFLAG Representative
2814 N. Mill Ave.
Bowling Green, KY 42104

Lexington PFLAG Chapter
P.O. Box 55484
Lexington, KY 40555-5484

Metro Louisville PFLAG Chapter, Inc.
P.O. Box 5002
Louisville, KY 40255-0002

Paducah PFLAG Chapter
2942 Clay St.
Paducah, KY 42001-4133

Baton Rouge PFLAG Chapter
P.O. Box 65398
Baton Rouge, LA 70896

Lafayette PFLAG Chapter
P.O. Box 31078
Lafayette, LA 70593

New Orleans PFLAG Chapter
P.O. Box 15515
New Orleans, LA 70175

Sappho's Circle
P.O. Box 57447
New Orleans, LA 70157

Shreveport PFLAG Representative
P.O. Box 8931
Shreveport, LA 71148

Augusta PFLAG Representative
23 Winthrop St.
Hallowell, ME 04347

Andy Valley PFLAG
6 Lemieux St.
Lewiston, ME 04240

Portland PFLAG Chapter
P.O. Box 8742
Portland, ME 04104

Waldoboro Area PFLAG Representative
P.O. Box O
Waldoboro, ME 04572-0916

Baltimore PFLAG Chapter
P.O. Box 5637
Baltimore, MD 21210-0610

Howard County PFLAG Representative
7303 Swan Point Way
Columbia, MD 21045

PFLAG of Maryland's Eastern Shore
P.O. Box 171
Stevensville, MD 21666

Amherst PFLAG Chapter
P.O. Box 2025
Amherst, MA 01004

Family & Parenting Program
Fenway Community Health Center
16 Haviland St.
Boston, MA 02115

Gay & Lesbian Advocates and Defenders
P.O. Box 218
Boston, MA 02112

Lesbians Choosing Children Network
Women's Center
46 Pleasant St.
Cambridge, MA 02139

Gardner PFLAG Representative
20 School St.
Gardner, MA 01440

Hingham PFLAG Chapter
510 Main St.
Hingham, MA 02043

Berkshire County / South PFLAG Chapter
29 Stringer Ave.
Lee, MA 01238-9569

Cape Cod / Brewster PFLAG Chapter
P.O. Box 1167
Orleans, MA 02653

Pioneer Valley PFLAG Chapter
P.O. Box 55
South Hadley, MA 01075-0055

Canton / Southeast PFLAG Chapter
P.O. Box 187
Stoughton, MA 02072

Concord Area PFLAG Chapter
P.O. Box 344
Stow, MA 01775

Metro-West, Framingham PFLAG Chapter
22 Caroline St.
Wellesley, MA 02181

Cape Cod / Falmouth PFLAG Chapter
P.O. Box 839
West Falmouth, MA 02574

Boston PFLAG Chapter
P.O. Box 44-4
West Somerville, MA 02144

Springfield PFLAG Chapter
P.O. Box 625
West Springfield, MA 01089

Worcester PFLAG Chapter
c/o United Congregational Church
6 Institution Rd.
Worcester, MA 01609

Ann Arbor PFLAG Chapter
P.O. Box 7471
Ann Arbor, MI 48107-7471

Bay City, Midland, Saginaw PFLAG Chapter
P.O. Box 834
Bay City, MI 48707-0834

Flint PFLAG Chapter
P.O. Box 90722
Burton, MI 48509

Carleton PFLAG Representative
3500 Kane Rd.
Carleton, MI 48117

Detroit PFLAG Chapter
P.O. Box 145
Farmington, MI 48332

Grand Rapids PFLAG Chapter
P.O. Box 6226
Grand Rapids, MI 49506-4823

Iron Mountain Area PFLAG Representative
305 W. "B" St.
Iron Mountain, MI 49801

Jackson PFLAG Chapter
P.O. Box 4065
Jackson, MI 49204

Mt. Pleasant PFLAG Representative
P.O. Box 272
Mt. Pleasant, MI 48804-0272

Lansing Area PFLAG Chapter
P.O. Box 35
Okemos, MI 48805

Port Huron PFLAG Representative
P.O. Box 611866
Port Huron, MI 48061-1866

Kalamazoo PFLAG Chapter
P.O. Box 1201
Portage, MI 49081-1201

Our Kids
c/o Pandora's Books & Music
226 W. Lovell
Kalamazoo, MI 49007

Sault Ste. Marie PFLAG Representative
1330 E. 3 Mile Rd.
Sault Ste. Marie, MI 49783-9376

Gay & Lesbian Parents Association
P.O. Box 2694
Southfield, MI 48037

Traverse City Area PFLAG Representative
229 1/2 W. 15th St.
Traverse City, MI 49684

Duluth PFLAG Chapter
612 1st Bank Pl.
Duluth, MN 55802-2056

Faribault PFLAG Representative
714 Valley View Rd.
Faribault, MN 55021

Queer Parents
P.O. Box 124
Mankato, MN 56002-0124

Alexandria PFLAG Chapter
12556 E. Lake Miltona Dr. N.E.
Miltona, MN 56354

PFLAG Saint Paul / Minneapolis
P.O. Box 8588
Minneapolis, MN 55408-0588

Northfield PFLAG Chapter
5048 Ebel Wy.
Northfield, MN 55057

Rochester / Southern Minnesota PFLAG Chapter
2205 Elton Hills Dr. N.W.
Rochester, MN 55901-1564

Saint Cloud PFLAG Chapter
402 8th Ave. S.
Saint Cloud, MN 56302

Minnesota Families
P.O. Box 11386
St. Paul, MN 55111

Gay & Lesbian Parents Coalition
6241 Blue Ridge Blvd.
Kansas City, MO 64113

Kansas City PFLAG Chapter
P.O. Box 414101
Kansas City, MO 64141-4101

Butte PFLAG Representative
P.O. Box 4815
Butte, MT 59702

Florence PFLAG Representative
5110 Hoblitt Ln.
Florence, MT 59833

Great Falls PFLAG Representative
P.O. Box 6416
Great Falls, MT 59406-

Helena PFLAG Representative
38 Sloway W.
St. Regis, MT 59866

Montana PFLAG Chapter
38 Sloway W.
St. Regis, MT 59866

Fullerton PFLAG Representative
P.O. Box 833
Fullerton, NE 68638

Hastings PFLAG Representative
721 N. Hastings
Hastings, NE 68901

Hendley PFLAG Representative
P.O. Box 427
Hendley, NE 68946

Holdrege / Kearney PFLAG Chapter
1320 8th Ave.
Holdrege, NE 68949

PFLAG Cornhusker
P.O. Box 4374
Lincoln, NE 68505-1819

Gay & Lesbian Parents Support Group
MCC
P.O. Box 3173
Omaha, NE 68103

Omaha PFLAG Chapter
2912 Lynwood Dr.
Omaha, NE 68123-1957

Carson City PFLAG Representative
1190 Sharrow Way
Carson City, NV 89703

Las Vegas PFLAG Chapter
P.O. Box 20145
Las Vegas, NV 89112-0145

Reno / Sparks PFLAG Representative
1685 Whitewood Dr.
Sparks, NV 89434

Concord Area PFLAG Chapter
158 Liberty Hill Rd.
Bedford, NH 03110

New Hampshire Gay Parents
P.O. Box 5981
Manchester, NH 03108

Seacoast Area PFLAG Chapter
5 Ash St.
Exeter, NH 03833

PFLAG (Monadnock Region)
RR 1, Box 703
Francestown, NH 03043

Seacoast Area PFLAG Chapter
18 Hobbs Rd.
Kensington, NH 03833-5510

Hanover NH / VT Upper Valley PFLAG Representative
P.O. Box 981
Lebanon, NH 03766

Concord PFLAG Chapter
P.O. Box 386
Manchester, NH 03105

PFLAG New Hampshire
P.O. Box 386
Manchester, NH 03105

Nashua PFLAG Representative
26 Deerwood Dr.
Nashua, NH 03063-1203

Monadnock Area PFLAG Chapter
Willard Farm Rd.
New Ipswich, NH 03071

Asbury Park Monmouth-Ocean PFLAG Chapter
P.O. Box 1542
Asbury Park, NJ 07712

Metuchen PFLAG Representative
P.O. Box 244
Belleville, NJ 07109-0244

North New Jersey PFLAG Chapter
P.O. Box 244
Belleville, NJ 07109-0244

Mays Landing PFLAG Chapter
103 Dover Ave.
Mays Landing, NJ 08330

Central New Jersey PFLAG
91 Mason Dr.
Metuchen, NJ 08840

Bergen County PFLAG Chapter
44 Kira Ln.
Ridgewood, NJ 07450

Albuquerque PFLAG Chapter
1907 Buena Vista S.E., #75
Albuquerque, NM 87106-4178

Santa Fe PFLAG Chapter
P.O. Box 16498
Santa Fe, NM 87506

Taos PFLAG Chapter
P.O. Box 3550
Taos, NM 87571

Albany PFLAG Chapter
P.O. Box 12531
Albany, NY 12212-2531

Binghamton PFLAG Chapter
P.O. Box 728
Westview Station
Binghamton, NY 13905-4631

Brooklyn PFLAG Chapter
7304 5th Ave., Suite 307
Brooklyn, NY 11209

Buffalo / Niagara Area PFLAG Chapter
P.O. Box 861
Buffalo, NY 14225

Long Island PFLAG Chapter
109 Browns Rd.
Huntington, NY 11743

Jamestown PFLAG Chapter
414 Palmer St.
Jamestown, NY 14701

Westchester County PFLAG Chapter
3 Leatherstocking Ln.
Mamaroneck, NY 10543

Center Kids
Lesbian and Gay Community Services Center
208 W. 13th St.
New York, NY 10011

New York City PFLAG Chapter
P.O. Box 553
Lenox Hill Station
New York, NY 10021

Rockland County PFLAG Representative
65 Lark St.
Pearl River, NY 10965

Poughkeepsie/Mid-Hudson PFLAG Chapter
P.O. Box 880
Pleasant Valley, NY 12569

Rochester PFLAG Chapter
179 Atlantic Ave.
Rochester, NY 14607

Schenectady PFLAG Representative
31 Lincoln Mall
Schenectady, NY 12309

Syracuse PFLAG Chapter
232 E. Onondaga St.
Syracuse, NY 13202

PFLAG of the Mohawk Valley
423 Fiore Dr.
Utica, NY 13502

Ithaca PFLAG Chapter
P.O. Box 24
Willeysville, NY 13864

Gay and Lesbian Parents and Their Kids
(GALPAK)
P.O. Box 5978
Asheville, NC 28813

Western North Carolina PFLAG Chapter
P.O. Box 5978
Asheville, NC 28813-5978

Boone PFLAG Representative
Route 5, Box 549-A
Boone, NC 28607

Gay & Lesbian Parents Coalition
P.O. Box 221841
Charlotte, NC 23222

Charlotte PFLAG Chapter
5815 Charing Pl.
Charlotte, NC 28211

Dallas, North Carolina / Western Piedmont PFLAG Chapter
P.O. Box 722
Dallas, NC 28034

Flat Rock / Hendersonville PFLAG Chapter
Route 2, Box 105-L
Flat Rock, NC 28731

Lesbian and Gay Parents and Their Kids
P.O. Box 393
Morgantown, NC 28655

Raleigh / Durham PFLAG Chapter
P.O. Box 10844
Raleigh, NC 27605-0844

Winston-Salem PFLAG Representative
2700 St. John's Pl.
Winston-Salem, NC 27106

Central Dakota PFLAG Chapter
P.O. Box 2491
Bismarck, ND 58502-2491

Fargo/ Moorhead PFLAG Chapter
1709 6th Ave. S.
Fargo, ND 58103

Grand Forks PFLAG Chapter
3210 Cherry
Grand Forks, ND 58501

Lorain County PFLAG Chapter
730 Park Ave.
Amherst, OH 44001

Ashtabula PFLAG Representative
1710 Walnut Blvd.
Ashtabula, OH 44004

Artificial Insemination for Lesbians
DINAH
P.O. Box 1485
Cincinnati, OH 45201

Greater Cincinnati PFLAG Chapter
P.O. Box 19634
Cincinnati, OH 45219-0634

Cleveland Lesbian Mothers Group
1828 W. 47th St.
Cleveland, OH 44102

Columbus PFLAG Chapter
P.O. Box 340101
Columbus, OH 43234

Gay & Lesbian Parenting Group of Central Ohio
P.O. Box 13179
Columbus, OH 43213

Momazons
P.O. Box 02069
Columbus, OH 43202

Akron PFLAG Chapter
P.O. Box 3204
Cuyahoga Falls, OH 44223

Miami Valley Northwest Ohio PFLAG Chapter
P.O. Box 45
Greenville, OH 45331-0045

Athens Area PFLAG Chapter
40011 Carpenter Hill Rd.
Pomeroy, OH 45769

Portsmouth PFLAG Chapter
11 Offnere St.
Portsmouth, OH 45662

Cleveland PFLAG Chapter
14260 Larchmere Blvd.
Shaker Heights, OH 44120

Toledo / Oregon Area PFLAG Chapter
1719 Greenwood
Toledo, OH 43605

Dayton PFLAG Chapter
175 Park Meadows Dr.
Yellow Springs, OH 45387

Youngstown PFLAG Chapter
2201 Goleta Ave.
Youngstown, OH 44504

Oklahoma City PFLAG Representative
2816 N. Ann Arbor Ave.
Oklahoma City, OK 73127-1818

Tulsa PFLAG Chapter
P.O. Box 52800
Tulsa, OK 74152

Ashland PFLAG Chapter
P.O. Box 13
Ashland, OR 97520

Bandon PFLAG Chapter
535 9th St., Suite A12
Bandon, OR 97411

Bend PFLAG Chapter
1937 N.W. West Hills Ave.
Bend, OR 97701

Linn-Benton PFLAG Chapter
1687 N.W. Division St.
Corvallis, OR 97330

Eugene / Springfield PFLAG Chapter
P.O. Box 11137
Eugene, OR 97440-3337

Rockaway Beach PFLAG Representative
P.O. Box 655
Garibaldi, OR 97118

Salem PFLAG Chapter
P.O. Box 121
Gates, OR 97346

Hood River PFLAG Chapter
P.O. Box 321
Hood River, OR 97031

Klamath Falls PFLAG Chapter
2306 Marina Dr.
Klamath Falls, OR 97601

LaGrande Area PFLAG Representative
P.O. Box 2995
La Grande, OR 97850

Lincoln County PFLAG Representative
P.O. Box 1156
Newport, OR 97365

Ontario PFLAG Chapter
450 Bar-O Dr.
Ontario, OR 97914

Pendleton PFLAG Chapter
1805 Southgate
Pendleton, OR 97801

Portland PFLAG Chapter
P.O. Box 8944
Portland, OR 97207-8944

Roseburg PFLAG Chapter
1567 N.W. Lester St.
Roseburg, OR 97470

Grants Pass PFLAG Chapter
P.O. Box 555
Wilderville, OR 97543

Yachats PFLAG Representative
P.O. Box 522
Yachats, OR 97498

Philadelphia PFLAG Chapter
3667 Mechanicsville Rd.
Bensalem, PA 19020

Franklin Area PFLAG Chapter
7430 Nyesville Rd.
Chambersburg, PA 17201

DuBois PFLAG Representative
1191 Treasure Lake
DuBois, PA 15801

PFLAG of Lehigh Valley
2040 Lehigh St., Suite 710
Easton, PA 18042

Erie PFLAG Chapter
1106 Oregon
Erie, PA 16505

Northeastern Pennsylvania PFLAG Chapter
107 Butler St.
Forty Fort, PA 18704

Central Pennsylvania PFLAG
3641 Brookridge Terr., Suite 201
Harrisburg, PA 17109

Gay Fathers of Central Pennsylvania
P.O. Box 114444
Federal Square Station
Harrisburg, PA 17108

Johnstown PFLAG Representative
Lutheran Social Ministries
797 Goucher St.
Johnstown, PA 15905

Lancaster Red Rose PFLAG Chapter
2112-13 Stone Mill Rd.
Lancaster, PA 17603-6073

Mechanicsburg PFLAG Chapter
960 Century Dr.
Mechanicsburg, PA 17055

Central Susquehanna PFLAG Chapter
RD 2, Box 1955
Milton, PA 17847

Pittsburgh PFLAG Chapter
P.O. Box 223
Monroeville, PA 15146

Philadelphia PFLAG Chapter
P.O. Box 15711
Philadelphia, PA 19103

Custody Action for Lesbians
(CALM)
P.O. Box 281
Navberth, PA 19143

Philadelphia Area Lesbian Mothers Group
4519 Larchwood Ave.
Philadelphia, PA 19143

York PFLAG Chapter
Lutheran Social Services
1050 Pennsylvania Ave.
York, PA 17404

Santurce, Puerto Rico PFLAG Representative
P.O. Box 116, Calle Loiza 1505
Santurce, PR 00911

East Bay Rhode Island PFLAG Chapter
85 Roseland Terr.
Tiverton, RI 02878

Charleston Area PFLAG Chapter
P.O. Box 30734
Charleston, SC 29417-0734

Columbia PFLAG Chapter
493 Hickory Hill Dr.
Columbia, SC 29210

Greenville PFLAG Chapter
801 Butler Springs Rd.
Greenville, SC 29615

Custer PFLAG Representative
Route 3, Box 94
Custer, SD 57730

Sioux Falls PFLAG Representative
300 N. Duluth
Sioux Falls, SD 57104

Greater Chattanooga PFLAG Chapter
P.O. Box 17252
Chattanooga, TN 37415

Memphis PFLAG Chapter
1303 Calais Rd.
Memphis, TN 38120

Nashville PFLAG Chapter
135 Holly Forest
Nashville, TN 37221-2226

Austin PFLAG Chapter
P.O. Box 9151
Austin, TX 78766-9151

The Treehouse
607 Nueces St.
Austin, TX 78701

Dallas PFLAG Chapter
P.O. Box 38415
Dallas, TX 75238

Denton PFLAG Chapter
P.O. Box 51096
Denton, TX 76206

El Paso PFLAG Chapter
P.O. Box 1761
El Paso, TX 79949

Fort Worth PFLAG Chapter
P.O. Box 48612
Fort Worth, TX 76148

Houston Gay & Lesbian Parents
1301 Richmond, #T10
Houston, TX 77006
Support services

Houston PFLAG Chapter
P.O. Box 692444
Houston, TX 77269-2444

Dallas GLPCI Parents Group
P.O. Box 820492
Hurst, TX 76182

Odessa / Midland PFLAG Representative
2741 N. Muskingum
Odessa, TX 79762

Gay & Lesbian Parents Coalition
2839 N.W. Military Dr., #508
San Antonio, TX 78231

San Antonio PFLAG Chapter
P.O. Box 790093
San Antonio, TX 78279

Waco PFLAG Representative
P.O. Box 23533
Waco, TX 76702-3533

Tarant County Parents Group
P.O. Box 48382
Watauga, TX 76148

Salt Lake City PFLAG Chapter
3363 Enchanted Hills Dr.
Salt Lake City, UT 84121-5465

Support Group for Lesbian Mothers
Utah Stonewall Center
450 South 900 East, Suite 140
Salt Lake City, UT 84102

Brattleboro PFLAG Chapter
409 Hillwinds
Brattleboro, VT 05301

Burlington PFLAG Chapter
23 Birchwood Lane
Burlington, VT 05401

Barre / Montpelier PFLAG Chapter
15 Vine St.
Northfield, VT 05663

Manchester / Rutland PFLAG Representative
11 North St.
Rutland, VT 05701

Charlottesville PFLAG Chapter
301 Monte Vista Ave.
Charlottesville, VA 22903

Dayton / Harrisburg PFLAG Representative
P.O. Box 607
Dayton, VA 22821

We Are Families
P.O. Box 935
Great Falls, VA 22066

Roanoke and Western VA PFLAG Chapter
12 Lakeshore Terrace
Hardy, VA 24101-3501

Lexington PFLAG Representative
3 Maple Lane
Lexington, VA 24450

Radford PFLAG Representative
567 Wisteria Dr.
Radford, VA 24141

Richmond PFLAG Chapter
P.O. Box 36392
Richmond, VA 23235-8008

Bremerton PFLAG Chapter (Kitsap County)
2880 N.E. 72nd St.
Bremerton, WA 98311

Lewis and Clark PFLAG Chapter
2220 2nd Ave.
Clarkston, WA 99403

Colville PFLAG Representative
North Star Farm
618 Monumental Rd.
Colville, WA 99114

Ellensburg PFLAG Chapter
1106 E. 3rd Ave.
Ellensburg, WA 98926

Ephrata PFLAG Chapter
165 "D" St. S.W.
Ephrata, WA 98823

Wenatchee Valley PFLAG Representative
217 Orchard St.
Leavenworth, WA 98826

Olympia PFLAG Chapter
P.O. Box 6123
Olympia, WA 98502

Richland PFLAG Chapter
648 Saint St.
Richland, WA 99352

Lavender Families Resource Network
P.O. 21567
Seattle , WA 98111
Jenny Sayward

Partners in Pregnancy
Lesbian Resource Center
1808 E. Bellevue, #204
Seattle, WA 98122

Seattle-Tacoma Metropolitan PFLAG Chapter
1202 E. Pike St., Suite 260
Seattle, WA 98122

Seattle-Snohomish Counties Gay / Lesbian Adoption Support Groups
800-398-1272

Spokane PFLAG Chapter
P.O. Box 40122
Spokane, WA 99202-0901

Vancouver PFLAG Chapter
12102 N.W. 21st Ave.
Vancouver, WA 98685

Yakima Valley PFLAG Chapter
732 Summitview #584
Yakima, WA 98902

Huntington PFLAG Representative
550 2nd St., Suite 3
Huntington, WV 25701

Parkersburg PFLAG Representative
1610 Park St.
Parkersburg, WV 26101

Wheeling PFLAG Representative
115 18th St.
Wheeling, WV 26003

Williamstown PFLAG Representative
502 1/2 Columbia Ave.
Williamstown, WV 26181

Galesville / Western Wisconsin PFLAG Representative
Box 399
Galesville, WI 54630

Appleton / Fox Cities PFLAG Chapter
P.O. Box 75
Little Chute, WI 54140-0075

Lesbian Parents' Network
P.O. Box 572
Madison, WI 53701

Madison PFLAG Chapter
P.O. Box 1722
Madison, WI 53711

Milton PFLAG Representative
50 N. John Paul Rd.
Milton, WI 53563

Milwaukee PFLAG Chapter c/o Lutheran Campus Ministries
3074 N. Maryland
Milwaukee, WI 53211

Lakeshore/ Sheboygan PFLAG Chapter
831 Union Ave.
Sheboygan, WI 53081

Casper PFLAG Chapter
404 S. McKinley St.
Casper, WY 82601-2916

Jackson PFLAG Chapter
P.O. Box 2704
Jackson, WY 83001

Rawlins PFLAG Representative
518 9th St.
Rawlins, WY 82301

Politics

Judy Abdo
Mayor of Santa Monica
1635 Main St.
Santa Monica, CA 90401

Roberta Achtenberg
Assistant Secretary for Housing & Urban Development
451 7th St. S.W., Rm. 5100
Washington, DC 20410

ACLU Chicago
203 N. LaSalle St., Suite 1405
Chicago, IL 60601
Legal services

ACLU of North Carolina Legal Foundation
PO Box 28004
Raleigh, NC 27611-8004
Legal services

Action Wisconsin
P.O. Box 342
Madison, WI 53701

African Ancestral Lesbians United for Societal Change
208 W. 13th St.
New York, NY 10011

AIDS Legal Assistance
800-828-6417
Austin, TX
Legal services

AIDS Legal Project
151 Spring St. N.W.
Atlanta, GA 30303
Chip Rowan, legal services

AIDS / HIV Housing Law Project
c/o Legal Assistance Foundation of Chicago
343 S. Dearborn, Suite 700
Chicago, IL 60604
Legal services

AIDS / HIV Legal Project
Legal Aid Society, Inc.
810 Barrett Ave., Suite 652
Louisville, KY 40204
Legal services

Alamance County Gay/Lesbian Alliance
P.O. Box 743
Haw River, NC 27250

Alaskans for Civil Rights
P.O. Box 26
Anchorage, AK 99520

Alice B. Toklas Democratic Club
P.O. Box 422698
San Francisco, CA 94142-2698
Matthew Rothschild

Allard Lowenstein Democratic Club
3775 Poinciana Ave.
Miami, FL 33133

Alliance for Equal Rights
P.O. Box 240423
Honolulu, HI 96824
Tom Humphrey

Amarillo Lesbian & Gay Alliance
P.O. Box 9361
Amarillo, TX 79105-9361
John Hintz, Director

American Civil Liberties Union (ACLU)
1401 Canal St.
Decatur, GA 30032
Legal services

American Civil Liberties Union AIDS Project
132 W. 43rd St.
New York, NY 10036
Matt Coles

American Civil Liberties Union Lesbian and Gay Rights Project
132 W. 43 St.
New York, NY 10036
Ruth Harlow, Legal services

Tom Ammiano
San Francisco Board of Supervisors
City Hall
San Francisco, CA 94102

Amnesty International Members for Lesbian & Gay Concerns
P.O. Box 8293
Santa Cruz, CA 95061-8293

Cal Anderson
Washington House
of Representatives
P.O. Box 40685
Olympia, WA 98504-0685

ANGLE
c/o Hitt
1734 N. Doheny
Los Angeles, CA 90069
David Mixner

Virginia Apuzzo
New York State Division
of Housing and Community
38-40 State St.
Albany, NY 12207

Arizona Human Rights Fund
P. O. Box 25044
Phoenix, AZ 85002
Bill McDonald, Executive Director

Arizonans for Fairness
P.O. Box 34766
Phoenix, AZ 85067-4766
Diane Post, Director

Arkansas Gay and Lesbian Taskforce
P.O. Box 45053
Little Rock, AR 72214

Arkansas Women's Political Caucus
P.O. Box 2494
Little Rock, AR 72203

Atlantic Coast Democratic Club
3273 Grove Rd.
Boynton Beach, FL 33435
Phil Carlson/Norman Aaron

Austin Lesbian and Gay Political Caucus
602 W. 7th St.
Austin, TX 78701

Tammy Baldwin
Wisconsin State Assembly
78th Assembly District
P.O. 8952
Madison, WI 53708

Baltimore Justice Campaign
P.O. Box 13221
Baltimore, MD 21203

Andrew E. Barrer
Office of the National AIDS Policy Coordinator
Executive Office of the President
750 17th St., N.W., Suite 1069
Washington, DC 20503

Deborah Batts
Foley Square Federal District Court
40 Center St., Rm. 2904
New York, NY 10007

Bay Area Municipal Elections Committee
P.O. Box 90070
San José, CA 95109

Roberta B. Bennett
Abbitt & Bennett
11755 Wilshire Blvd., #1450
Los Angeles, CA 90025
Certified Family Law Specialist

Bisbee Gay and Lesbian Alliance
P.O. Box 818
Bisbee, AZ 85603
Carol Parks

Bisexual and Radical Feminist (BARF)
1400 "L" St. N.W., PO Box 34086
Washington, DC 20043

Bisexual Political Action Coalition (BiPAC)
2863 N. Clark
Chicago, IL 60657

Bisexuals Engaging in Politics
P.O. Box 594
Northfield, OH 44067
Barbara Nicely

Black Gay and Lesbian Leadership Forum
1219 S. La Brea Ave.
Los Angeles, CA 90019

Keith Boykin
Special Assistant to the President
The White House
1600 Pennsylvania Ave.
Washington, DC 20500

David Braff
Sullivan & Cromwell
125 Broad St.
New York, NY 10004
Partner; does pro-bono civil rights work

Bronx Lesbians United in Sisterhood
P.O. Box 1738
Bronx, NY 10451
Lisa Winters

Tom Brougham
Peralta Community College Board
1725 Berkeley Way, #8
Berkeley, CA 94703

California Capital PAC
1008 10th St., Suite 255
Sacramento, CA 94117

Steven A. Camara
Fall River City Council
199 Purchase St.
Fall River, MA 02720-3222

Cambridge Lavender Alliance
P.O. Box 884
Cambridge, MA 02238
Sue Hyde

Col. Margarethe Cammermeyer
c/o Patricia Kelly
Viking Publicity
375 Hudson St., 4th Floor
New York, NY 10014
Author

Chuck Carpenter
State House of Representatives
State Capitol
Salem, OR 97310

Kevin Cathcart
Lambda Legal Defense and Education Fund
666 Broadway
New York, NY 10012

The Center for Anti-Violence Education
421 5th Ave.
Brooklyn, NY 11215
Annie Ellman, Executive Director
Anti-violence organization

Center for Constitutional Rights
666 Broadway
New York, NY 10012

Champaign County Lesbian, Gay, & Bisexual Task Force
P.O. Box 2511, Station A
Champaign, IL 61825-2511

Kent Cheuvront
Arizona House of Representatives
P.O. Box 17043
Phoenix, AZ

Tom Chiola
Circuit Court Judge
2600 Richard J. Daley Center
Chicago, IL 60602

Christopher St. South
P.O. Box 2752
Pensacola, FL 32513-2752
Andy Anderson, President

Citizens Alliance for Gay and Lesbian Civil Rights
P.O. Box 816
Concord, NH 03302

Citizens for Equal Protection
P.O. Box 55548
Omaha, NE 68155-0548
M.J. McBride/Neva Cozine

Citizens for Equal Rights Fund PAC
P.O. Box 301
Upton, NY 11973
Sharon Randall

Citizens for Justice
1487 W. 5th Ave., Box 226
Columbus, OH 43212

Citizens United Against Discrimination
380 E. 40th St., #107
Eugene, OR 97405
Kelly Weigel

Karen Clark
Minnesota House of Representatives
2633 19th Ave. S.
Minneapolis, MN 55407

President Bill Clinton
1600 Pennsylvania Ave., N.W.
Washington, DC 20500

Coalition for Gay and Lesbian Civil Rights
P.O. Box 94882
Lincoln, NE 68509

Coalition for Human Dignity
P.O. Box 40344
Portland, OR 97240
Steve Gardner

Coalition for Lesbian & Gay Civil Rights
State House P.O. Box 206
Boston, MA 02133
David LaFontaine

Coalition for Lesbian & Gay Rights
208 W. 13th St.
New York, NY 10025
Eleanor Cooper

COHAB
600 W. College, Box 432
Springfield, MO 68506

Colorado Legal Initiatives Project
P.O. Box 44447
Denver, CO 80201-4447
Legal services

Kelli Conlon
National Abortion &
Reproductive Rights Action
League, New York State Affiliate
462 Broadway, Suite 540
New York, NY 10013

Connecticut Coalition for Lesbian & Gay Civil Rights: Fairfield County
P.O. Box 4161
East Norwalk, CT 06855

Connecticut Coalition for Lesbian and Gay Civil Rights
P.O. Box 141025
Hartford, CT 06114
Charlotte Kinlock

Cook County Commission on Human Rights
118 N. Clark St., Rm. 624
Chicago, IL 60602-1304

Bill Crews
Mayor, Melbourne
P.O. Box 1994
Melbourne, IA 50162

David Cruise
Director of Intergovernmental
Relations
U.S. Department of Commerce
14th St./Constitution Ave. N.W.
Washington, DC 20230

Dade ActionPAC
P.O. Box 431151
Miami, FL 33243-1151
Shari McCartney/Greg Baldwin

Dan Bradley Democratic Club
P.O. Box 107
Coconut Grove, FL 33233
Alex Sanchez/Jack Campbell

D.C. Coalition of Black Lesbians and Gay Men
P.O. Box 21543
Washington, DC 20009

Dennis deLeon
Human Rights Commissioner
337 W. 14th St.
New York, NY 10014

Democratic Socialists of America, Lesbian / Gay / Bisexual Commission
Chicago DSA
1608 N. Milwaukee, #403
Chicago, IL 60647

Department of Defense
The Pentagon
Washington, DC 20301
William J. Perry

Department of Health & Human Services
200 Independence Ave. S.W.
Washington, DC 20201
Donna Shalala

Department of Justice
10th St. / Constitution Ave.
Washington, DC 20530
Janet Reno, Attorney General

Des Moines Gay & Lesbian Democratic Club
3500 Kingman Blvd.
Des Moines, IA 50311

Romulo Diaz, Jr.
Deputy Assistant Secretary
for International Affairs
U.S. Department of Energy
Rm. 7B-164
1000 Independence Ave. S.W.
Washington, DC 20585

Digital Queers
584 Castro St. #150
San Francisco, CA 94114
Tom Rielly

Beatrice Dohrn
Lambda Legal Defense
and Education Fund
666 Broadway
New York, NY 10012
Legal Director

Dolphin Democratic Club
P.O. Box 4646
Fort Lauderdale, FL 33338-4646
Sue Messinger

Mary Dorman
584 Broadway, Suite 1006
New York, NY 10012
Activist Attorney

Tom Duane
New York City Council
275 7th Ave., 12th Fl.
New York, NY 10001

Helen Dunlap
Deputy Assistant Secretary
for Multi-Family Housing Program
U.S. Department of Housing
and Urban Development
451 7th St. S.W., Rm. 5100
Washington, DC 20410

East Bay Lesbian and Gay Democratic Club
P.O. Box 443
Berkeley, CA 94701

East End Gay Organization
P.O. Box 708
Bridgehampton, NY 11932-0077
Sandy Papp

George Eighmey
Oregon State Assembly
1423 S.E. Hawthorne Blvd.
Portland, OR 97214

Eleanor Roosevelt Democratic Club
P.O. Box 2180
Albany, NY 12220-2180

Electronic Political Action in the Gay Environment
P.O. Box 19851
Portland , OR 97280-0851

Emily's List
1112 16th St. N.W., Suite 750
Washington, DC 20036
Ellen Malcolm

Empire State Pride Agenda
611 Broadway, #907A
New York, NY 10012
Dick Dadey

Equal Opportunity Commission
1801 "L" St.., N.W.
Washington, DC 20507

Equality Cincinnati
P.O. Box 271
Cincinnati, OH 45201-0271
Steve Segal and Doreen Quinn

Equality Kansas
P.O. Box 116
Topeka, KS 66601

Angie Fa
San Francisco Board of Education
135 Van Ness Ave.
San Francisco, CA 94102

Susan Farnsworth
Maine House of Representatives
222 Water St.
Hallowell, ME 04347

Federal Information Center
800-726-4995
Washington, DC

John Fiore
Wilton Manors City Council
2450 N.E. 15th Ave., #210
Wilton Manors, FL 33305

Will Fitzpatrick
Rhode Island State Senate
187 Narragansett St.
Cranston, RI 02905-4109

Flathead Valley Alliance
P.O. Box 2730
Kalispell, MT 59903
Dan Howard

Tom Fleury
Vermont State Assembly
12 Avenue A
Burlington, VT 05401

Floridians Respecting Everyone's Equality
P.O. Box 20021
Tallahassee, FL 32316
Jeff Peterson

Barney Frank
U.S. Congressman (D/MA)
2404 Rayburn House Office Bldg.
Washington, DC 20515

Free State Justice Campaign
P.O. Box 13221
Baltimore, MD 21203
John Hannay

GAPAC
P.O. Box 8420
Atlanta, GA 30306
Ed Stansell

Roslyn Garfield
Provincetown Town Moderator
City Hall, 260 Commercial St.
Provincetown, MA 02667

Gay Activists Alliance of New Jersey
P.O. Box 1734
South Hackensack, NJ 07606

Gay and Lesbian Action Alliance
P.O. Box 7293
Santa Cruz, CA 95061

Gay and Lesbian Action Delegation
P.O. Box 2897
Fayetteville, AR 72702

Gay and Lesbian Alliance Against Defamation
150 W. 26th St., Suite 503
New York, NY 10001

Gay and Lesbian Americans
2001 "O" St. N.W.
Washington, DC 20036
Michael Petrelis

Gay and Lesbian Democratic Caucus
P.O. Box 8342
Jackson, MS 39284-8342

Gay and Lesbian Political Action & Support
P.O. Box 11406
New Brunswick, NJ 08916-2536

Gay and Lesbian Utah Democrats
P.O. Box 11311
Salt Lake City, UT 84147

Gay and Lesbian Visibility Alliance
P.O. Box 1403
Madison, WI 53701-1403

Gay & Lesbian Activists Alliance
1734 14th St. N.W., 2nd Fl.
Washington, DC 20009
Jeff Courtier

Gay & Lesbian Alliance
2701 Reagan St.
Dallas, TX 75219
CeCe Cox, President

Gay & Lesbian Education & Advocacy
P.O. Box 37083
Honolulu, HI 96837-0083

Gay & Lesbian Independent Democrats
208 W. 13th St.
New York, NY 10025
Laura Morrison

Gay & Lesbian Interest Consortium
c/o 2101 Bucknell Terrace
Silver Spring, MD 20902
John Burlison, contact

Gay & Lesbian Rights Project, ACLU of Illinois
203 N. LaSalle St., Suite 1405
Chicago, IL 60601
Legal services

Gay & Lesbian United Effort PAC
Post Office Box 2004
Newport, OR 97365
Muril Demory

Gay & Lesbian Victory Fund
1012 14th St. NW, Suite 707
Washington, DC 20005
William Waybourne, Executive Director

Gay, Lesbian, and Bisexual Veterans of America
1350 N. 37th Pl.
Milwaukee, WI 53208

Gay Rights Task Force
P.O. Box 37083
Honolulu, HI 96837-0083

Gay Veterans Association
346 Broadway, #814
New York, NY 10013

Gay / Lesbian Human Rights Caucus
P.O. Box 1926
St. Louis, MO 63118
David Weeda

Gays & Lesbians for Individual Liberty
P.O. Box 65743
Washington, DC 20035
David Morris, President

Gays & Lesbians United for Equality
P.O. Box 992
Louisville, KY 40201-0992

Robert Gentry
Laguna Beach City Council
1475 Pacific Ave.
Laguna Beach, CA 92651
Councilmember

Georgia Political Awareness Coalition
P.O. Box 8420
Atlanta, GA 30306

Gertrude Stein Democratic Club
P.O. Box 21067
Washington, DC 20009

Deborah Glick
New York State Assembly
District Office
853 Broadway, Suite 2120
New York, NY 10003

Suzanne Goldberg
Lambda Legal Defense and Education Fund
666 Broadway
New York, NY 10012

Jackie Goldberg
Los Angeles City Council
City Hall, Rm. 240
Los Angeles, CA 90012

Ricardo Gonzalez
Madison Common Council
504 Wisconsin Ave., #1
Madison, WI 53703

Richard Gordon
San Mateo County Board of Education
101 Twin Dolphin Dr.
Redwood City, CA 94065-1064

Albert Gore
Vice President
Old Executive Office Building
Washington, DC 20500

Governor's Commission on Gay & Lesbian Youth
State House Rm. 111
Boston, MA 02133
David LaFontaine

Grass Roots Gay Rights Fund
533 Columbus Ave., #11
Boston, MA 02118
Jeff Lane

Greater Boston Lesbian & Gay Political Alliance
P.O. Box 65, Back Bay Annex
Boston, MA 02117
Don Gorton

Greater Cincinnati Gay and Lesbian Coalition
P.O. Box 19158
Cincinnati, OH 45219

Green Party Lesbian, Bisexual, Gay & Questioning Queer Caucus
691 Union St., #3L
Brooklyn, NY 11215

Guilford Alliance for Gay / Lesbian Equality
P.O. Box 5213
Greensboro, NC 274-2100

Gulf Alliance for Equality
1102 Ginion Circle
Mobile, AL 36605

Steve Gunderson
U.S. Congressman (R/WI)
2185 Rayburn HOB
Washington, DC 20515

Kenneth P. Hahn
Los Angeles County Assessor
500 W. Temple St., Rm.320
Los Angeles, CA 90012

Hands Off Washington / Washington Citizens for Fairness
1535 11th Ave. E.
Seattle, WA 98104
Charlie Brydon, Board President
Gloria Metz, Campaign Director

Edward Harrington
Controller
City Hall, Rm. 109
San Francisco, CA 94102

Jill Harris
New York City School Board
District 15
175 Remsen St.
Brooklyn, NY 11201

Sherry Harris
Seattle City Council
Municipal Building, 11th Fl.
Seattle, WA 98104

Harvard Law School Lambda Research Project
23 Everett St.
Cambrdge, MA 02138

Harvey Milk Lesbian & Gay Democratic Club
P.O. Box 14368
San Francisco, CA 94114-0368

Harvey Muggy Lesbian & Gay Democrats
1202 E. Pike St. #1196
Seattle, WA 98122-3934

Bob Hattoy
Assistant Deputy Secretary and White House Liaison
U.S. Department of the Interior
1849 "C" St., N.W., Rm. 5100
Washington, DC 20240-5100

Hawaii Equal Rights Marriage Project
c/o GLCC
1820 University Ave., Rm. 8
Honolulu, HI 96822

John Heilman
West Hollywood City Council
8611 Santa Monica Blvd.
West Hollywood, CA 90069-4109

Alan Hergott
Bloom, Dekom, Hergott & Cook
150 S. Rodeo Dr., 3rd Fl.
Beverly Hills, CA 90212

Nancy Hoff
Goshen Board of Selectmen
P.O. Box 109
Goshen, MA 01032

Homecoming
c/o American Friends Service Committee
814 N.E. 40th St.
Seattle, WA 98105
Arlis Stewart

Jeff Horton
Los Angeles Board of Education
P.O. Box 3307
Los Angeles, CA 90051

The United States House of Representatives
Washington, DC 20515

Housing Works Inc.
594 Broadway, Suite 700
New York, NY 10012
Keith Cylar

Houston Gay & Lesbian Political Caucus
P.O. Box 66664
Houston, TX 77266
Terri Richardson

Human Rights Bar Association of DePaul
De Paul University College of Law
25 E. Jackson
Chicago, IL 60604
Legal services

Human Rights Campaign Fund
1012 14th St. NW, Suite 607
Washington, DC 20005
Elizabeth Birch, Executive Director

Human Rights Council, Palm Beach County
3273 Grove Rd.
Boynton Beach, FL 33435
Norman Aaron

Human Rights Council of North Central Florida
P.O. Box 2112
Gainesville, FL 32602

Human Rights League for Lesbians & Gays
P.O. Box 92674
Milwaukee, WI 53202

Human Rights PAC
7230B Raytown Rd.
Raytown, MO 64135

Human Rights Project
P.O. Box 32812
Kansas City, MO 64171-7812

Human Rights Task Force of Florida
4915 Suwannee Ave.
Tampa, FL 33603
Nadine Smith/Todd Simmons

Nan Hunter
Office of the General Council,
Department of Health and Human Services
722-A Humphrey Bldg.
200 Independence Ave. S.W.
Washington, DC 20201

Susan Hyde
Hartford City Council
52 Lincoln St.
Hartford , CT 06106

Idaho for Human Dignity
P.O. Box 797
Boise, ID 83701-0797
Brian Bergquist Co-chair

Idaho Voices for Human Rights
967 E. Park Center Blvd. #250
Boise, ID 83706
Mary Rolfing, Executive Director

Impact
909 W. Belmont, Suite 201
Chicago, IL 60657

International Gay and Lesbian Human Rights Commission
1360 Mission St., Suite 200
San Francisco, CA 94103
Julie Dorf/Jorge Cortinas

International Lesbian and Gay Association
208 W 13th St.
New York, NY 10011
Mark Unger

International Network of Lesbian & Gay Officials
3801 26th St. E.
Minneapolis, MN 55406-1857
Tim Cole

Patricia Ireland
National Organization of Women
1000 16th St. N.W., Suite 700
Washington, DC 20036

Jerry Mayer Democratic Club
1227 Neil Ave.
Columbus , OH 43201
Lynn Greer

Justice
P.O. Box 2387
Indianapolis, IN 46206

Christine Kehoe
San Diego City Council
2515 Meade Ave.
San Diego, CA 92116

Kentucky Fairness Alliance
P.O. Box 1523
Frankfort, KY 40602

Key West Business Guild
P.O. Box 1208
Key West, FL 33041

Sheila Kuehl
California State Assembly Member
State Capitol
Sacramento, CA

Lesbian & Gay Democrats of Montgomery County
2101 Bucknell Terrace
Silver Spring, MD 20902
John Burlison

Lambda Democratic Caucus
P.O. Box 77389
Tuscon, AZ 85703
Deborah Broner

Lambda Independent Democrats
309 5th Ave., #434
Brooklyn , NY 11215
Liz Schalet

Lambda Legal Defense & Education Fund
666 Broadway, 12th Fl.
New York, NY 10012
Legal services

Lambda Legal Defense & Education Fund (Midwest Regional Office)
17 E. Monroe, Suite 212
Chicago, IL 60603
Legal services

Lambda Legal Defense & Education Fund (Western Regional Office)
6030 Wilshire Blvd., Suite 200
Los Angeles, CA 90036-3617
J. Craig Fong, legal services

Lambda Rights Network
P.O. Box 93252
Milwaukee, WI 53203

League of Gay & Lesbian Voters
P.O. Box 3063
Erie, PA 16508

League of Gay & Lesbian Voters
Penn West Building
909 West St., Suite 150
Pittsburgh, PA 15221
Chris Young

Susan Leal
San Francisco Board of Supervisors
4115 26th St.
San Francisco, CA 94131

Legal Advocates for Children and Youth
111 W. St. John, Suite 315
San José, CA 95113
Legal services

Bruce Lehman
Assistant Secretary of Commerce and Commissioner of Patents and Trademarks
U.S. Department of Commerce
Patents and Trademarks Office
14th St./Constitution Ave. N.W.
Washington, DC 20231

Lesbian Alliance Metro Milwaukee
P.O. Box 93323
Milwaukee, WI 53203

Lesbian and Gay Democrats of Texas
P.O. Box 190933
Dallas, TX 75219

Lesbian and Gay Political Coalition of Dallas
P.O. Box 224424
Dallas, TX 75222
Steve Atkinson

Lesbian Avengers / Austin
44 East Ave., Suite 300, Box 69
Austin, TX 78701

Lesbian Avengers / New Orleans
P.O. Box 791375
New Orleans, LA 70179-1375

Lesbian Avengers / New York
208 W. 13th St.
New York, NY 10011

Lesbian & Gay Caucus of the California Democratic Party
c/o 910A Steiner St.
San Francisco, CA 94117
Robert Barnes

Lesbian & Gay Caucus, Oregon Democratic Party
1703 S.W. Montgomery Dr.
Portland, OR 97201

Lesbian & Gay Community Mediation Project
Lawyers for Human Rights and
Lambda Legal Defense
1625 N. Schrader Ave.
Los Angeles, CA 90028-9998
Dorothy Lank

Lesbian & Gay Democratic Club
P.O. Box 36
Sherwood, OR 97140
Robert Ralphs

Lesbian & Gay Pride of the Delaware Valley
P.O. Box 395
Philadelphia, PA 19105

Lesbian Rights Task Force
National Organization for Women
P.O. Box 80292
San Diego, CA 92138

Lesbian / Gay Political Action Network
P.O. Box 3775
Grand Rapids, MI 49501-3775

Lesbian / Gay Rights Lobby of Texas
P.O. Box 2579
Austin, TX 78768-2579
Dianne Hardy-Garcia

Lesbians and Gays of African Descent for Democratic Action
Box 584, Castro St., #30
San Francisco, CA 94114

Linda T. Leslie
Village Trustee
P.O. Box 511
Douglas, MI 49406

LGLA Low Country Gay and Lesbian Alliance
P.O. Box 98
Charleston, SC 29402
Mark Schwartzot and Frances Wright

LIFE AIDS Lobby
926 "J" St., Suite 522
Sacramento, CA 95814
Laurie McBride, Executive Director

LLEGO (National Latino / a Lesbian & Gay Organization
P.O. Box 44483
Washington, DC 20026
Letitia Gomez

LLEGO California
P.O. Box 40816
San Francisco, CA 94140

Log Cabin Atlanta
P.O. Box 930396
Norcross, GA 30093

Log Cabin Austin
P.O. Box 50484
Austin, TX 78763

Log Cabin Broward County
P.O. Box 1281
Ft. Lauderdale, FL 33302

Log Cabin California
932 Rembrandt Dr.
Laguna Beach, CA 92651

Log Cabin Capital Area
P.O. Box 90201
Washington, DC 20090-0201

Log Cabin Central Michigan
P.o. Box 10037
Lansing, MI 48901

Log Cabin Cincinnati
P.O. Box 19472
Cincinnati, OH 45219

Log Cabin Club
P.O. Box 869
Oldsmar, FL 34677

Log Cabin Club / Los Angeles
P.O. Box 480336
Los Angeles, CA 90048
Ritch Colbert

Log Cabin Connecticut
130 Maple St.
New Britain, CT 06050

Log Cabin Denver
1313 Williams St. #1202
Denver, CO 80218

Log Cabin Federation
53 Rutland St. #3
Boston, MA 02118
Abner Mason, President

Log Cabin Houston
P.O. Box 131104
Houston, TX 77219

Log Cabin Idaho
1117 Kimberly Ln.
Boise, ID 83712

Log Cabin Kentucky
1556 Alexandria Dr., #4B
Lexington, KY 40504

Log Cabin Las Vegas
P.O. Box 13439
Las Vegas, NV 89112

Log Cabin Louisiana
P.O. Box 70744
New Orleans, LA 70172

Log Cabin Maine
137 York St.
Portland, ME 04101

Log Cabin Massachusetts
Back Bay Annex
P.O. Box 1465
Boston, MA 02117-1465

Log Cabin Minnesota Independent Republicans
2732 Grand Ave. S., #201
Minneapolis, MN 55408

Log Cabin North San Diego County
1035 E. Vista Way, #142
Vista, CA 92084

Log Cabin New Jersey
P.O. Box 4102
Wayne, NJ 07474

Log Cabin New York City
P.O. Box 1690
Madison Square Garden Station
New York, NY 10159-1690

Log Cabin Northeast Ohio
Suite 1, Leader Bldg.
P.O. Box 94110
Cleveland, OH 44101-6100

Log Cabin Orange County
4482 Barranca Pkwy., #180-115
Irvine, CA 92714

Log Cabin Philadelphia
P.O. Box 34704
Philadelphia, PA 19101

Log Cabin Republicans
558 S. Meyer
Tucson, AZ 85701
Ron St. John

Log Cabin Riverside County
2284 Temple Hills Dr.
Laguna Beach, CA 92651

Log Cabin Sacramento
2025 23rd St.
Sacramento, CA 95818-1717

Log Cabin San Diego
P.O. Box 3242
San Diego, CA 92163-3242

Log Cabin San Francisco
P.O. Box 14174
San Francisco, CA 94114

Log Cabin San Luis Obispo
P.O. Box 608
Avila Beach, CA 93424

Log Cabin Santa Clara
P.O. Box 1007
Santa Margarita, CA 93453

Log Cabin Southeast Michigan
18530 Mack Ave., #113
Grosse Pte. Farms, MI 48236

Log Cabin Washington
14302 S.E. 18th, #A2
Bellevue, WA 98007

Log Cabin West Michigan
9654 84th St. SE
Alto, MI 49302

Log Cabin Wisconsin
913 E. Kilbourne, #1
Milwaukee, WI 53202

Long Beach Lambda Democratic Club
P.O. Box 14454
Long Beach, CA 90803

Louisiana Electorate of Gays and Lesbians
P.O. Box 70344
New Orleans, LA 70172

Louisiana Lesbian and Gay Political Action Caucus
P.O. Box 53705
New Orleans, LA 70153
Jim Wiltberger

Mark Loveless
Community Representative,
Pulaski School Board
2130 W. McLean, Apt. 1
Chicago, IL 60647

Sandy Lowe
240 Prospect Place
Brooklyn, NY 11238
Activist Attorney

Madison Community United
14 E. Mifflin
Madison, Wisconsin 53703
Jane Vanderbosch

Maine Civil Liberties Union
97A Exchange St.
Portland, ME 04104
Pat Beard, legal services

Maine Lesbian and Gay Political Alliance
72 High St., #2
Portland, ME 04101
Karen Geraghty

Tim O. Mains
Rochester City Council
413 Broadway
Rochester, NY 14607

Steve Martin
West Hollywood City Council
812 N. Huntley Dr.
West Hollywood, CA 90069

Phillip Martin
Ward Chairman
340 Ohio Union, 1739 N. High St.
Columbus, OH 43210

David Martin
Assistant to the Assistant
Secretary for Legislative
and Intergovernmental Affairs
U.S. Department of Commerce
Rm. 5422
14th St./Constitution Ave. N.W.
Washington, DC 20230

Massachusetts Gay & Lesbian Political Caucus
P.O. Box 246
State House
Boston, MA 02133
Arlene Isaacson

Glen Maxey
Texas House of Representatives
P.O. Box 2910
Austin, TX 78768

Dale McCormick
Maine State Senate
RFD 1, Box 697
Monmouth, ME 04259

Scott McCormick
Dane County Board of Supervisors
633 Langden St., #322
Madison, WI 53703

Craig McDaniel
Dallas City Council
1500 Marilla St.
Dallas, TX 75201

Jim McGill
Wilkinsburg Borough Council
800 Ross Ave., #1
Pittsburgh, PA 15221-2356

Larry McKeon
Mayor's Liaison to Gay/Lesbian Community
500 N. Pestigo, Suite 6A
Chicago, IL 60611

Memphis Gay Coalition
P.O. Box 3038
Memphis, TN 38173-0038

Ben Merrill
Special Assistant
White House Office of AIDS Policy
The White House
1600 Pennsylvania Ave. N.W.
Washington, DC 20500

Metroplex Republicans
P.O. Box 191033
Dallas, TX 75219-8033

Michigan Campaign for Human Dignity
P.O. Box 27363
Lansing, MI 48909-7363
Linda Shapanka

Michigan Coalition for Human Rights
4800 Woodward Ave.
Detroit, MI 48201
Katherine Savoie

Michigan Lesbian & Gay Democratic Caucus
P.O. Box 1708
Royal Oak, MI 48068

Michigan Organization for Human Rights
P.O. Box 27383
Lansing, MI 48909-7383
Victor Estevez

Carole Migden
San Francisco Board of Supervisors
City Hall, Rm. 235
San Francisco, CA 94102

Military Law Task Force
1168 Union St., Suite 201
San Diego, CA 92101
Kathleen Gilberd/ Harold Jordan, Co-Chairs

Gary Miller
Robla School Board
363 Berthoud St.
Sacramento, CA 95838-1699

Minnesota Independent Republican Club
2518 Blaisdell Ave. S.
Minneapolis, MN 55404

Mississippi Gay and Lesbian Task Force
311 Caillavet St.
Biloxi, MS 399530

Mississippi Gay and Lesbian Task Force
P.O. Box 7737
Jackson, MS 39284-7737

Missourians for Freedom and Justice
P.O. Box 50225
Clayton, MO 63105
The Very Rev. J.C. Michael Allen

David Mixner
ANGLE
356 Huntley Dr.
West Hollywood, CA 90048

Michael Morand
New Haven Board of Alders
P.O. Box 6537
New Haven, CT 06520

Howard Moses
Deputy Assistant Secretary for Special Education and Rehabilitative Services
Department of Education
400 Maryland Ave. S.W.
Washington, DC 20202

Moving On Coalition
P.O. Box 7534
Columbia, MO 65205-7534

Scot Nakagawa
National Gay and Lesbian Task Force
522 S.W. 5th Ave., Suite #1023
Portland, OR 97204

Jon Nalley
New York City School Board
District 2
330 W. 18th St.
New York, NY 10011

National Center for Lesbian Rights
462 Broadway, Suite 500A
New York, NY 10013
Paula Brantner, Legal Director

National Center for Lesbian Rights
1663 Mission St., #550
San Francisco, CA 94103
Liz Hendrickson, Executive Director

National Coming Out Day
P.O. Box 34640
Washington, DC 20043-4640

National Gay and Lesbian Task Force
2320 17th St. N.W.
Washington, DC 20009-2702
Melinda Paras, Executive Director

National Organization of Women
1000 16th St., N.W., Suite 700
Washington, DC 20036
Patricia Ireland

NCARRV
P.O. Box 240
Durham, NC 27702
Anti-violence group

Michael Nelson
Carrboro City Council
501 W. Poplar Ave.
Carrboro, NC 27510

Network of Rhode Island
P.O. Box 1474
Pawtucket, RI 02862-1474

New Hampshire Coalition to End Discrimination
P.O. Box 74
Concord, NH 03302-0074
Chris Margetou

New Mexico Lesbian & Gay Political Alliance
P.O. Box 25191
Albuquerque, NM 87125

New York City Gay & Lesbian Anti-Violence Project
647 Hudson St.
New York, NY 10014

Zoon Nguyen
Special Assistant
to the Assistant Secretary
U.S. Department of Housing
and Urban Development
451 7th St. S, Rm. 5100
Washington, DC 20410

North Carolina Coalition for Gay and Lesbian Equality
P.O. Box 61392
Durham, NC 27715
Kenda Kirby, Executive Director

North Carolina Coalition for Gay and Lesbian Equality
P.O. Box 15533
Winston-Salem, NC 27113

North Carolina Gay / Lesbian Political Action
2009 Chapel Hill Rd.
Durham, NC 27707

North Carolina Human Rights Fund
P.O. Box 10782
Raleigh, NC 27605

North Carolina Pride PAC
P.O. Box 813
Carrboro, NC 27510

Northeast Vermonters for Gay & Lesbian Rights
c/o Umbrella
1 Prospect St.
Saint Johnsbury, VT 05819

Office of Lesbian & Gay Concerns
NYS Executive Chamber
State Capitol
Albany, NY 12224
Sheila Healy, government

Ohio Human Rights Bar Association
PO Box 10655
Columbus, OH 43201

Oklahoma Gay & Lesbian Political Caucus
P.O. Box 611886
Oklahoma City, OK 73146
Paul Thompson

Orange Lesbian / Gay Association
P.O. Box 307
Chapel Hill, NC 27514
Doug Ferguson

Out Voice
1487 W. 5th Ave., Box 226
Columbus, OH 43212

Ozarks Human Rights Coalition
P.O. Box 901
West Plains, MO 65775

Antonio Pagan
New York City Council
New York City Hall
New York, NY 10007

Jay Pagano and Larry Ray
Advisory Neighborhood Committee 2B 01
1825 "T" St. N.W., Suite 404
Washington, DC 20009

Joe Pais
Key West City Commission
P.O. Box 4381
Key West, FL 33041-4381

Partners Task Force for Gay & Lesbian Couples
Box 9658
Seattle, WA 98109-9685
Steve Bryant

Pennsylvania Justice Campaign for Lesbian & Gay Rights
P.O. Box 614
Harrisburg, PA 17108
Patrick Wallen

People for the American Way
2000 "M" St. N.W., Suite 400
Washington, DC 20036
Arthur Kropp

People for the American Way / Florida
P.O.Box 310
Indian Rocks Beach, FL 34635
Susan Glickman

Philadelphia Equal Rights Coalition
4519 Osage
Philadelphia, PA 19143

Philadelphia Lesbian & Gay Task Force
1616 Walnut St., Suite 105
Philadelphia, PA 19103
Rita Adessa

Mark Pocan
Dane County Board of Supervisors
1 E. Gilman, #206
Madison, WI 53703

Nancy Polikoff
American University Law School
4400 Massachusetts Ave., N.W.
Washington, DC 20016
Professor of Family Law

Prairie Lesbian & Gay Community
P.O. Box 83
Moorhead, MN 56560

Pride Montana
P.O. Box 775
Helena, MT 59624
Diane Sands

Prince Georgians for Equal Rights
c/o 7024 Hanover Parkway, #B2
Greenbelt, MD 20770
Kevin Watkins

Privacy Fund
1202 E. Pike St., #1196
Seattle, WA 98122-3934

Privacy Rights Education Project
P.O. Box 24106
St. Louis, MO 63130
Leah Edelman, Administrative Director

Pro-Life Alliance of Gays & Lesbians
P.O. Box 33292
Washington, DC 20033-0292

Project Rainbow
c/o GLCSC
1625 N. Hudson Ave
Los Angeles, CA 90028-9998

Public Awareness Project
3136 N. 3rd Ave.
Phoenix, AZ 85013
Peter Crozier

Queens Gays and Lesbians United
P.O. Box 4669
Sunnyside, NY 11104
Ed Sedarbaum

Queer Nation
P.O. Box 34463
Omaha, NE 68134-0463

Irene Rabinowitz
President, Provincetown Board of Selectmen
7 Washington Ave.
Provincetown, MA 02657

Radical Women—National Office
523-A Valencia St.
San Francisco, CA 94110
Nancy Reiko-Kato, National Organizer

Rainbow Coalition
P.O. Box 70811
New Orleans, LA 70153

Rainbow Democratic Club
P.O. Box 532041
Orlando, FL 32853-2041
Bob Spears

Kenneth E. Reeves
Mayor of Cambridge
City Hall
Cambridge, MA 02139

Republicans for Individual Freedoms
P.O. Box 13162
Atlanta , GA 30324
Gary Bastien

Rhode Island Alliance for Gay and Lesbian Civil Rights
P.O. Box 5758
Weybosset Hill Station
Providence , RI 02903

R. Paul Richard
Deputy Staff Secretary
The White House
1600 Pennsylvania Ave. N.W.
Washington, DC 20500

Right to Privacy PAC
921 S.W. Morrison, #518
Portland , OR 97205
Greg Jackson

Hedy Rijken
Oregon State Representative
State House of Representatives
State Capitol
Salem, OR 97310

River City Democratic Club
P.O. Box 161958
Sacramento, CA 95816-1958

Tom Roberts
Santa Barbara City Council
P.O. Box 1990
Santa Barbara, CA 93102

Rochester Lesbian & Gay Political Caucus
179 Atlantic Ave.
Rochester, NY 14607-1255
Bill Pritchard

Angelica Rovira
New York City School Board
District 1
80 Montgomery St., Rm. 2
New York, NY 10002

Rural Organizing Project
P.O. Box 919
Scappoose, OR 97056
Marcy Westerling, Coordinator

San Antonio Equal Rights Political Caucus for Lesbians, Gays, Bisexuals and Transgendered (SAERPC)
P.O. Box 12571
San Antonio, TX 78212
Tere Frederickson

San Diego Democratic Club
P.O. Box 80193
San Diego, CA 92138

San Francisco School Board
135 Van Ness Ave.
San Francisco, CA 94110

SC-NOW
1009 Oak Creek Dr.
Spartanburg, SC 29302
Liz Clarke

Seattle Municipal Elections Committee for Gays, Lesbians, and Bisexuals
1202 E. Pike, #901
Seattle, WA 98122-3934

The United States Senate
Washington, DC 20510

Servicemembers Legal Defense Network
PO Box 53013
Washington, DC 20009
Michelle Beneike, legal services

Gail Shibley
Oregon State Assembly
c/o Friends of Gail Shibley
P.O. Box 6805
Portland, OR 97228

Simply Equal
P.O. Box 61305
Oklahoma City, OK 73146

Nadine Smith
Human Rights Task Force of Florida
4915 Suwannee Ave.
Tampa, FL 33603
Executive Director

Richard Socarides
White House Liaison
U.S. Department of Labor
200 Constitution Ave. N.W.
Rm. S-1004
Washington, DC 20210

South Carolina Gay & Lesbian Pride Movement
P.O. Box 12648
Columbia, SC 29211
Matt Tischler and Kristen Gregory

South Carolina Women's Consortium
P.O. Box 3099
Columbia, SC 29230
Marvella Peoples

Southern Oregon Lambda Association
P.O. Box 4387
Medford, OR 97501

Allan Spear
President, Minnesota Senate
Rm. G-27 Capitol
St. Paul, MN 55155

Keith C. St. John
Albany Common Council
116 Philip St.
Albany, NY 12202-1727

Liz Stefanics
New Mexico State Senate
P.O. Box 1301
Santa Fe, NM 87504-1301

Stonewall Cincinnati
P.O. Box 954
Cincinnati, OH 45201
Kelly Malone

Stonewall Cleveland
P.O. Box 5936
Cleveland, OH 44101

Stonewall Committee for Lesbian and Gay Rights
6727 Seward Park Ave. S.
Seattle, WA 98118
Chris Smith
Brice Peyre

Stonewall Democratic Club
P.O. Box 26367
Los Angeles, CA 90026
Eric Bauman/Al Rodriguez

Stonewall Democratic Club
P.O. Box 1750
Old Chelsea Station
New York, NY 10011

Stonewall Gay Democratic Club
150 Eureka St.
San Francisco, CA 94114

Stonewall of Ohio PAC
P.O. Box 10095
Columbus, OH 43201
B. Scott Sanchez

Stonewall Union
P.O. Box 10814
Columbus, OH 43201-7814

Gerry Studds
U.S. Congressman (D/MA)
237 Cannon House Office Bldg.
Washington, DC 20515-2110

Support Our Communities PAC
P.O. Box 40625
Portland, OR 97240
Julie Davis

Wallace Swan
Minneapolis Board of Estimate and Taxation
15 S. 1st St.
Minneapolis, MN 55401

Rich Tafel
Log Cabin Republicans
1012 14th St N.W., #703
Washington, DC 20005
Executive Director

Tennessee Gay and Lesbian Alliance
P.O. Box 41305
Nashville, TN 37204-1305

Texas Human Rights Foundation
PO Box 49740
Austin, TX 78765
Legal services

The Agora
PO Box 66403
Houston, TX 77266
Bart Loeser, President

Thompson & Wheatley
2005 Massachusetts Ave. N.W.
Washington, DC 20036-1011
Law Firm

Tri-PAC
414 S. Craig St., #282
Pittsburgh, PA 15213

Triangle Coalition
AO22 Brady Commons
University of Missouri
Columbia, MO 65211
Jeff Passmore

Triangle Foundation
19641 W. Seven Mile Rd.
Detroit, Michigan 48219
Jeffrey Montgomery

Triangle Lesbian / Gay Alliance
P.O. Box 3295
Durham, NC 27705

Katherine Triantifillou
Cambridge City Council
Cambridge City Hall
Cambridge, MA 02139

Tucson Lesbian and Gay Alliance
P.O. Box 40301
Tucson, AZ 85717
John Haase, Director

Tulsa Oklahomans for Human Rights
P.O. Box 52729
Tulsa, OK 74152

Gerald Ulrich
Mayor of Bunceton
City Hall, P.O. Box 200
Bunceton, MO 65237

Uptown Democratic Club
P.O. Box 3113
San Diego, CA 92163

Utah Log Cabin Club
P.O. Box 3493
Salt Lake City, UT 84110-3493

Urvashi Vaid
P.O. Box 103
Provincetown, MA 02657

Tim van Zandt
Missouri House of Representatives
P.O. Box 45682
Kansas City, MO 64111

Braulio (Brad) Veloz
230 W. Craig Place
San Antonio, TX 78212

Vermont Coalition for Lesbians & Gay Men
P.O. Box 1125
Montpelier, VT 05602

Virginia Partisan Gay and Lesbian Democratic Club
P.O. Box 20633
Alexandria, VA 223020
Adam Ebbin

Virginia Political Action Network
2036 Peach Orchard, #21
Falls Church, VA 22043
Ken Stillson

Virginians for Justice
P.O. Box 342, Capital Station
Richmond, VA 23202
Janice Conard

Voter Registration Project
The Center
208 W. 13th St.
New York, NY 10011

Voters United for Equality
P.O. Box 8381
Greenville, SC 29604
Jim Fowler and Susan Stallard

Richard Wagner
Dane County Board of Supervisors
739 Jennifer St.
Madison, WI 53703

Washington Freedom Coalition
P.O. Box 7703
Olympia, WA 98507

West Hollywood Democratic Club
P.O. Box 691005
West Hollywood, CA 90069

Bruce Williams
Tacoma Park City Council
326 Lincoln Ave.
Tacoma Park, MD 20912

Chris Wilson
Oakland Park City Council
P.O. Box 70187
Oakland Park, FL 33307

Tim Wolfred
San Francisco County College
Governing Board
975 Duncan St.
San Francisco, CA 94131

Cynthia Wooten
State House of Representatives
State Capitol
Salem, OR 97310

Ken Yeager
San José Community College
Trustee
1925 Cleveland Ave.
San José, CA 95126

Your Family, Friends, and Neighbors
P.O. Box 768
Boise, ID 83701
John Hummel

Professional

Alliance for Gay and Lesbian Artists in theEntertainment Industry
P.O. Box 69A18
West Hollywood, CA 90069

American Public Health Association, Lesbian & Gay Caucus
1345 N. Hayworth Ave.
West Hollywood, CA 90046
Marc Wynne

Apple Lambda
20525 Mariani Ave.
Cupertino, CA 95014
Bennet Marks

Association for Gay, Lesbian & Bisexual Issues in Counseling
(AGLIBC)
P.O. Box 216
Jenkintown, PA 19046

Association of Gay & Lesbian Psychiatrists
c/o Diana Miller, M.D.
3331 Ocean Park Blvd., #201
Santa Monica, CA 90405

Bar Association for Human Rights
P.O. Box 1899
Grand Central Station
New York, NY 10163

Capital Cities/ABC Gay and Lesbian Organization of Employees
(GLOE)
1383 12th Ave.
San Francisco, CA 94122

EAGLE (Omaha)
1314 Douglas, 8th Fl.
Omaha, NE 68102
Organization for employees at U.S. West

EAGLE (Spokane)
501 W. 2nd Ave., Rm. 201
Spokane, WA 99204
Organization for employees at U.S. West

Federal Globe
c/o Leonard Hirsch
S. Dillon Ripley Center
1199 Jefferson Dr. S.W., Suite 3123
MRC 705
Washington, DC 20560
Federal employees

Gay and Lesbian Association of Xerox Employees
(GALAXE)
P.O. Box 25382
Rochester, NY 14625-0382

Gay and Lesbian Employees of the Red Cross
1197 N. Decatur Rd. N.E.
Atlanta, GA 30306-2362

Gay and Lesbian Medical Association / American Association of Physicians for Human Rights
2940 16th St., #105
San Francisco, CA 94103
Ben Schatz

Gay and Lesbian PEN
P.O. Box 580397
Minneapolis, MN 55458-0397
Postal employees

Gay and Lesbian Task Force of the American Library Association's Social Responsibilities Round Table
Schlesinger Library, Radcliffe College
10 Garden St.
Cambridge, MA 02138

Gay and Lesbian United Airlines Employees Coalition
2261 Market St., Suite 293
San Francisco, CA 94103

Gay, Lesbian and Bisexual Employees of Ameritech
P.O. Box 14308
Chicago, IL 60614

Gay & Lesbian Press Association
P.O. Box 8185
Universal City, CA 91608-0185

Gay & Lesbian Resource Network of the American Red Cross
9706 Dilston Rd.
Silver Spring, MD 20903

Gay & Lesbian Statisticians Caucus
c/o David Wijp, Department of Biostatistics, Harvard University
677 Huntington Ave.
Boston, MA 02115

Gay & Lesbian University Employees
University of Washington (Seattle)
P.O. Box 23164
Seattle, WA 98102-0464

Gay Officers Action League
P.O. Box 2038
Canal Street Station
New York, NY 10013

Gay Pilots Association
P.O. Box 1291
Alexandria, VA 22313

Gays & Lesbians in Foreign Affairs
P.O. Box 18774
Washington, DC 20036-8774

Gays & Lesbians in Urban Planning & Policy
1705 Lanier Pl. N.W. #402
Washington, DC 20009

GLEAM-Gay and Lesbian Employees at Microsoft
1 Microsoft Way, Bldg. 1-1
Redmond, WA 98052-6399
Jeff Howard

GLOBAL: Gay & Lesbian Organizations Bridging Across the Land
P.O. Box 42406
Philadelphia, PA 19101-2406

Group Health
(Gay & Lesbian Employees)
83 S. King St., Suite 515
Seattle, Washington 98104-2848
Laura Lea Smith

High Tech Gays
P.O. Box 6777
San José, CA 95150
A. J. Alfieri

Labor Pride of Philadelphia
c/o Temple AFSCME
1606 Walnut St.
Philadelphia, PA 19103

Lambda Labor
P.O. Box 65893
Washington Square Station
Washington, DC 20035-5893
David White

Lawyers for Human Rights
P.O. Box 480318
Los Angeles, CA 90048
Shedrick O. Davis and Cynthia Juno

Lesbian and Gay Bar Association of Chicago
P.O. Box 06498
Chicago, IL 60606-0498

Lesbian & Gay Child & Adolescent Psychiatrists
P.O. Box 570
Glen Oaks, NY 11004

Lesbian and Gay Congressional Staff Association
U.S. House of Representatives
Miscellaneous Mails
Washington, DC 20515

Lesbian and Gay Labor Network
P.O. Box 1159
Peter Stuyvesant Station
New York, NY 10009
Publishes Pride at Work

Lesbian, Bisexual & Gay United Employees at AT&T
(LEAGUE)
c/o Margaret Burd
11900 N. Peros St., Room 30H78
Denver, CO 80234

Lesbian & Gay Labor Alliance
763 14th St.
San Francisco, CA 94114

Lesbian Visual Artists
3543 18th St. #5
San Francisco, CA 94110

Los Angeles Lesbian And Gay Labor Coalition
c/o SEIU Local 399
1247 West St.
Los Angeles, CA 90017

Midwest Association of Lesbian & Gay Psychologists
Box 199
3023 N. Clark
Chicago, IL 60657

National Gay & Lesbian Nurses: The Lavender Lamps
208 W. 13th St.
New York, NY 10011

National Gay Pilots Association
P.O. Box 27542
Washington, DC 20038-7542

National Association of Social Workers
7981 Eastern Ave.
Silver Springs, MD 20910
The national committee on lesbian & gay issues

National Lesbian and Gay Labor Organization
125 Barclay St., Rm. 784
New York, NY 10007

National Lesbian and Gay Law Association
P.O. Box 77130,
National Capitol Station
Washington, DC 20013-7130

National Lesbian & Gay Journalists Association
P.O. Box 423048
San Francisco, CA 94142-3048
Robin Stevens

National Lesbian & Gay Law Association
P.O. Box 120795
Nashville, TN 37212-0795

National Organization of Gay and Lesbian Scientists & Technicians
P.O. Box 91803
Pasadena, CA 91109

NBC Gay and Lesbian Employees
c/o Mike Schreiberman
30 Rockefeller Plaza
New York, NY 10112

Northwest GLEN (Gay & Lesbian Employee Network)
830 19th Ave.
Seattle, WA 98122

Organization of Lesbian and Gay Architects & Designers
P.O. Box 927
Old Chelsea Station
New York, NY 10113

Out at Work
P.O. Box 359
Chicago, IL 60690-0359
Jason Cohen

Out Front Labor Action Committee
c/o B. Capoferri
2003 S.E. 54th St.
Portland, OR 97215

Publishing Triangle
P.O. Box 114
Prince Street Station
New York, NY 10012

San José State University Staff for Individual Rights
P.O. Box 3431
San José, CA 95156-3431

Society for the Psychological Study of Gay & Lesbian Issues
1200 17th St. N.W.
Washington, DC 20036
American Psychological Association affinity group

Utah Coalition of Gay, Lesbian and Bi Union Activists & Supporters
c/o Utah State AFL-CIO
2261 S. Redwood Rd.
Salt Lake City, UT 84119

Walt Disney League and Alliance
500 S. Buena Vista St.
Burbank, CA 91521
Garret Hicks

The Wandering Eye Society
1459 18th St. #178
San Francisco, CA 94107
Gay and lesbian ophthalmologists

Publications

10 Percent Magazine
54 Mint St., Suite 200
San Francisco, CA 94103-1819
Sara Hart, Editor-in-chief

ACHE—A Journal for Lesbians of African Descent
P.O. Box 6071
Albany, CA 94706
Lisbet, Editor-in-chief

The Advocate
6922 Hollywood Blvd, 10th Fl.
Los Angeles, CA 90028
Jeff Yarborough, Editor-in-chief

AIDS Treatment News
P.O. Box 411256
San Francisco, CA 94141
John S. James, Editor

Alabama Forum
P.O.Box 55894
Birmingham, AL 35255-5894
June Holloway, Editor

Alive & Kicking! We the People
425 S. Broad St.
Philadelphia, PA 19147-1126
Gregory Webb, Editor

Alternative Expressions
P.O. Box 446
Buffalo, NY 14205-0446

Alternatives
NLGJA
P.O. Box 423048
San Francisco, CA 94142
Robin Stevens, Editor

AMbush Magazine
P.O.Box 71291
New Orleans, LA 70172-1291
R. Rip Naquin, Editor

Amethyst Newsletter
P.O.Box 728, Westview Station
Binghamton, NY 13905

Anything That Moves: Beyond the Myths of Bisexuality
c/o Bay Area Bisexual Network
2404 California St., Box 24
San Francisco, CA 94115

Ariel
P.O.Box 1011
Ashland, OR 97520

PUBLICATIONS

Art & Understanding
25 Monroe St., Suite 205
Albany, NY 12210-2743
David L. Waggoner, Editor-in-chief

Attitude
617 St. Remi, #205
Montreal, PQ H4C 3G7 Canada
David Verchere, Editor

Au Courant
P.O. Box 42741
Philadelphia, PA 19101-2741
M. Scott Nallinger, Editor

Babble
3223 N. Sheffield
Chicago, Illinois 60657
Malone, Editor-in-chief

Balm Publishing
P.O. Box 1981
Costa Mesa, CA 92628
Marsha Stevens, Publisher

Baltimore Alternative
6619 Frederick Rd.
Baltimore, MD 21228-3530
Charles Mueller, Editor-in-chief

Bay Area Reporter
395 9th St.
San Francisco, CA 94103-3831
Bob Ross, Editor-in-chief

Bay Press
115 W. Denny Way
Seattle, WA 98119
Kimberly A. Barnett, Editor-in-chief

Bay Windows, Inc.
1523 Washington St.
Boston, MA 02118
Jeff Epperly, Editor

Bent Communications
1108 N.E. Going
Portland, OR 97211
Jack Cox, contact person

Bi Centrist Alliance Newsletter
P.O. Box 2254
Washington, DC 20013-2254

BiFocus
P.O. Box 30372
Philadelphia, PA 19103
Cappy Harrison, Editor

BiGALA
University of Pittsburgh
502 WPU
Pittsburgh, PA 15260
Chris Koch, Editor

Black Lace
P.O. Box 83912
Los Angeles, CA 90083-0912
Erotica

BLK
P.O. Box 83912
Los Angeles, CA 90083-0912
Alan Bell, Editor

Blue Ridge Lambda Press
P.O. Box 237
Roanoke, VA 24002
Tom Winn, Editor

Boehs Printing & Publishing
4624 N. State St.
Jackson, MS 39206

Bondings New Ways Ministry
4012 29th St.
Mt. Rainier, MD 20712
John Gallagher, Editor-in-chief

The Boston Phoenix
126 Brookline Ave.
Boston, MA 02215
Peter Kadzis, Editor-in-chief

Bottom Line
1243 N. Gene Autry Trail
Suite 121-122
Palm Springs, CA 92262
James J. Suguitan, Editor

Bravo!
P.O. Box 34646
San Diego, CA 92103

The Bulletin
126 E. Haley, Suite A-17
Santa Barbara, CA 93101
Rob Vargas, Managing Editor

The Call and Post
128-D Baldwin St.
Youngstown, OH 44505
Tuam Bustamante, Editor-in-chief

Camp Rehoboth
39 Baltimore Ave.
Rehoboth Beach, DE 19971
Steve Elkins, Editor

Caribbean Publishing, Inc.
106 de Diego Ave.
Box 78 Santurce, PR 00907
Miguel Marzial, Publisher

Chi Rho Press
P.O. Box 7864
Gaithersburg, MD 20898
Adam Debaugh, Editor

Children of Lesbians and Gays Everywhere
2350 Market St., Box 165
San Francisco, CA 94114
Publishes newsletter

Christopher St.
P.O. Box 1475
New York NY 10008-1475
Tom Steele, Editor

ColorLife! Magazine
2840 Broadway, Box 287
New York, NY 10025
Marianna Romo Carmona

Coming Up!
592 Castro St.
San Francisco, CA 94117
Kim Corsaro, Editor

Common Lives/Lesbian Lives
P.O. Box 1553
Iowa City, IA 52244
The Collective

Community Connections Publications
P.O. Box 18088
Asheville, NC 28814

Community Directories
P.O. Box 2270
Boulder, CO 80306-2270

Community News
P.O. Box 663
Salem, OR 97308
Chuck Simpson, Editor

Community News
P.O. Box 14682
Tallahassee, FL 32317-4682
Ian Granick, Managing Director

Community Voice
P.O. Box 17975
West Palm Beach, FL 33416
Susan Harris, Editor

Community Yellow Pages
2305 Canyon Dr.
Los Angeles, CA 90068
Jeanne Cordova, Publisher

Compass
P.O. Box 1586
Hollywood, CA 90078

CTN Magazine
P.O. Box 14431
San Francisco, CA 94114
Deaf lesbian and gay magazine

Current News
16 E. 39th St.
Kansas City, MO

Dallas Voice
3000 Carlisle, Suite 200
Dallas, TX 75204-1131
Dennis Vercher, Editor

Dare
P.O. Box 40422
Nashville, TN 37204-0422

David Magazine
801 S.W. 27th Ave.
Fort Lauderdale, FL 33312-2907
Jerry Byers, Editor

Deneuve
2336 Market St., Suite 15
San Francisco, CA 94114
Francis Stevens, Editor

Dimensions
P.O. Box 856
Lubbock, TX 79408
Kelle Chambers, Editor

Dinah
P.O. Box 1465
Cincinnati, OH 45201
Media

Diseased Pariah News
c/o Men's Support Center
P.O. Box 30564
Oakland, CA 94604

Diversity
P.O. Box 323
Boise, ID 83701
Rich Keefe, Editor

Dyke Review Magazine
584 Castro St., #456
San Francisco, CA 94114
Christie Carr

Ecce Queer
1925 8th Ave., Floor 2
Seattle, WA 98101

Echo
313 E. Thomas Rd., Suite 206
Phoenix, AZ 85012
Bill Orovan, Editor

EDGE Magazine
6434 Santa Monica Blvd.
Hollywood, CA 90038
Michael Jones, Editor-in-chief

Empowerment Times
c/o Gay & Lesbian Community
Services Center
1625 N. Hudson Ave.
Los Angeles, CA 90028-9998

Empty Closet
179 Atlantic Ave.
Rochester, NY 14607-1255
Susan Jordan, Editor

Equality Public News Service
7239 S. 43rd Pl.
Phoenix, AZ 85040-6318

Essence Magazine
1500 Broadway, 6th Fl.
New York, NY 10036
Linda Villarosa, Senior Editor

esto no tiene nombre
4700 N.W. 7th St., #463
Miami, Florida 33126
Tatiana de la Tierra, Editor

Etcetera
P.O. Box 8916
Atlanta, GA 30306
Jack Pelham, Editor

Family Next Door
P.O. Box 21580
Oakland, CA 94620
Lisa Orta, Editor

Ferrari Publications
P.O. Box 37887
Phoenix, AZ 85069
Marianne Ferarri, Publisher

Fountain Magazine
2221 Wilton Dr.
Ft. Lauderdale, FL 33305
Anna Fuentes, Editor-in-chief

Freedom Writer
Institute for First Amendment
Studies
P.O. Box 589
Great Barrington, MA 01230
Barbara/Skipp, Editors

The Front Page
P.O. Box 27928
Raleigh, NC 27611
Jim Baxter, Editor/Publisher

Frontiers Newsmagazine
P.O. Box 46367
West Hollywood, CA
90046-0637
David, Editor

Gay and Lesbian Almanac Project
P.O. Box 460909
San Francisco, CA 94146
Lynn Witt, Sherry Thomas, Eric Marcus, Editors

The Gay and Lesbian Quarterly
459 Boulevard Way
Oakland, CA 94610
Christopher J. Alexander, PhD, Editor-in-chief

Gay Chicago Magazine
3121 N. Broadway
Chicago, IL 60657-4522
Ralph Gernhardt, Editor

Gay Community News
P.O. Box 623
Waimanalo, HI 96795

Gay Community News
25 West St.
Boston, MA 02111-1213
Marla Erlien, Editor

Gay Community News
P.O. Box 37803
Honolulu, HI 96837
William E. Woods, Editor

GAY GAIA
267 Sanford St.
New Brunswick, NJ 08901

Gay & Lesbian International News Network
1618 N. Jackson St.
Milwaukee, WI 53202-2004

Gay & Lesbian Times
P.O. Box 34624
San Diego, CA 92163
Jeri Dilno, Editor

Gay People's Chronicle
P.O. Box 5426
Cleveland, OH 44101
Doreen Cudnik, Editor

Gay Perspectives
P.O. Box 8518
Silver Spring, MD 20907-8518

GayBeat
772 N. High St., Suite 103
Columbus, OH 43215
Josh Thomas, Editor

Gayellow Pages
P.O. Box 533
New York, NY 10014-0533
Francis Green, Editor

Gayly Oklahoman
P.O. Box 60930
Oklahoma City, OK 73146
Don Hawkins, Editor

Gaze Magazine
2344 Nicollet Ave., Suite 130
Minneapolis, MN 55404-3370

GenderTrash
P.O. Box 500-62
552 Church St.
Toronto, Ontario M4Y 2E3
Canada
Mirha Soleil, Editor

Genre
8033 Sunset Blvd., Suite 261
Los Angeles, CA 90046
Richard Settles, Editor-in-chief

Girljock Magazine
P.O. Box 882723
San Francisco, CA 94188-2723
Roxxie, Editor

GLAAD / SFBA Update
The Gay & Lesbian Alliance
Against Defamation
1360 Mission St, 200
San Francisco, CA 94103
Kathleen Wilkinson, Editor

The GLC Voice
2103 Pleasant Ave S., Suite 1
Minneapolis, MN 55404-2321
Tim Campbell, Editor

GO INFO
P.O. Box 2919, Station D
Ottawa, Ontario K1P 5W9
Canada
Kerry Beckett, Editor

The Guide
P.O. Box 593
Boston, MA 02199
French Wall, Editor

Hag Rag
P.O. Box 93243
Milwaukee, WI 53203

Harvard Gay & Lesbian Review
P.O. Box 180722
Boston, MA 02118
Richard Schneider, Jr., Editor

Hera Newspaper & Eventline
P.O. Box 354
Binghamton, NY 13902-0354
Peg Johnston, Editor

Heresies
P.O. Box 1306
Canal St. Station
New York, NY 10013

Herland Voice
Herland Sister Resources
2312 N.W. 39th
Oklahoma City, OK 73112

Hers
P.O. Box 8362
Longboat Key, FL 34228
Susan Fernandez & Diane Mason, Editors-in-chief

Hommenage
117 W. Harrison Building
6th Fl., Suite 385H
Chicago, IL 60605

HomoXtra
19 W. 21st St., #105
New York, NY 10010
Austin Downey, Editor

Hotlines Newsletter
P.O. Box 167
Lorain, OH 44052

Houston Voice
811 Westheimer, Suite #105
Houston, TX 77067
Sheri Darbonne, Editor

Impact
P.O. Box 52079
New Orleans, LA 70152
Jon Newlin, Editor

In Newsweekly
258 Shawmut Ave.
Boston, MA 02118
Trixi Burke, Editor

In Step Magazine
225 S. 2nd St.
Milwaulkee. WI 53204-1412
Ron Geiman

Information Express
Richmond Lesbian & Gay Pride Coalition
P.O. Box 14747
Richmond, VA 23221
Brenton Lago

Inside Out
P.O. Box 406268
San Francisco, CA 94146-0268
Arwyn, Editor

Inside OUT YOUTH
University YWCA
2330 Guadalupe St.
Austin, TX 78705
Lisa, Program Director

Iris Literary Review
P.O. Box 7263
Atlanta, GA 30357

Island Lifestyle Magazine
2851A Kihei Place
Honolulu, HI 96816

James White Literary Review
P.O. Box 3356
Butler Quarter Station
Minneapolis, MN 55403
Phil Wilkie, Editor-in-chief

Just for the Record
P.O. Box 353730
Dallas, TX 75235-0373
Valda Lewis, Editor

Just for You
262 St. James Place, Suite 4B
Brooklyn, NY 11238

Just Out
P.O. Box 15117
Portland, OR 97215
Renee LaChance, Editor

Kill the Robot
P.O. Box 296
Yellow Springs, OH 45387-0296

Kuumba
P.O. Box 83912
Los Angeles, CA 90083-0912
G. Winston James, Terri Jewell

La Gazette
P.O. Box 671
Santa Cruz, CA 95061
Tracye Lea Lawson, Editor

Lambda Book Report
1625 Connecticut Ave. N.W.
Washington, DC 20009-1013
Jim Marks, Editor

The Lambda Report
712 W. 9th Ave.
Denver, CO 80204

Las Vegas Bugle
P.O. Box 14580
3131 Industrial Rd.
Las Vegas, NV 89114-4580
Rob Schlegel, Editor

Las Vegas Review-Journal
1111 W. Bonanza Rd.
P.O. Box 70
Las Vegas, NV 89125-0070
Tom Mitchell, Editor

The Latest Issue
P.O. Box 160584
Sacramento, CA. 95816
Kate Moore, Editor

Lavender Reader
P.O. Box 7293
Santa Cruz, CA 95061-7293
Scotty Brookie

The Leather Journal
7985 Santa Monica Blvd.
Suite 109-368
West Hollywood, CA 90046
Dave Roads, Editor

Lesbian and Gay News-Telegraph
P.O. Box 10085
Kansas City, MO 64171
Lisa Church, Editor

Lesbian and Gay News-Telegraph
P.O. Box 14229-A
St. Louis, MO 63178-1229
Jim Thomas, Editor

Lesbian Connection
Ambitious Amazons
P.O. Box 811
East Lansing, MI 48826
Sandy Taylor

Lesbian, Gay, Bisexual, Queer, Transgendered & Beyond Labels: Community News for the Central Coast
c/o Santa Cruz Lesbian, Gay, Bisexual & Transgendered Community Center
P.O. Box 8280
Santa Cruz, CA 95061-8280

The Lesbian News
P.O. Box 55
Torrance, CA 90501
Katie Cotter

Lesbian Resource Center Community News
1808 Bellevue Ave., Suite 204
Seattle, WA 98122
Terri L. Smith, Editorial Coordinator

Lesbian Sisters
3729 Cahuenga Blvd. W.
North Hollywood, CA 91604

Lesbian / Gay / Bisexual / Transgender Information Exchange
676 Ideal Way
Charlotte, NC 28203

Lexicon
P.O. Box 459, Station P
Toronto, Ontario M5S 2S9
Canada
Steven Minuk, Editor

LGLC Newsletter
(Libertarians for Gay and Lesbian Concerns)
P.O. Box 447
Chelsea, MI 48118

LGNY
601 E. 11th St.
New York, NY 10009
Irene Elizabth Stroud, Editor

Life In Out Publications
602 Washington Ave.
Girard, OH 44420-2267

Lifestyle
P.O. Box 8101
Westfield, MA 01086-8101

Lifetimes 2
c/o Stadtlanders Pharmacy
Suite 2112
Pittsburgh, PA 15235-5810

The List
135 W. 20th St., 30th Fl.
New York, NY 10011

METRA
P.O. Box 71844
Madison Heights, MI 48071-0844
Garry Hoffman, Editor

Metro Arts & Entertainment Weekly
724 9th St. N.W., Suite 429
Washington, DC 20001
Randy Schulman, Editor

Metro Times-Alternative Weekly
743 Beauvine
Detroit, MI 48226
Desiree Cooper, Editor

Metroline
1841 Broad St., 2nd Floor
Hartford, CT 06114-1780
Blake W., Managing Editor

Mom Guess What?
1725 "L" St.
Sacramento, CA 95814-4038
Linda Birner, Editor

Montrose Voice
811 Westheimer, Suite 105
Houston, TX 77006
Sheri Darbonne, Editor

Nashville Women's Alliance Newsletter
703 Berry Rd.
Nashville, TN 37204

Network
2 Julie Dr.
Edison, NJ 08820
Mary Ellen Carney, Editor-in-chief

The New Republic
1220 19th St. N.W., Suite 600
Washington, DC 20036
Andrew Sullivan, Editor-in-chief

The New Voice of Nebraska
P.O. Box 3512
Omaha, NE 68103
Sharon Van Butsel, Editor- in- chief

New York Native
P.O. Box 1475
Church Street Station
New York, NY 10008-1475
Neenyah Ostrom, Editor

News of the Columbus Gay / Lesbian Community
P.O. Box 8296
Columbus, OH 43201-0296
H. Herman, Editor

Next
101 Lafayette, 5th Floor
New York, NY 10013
Scott Hess, Editor

NGLTF Activist Alert
NGLTF Policy Institute
1734 14th St. N.W.
Washington, DC 20009-4309
Beth Barrett, Editor

Nightlife
6363 Santa Monica Blvd.
Suite 200
West Hollywood, CA 90038
Victor Bonito, Editor

Nightlines
3059 N. Southport
Chicago, IL 60657
Tracy Baim, Publisher

Nouveau Magazine
P.O. Box 3176
Cincinnati, OH 45201
Ed Hicks, Editor

Observer
P.O. Box 50733
Tucson, AZ 85703-1733
Bob Ellis, Editor

off our backs
2423 18th St., N.W., 2nd Fl.
Washington, DC 20009
Monthly news for lesbians/feminists

On Our Backs
1537 4th St., Suite 234
San Rafel, CA 94101
Bayla Travis; bi-monthly erotica for lesbians

On the Wilde Side
106 Cain Dr.
Brentwood, NY 11717
Anthony D'Aguanno,

Open Hands
3801 N. Keeler Ave.
Chicago, IL 60641
Mary Jo Osterman, Editor

Options
P.O. Box 27444
Providence, RI 02907
Gary Richards, Editor

Orange County Blade
P.O. Box 1538
Orange, CA 92652
David F. Etheridge, Editor

Other Countries
P.O. Box 3142,
Church Street Station
New York, NY 10008-3142
B. Michael Hunter, Editor

Our Own Community Press
739 Yarmouth St.
Norfolk, VA 23510
Kathleen Vickery

Our Paper
P.O. Box 23387
San José, CA 95153-0387
R.J. Nichols, Editor

Our World Magazine
1104 N. Nova, Suite 251
Daytona Beach FL 32117
Wayne Whiston, Editor

Out
The Soho Building
110 Greene St., Suite 600
New York, NY 10012
Michael Goff and Sarah Pettit, Editors

Out
747 South Ave.
Pittsburgh, PA 15221
Jeff Howells, Editor

Out!
P.O. Box 323
Boise, ID 83701
Brian Bergquist, Editor

Out!
P.O. Box 27237
Albuquerque, NM 87125
Roy Reini, Editor

Out and About
LGCA
P.O. Box 27061
Jacksonville, FL 32205
David Alport, Editor

Out and About, Inc.
P.O. Box 120122
Norfolk, VA 23502
Henry Edgar, Editor

Out & About
542 Chapel St.
New Haven, CT 06511
Billy Kolber, Editor

Out Front
244 Washington
Denver, CO 80203
Sam Gallegos, Editor

Out in the Mountains
P.O. Box 177
Burlington, VT 05402
Fred Kuhr, Media

Out Looks / In Front /
430 Oak Grove, Suite 230-B
Minneapolis, MI 55403
Craig Lindhal-Urben, Media

OUT Smart
3406 Audobon Pl.
Houston, TX 77006
Eric Roland, Editor

Outlines
P.O. Box 4701
Ithaca, NY 14852-4701
Jeff Popow, Editor

Outlines
3059 N. Southport
Chicago, IL 60657
Tracy Baim, Publisher

Outlines News
1200 W. Smith St.
Watseka, IL 60970
Tracy Baim, Publisher

OutNOW!
45 N. 1st St., Suite 124
San José, CA 95113
Chris Thomas

OUTwords
P.O. Box 443
Buffalo, NY 14209-0443
Karl Scheitheir

OutYouth
Youth Enrichment Services / BI-GLYNY LGCSC
208 W. 13th St.
New York, NY 10011-7799

PFLAG Newsletter
1012 14th St. N.W., Suite 700
Washington, DC 20005
Media - Newsletter

Philadelphia Gay News
254 S. 11th St.
Philadelphia, PA 19107
Al Patrick, Editor

Playland Magazine
1702-H Meridian Ave., #112
San José, CA 95125
Matthew Sonsola, Editor

PM Entertainment
P.O. Box 430
Babylon, NY 11702
Bill Hefter, Owner

Positively Aware
Test Positive Aware Network
1340 W. Irving Park Ave., Box 259
Chicago, IL 60613
Steve McGuire, Media

The Post
409 E. 4th
Long Beach, CA 90802
Don Reed, Editor

Poz Magazine
Box 1279, Old Chelsea Station
New York, NY 10113-1279
Sean Strub

pride nooz
P.O. Box 775
Helena, MT 59624-0775

Pride Path Magazine
266 Elmwood Ave., Suite 117
Buffalo, NY 14222
Carol Speser

Provincetown Advocate
P.O. Box 93
Provincetown, MA 02657
Peter A. Steele

Q Notes
4037 E. Independence Blvd.
Suite 611
Charlotte, NC 28205
Jim Yarbrough, Editor

The Queer Journal
WPTS
411 William Pitt Union
Pittsburgh, PA 15260
Sharon Davis, Editor

Queer Zine Explosion
P.O. Box 590488
San Francisco, CA 94159-0488
Larry - Bob

Query
Pyramid Publishing
P.O. Box 40422
Nashville, TN 37204-0422
Jeff Ellis, Editor

Quest
432 S. Broadway
Denver, CO 80209
Shawn Turney, Editor

The Reno Informer
5150 Mae Anne Ave., #213-185
Reno, NV 89523

Resolutions Advocacy
961 Terrace Ave., Suite 49
Los Angeles, CA 90042

Rhode Island Gay & Lesbian News Bureau
187 Narragansett St.
Cranston, RI 02905-4109
David C. Anderson, Director

Rubyfruit Journal
517 E. Gay St.
Tucson, AZ 85705

San Francisco Bay Times
288 7th St.
San Francisco, CA 94103
Kim Carsaro, Editor

San Francisco Sentinel
285 Shipley St.
San Francisco, CA 94107
Ray Chalker, Editor

Sappho's Isle
960 Willis Ave.
Albertson, NY 11507-1938

Seattle Gay News
1605 12th Ave., Suite 31
Seattle, WA 98122
Jim Burke

The Second Stone
P.O. Box 8340
New Orleans, LA 70182-8340
James Bailey, Editor

Shamakami
P.O. Box 460456
San Francisco, CA 94146-0456

Sierra Voice
P.O. Box 1191
Reno, NV 89504

Sinister Wisdom
P.O. Box 3252
Berkeley, CA 94703
Elana Dykewomon

slant
P.O. Box 629
Corte Madera, CA 94976
Ed Wright, Publisher

Sojourner—The Women's Forum
42 Seaverns Ave.
Boston, MA 02130
Karen Kahn, Editor

SoMo News Connection
Route 3, Box 6B2
Tecumseh, MO 65760
Mike Bromberg, Editor

Sound Out
P.O. Box 1844
Olympia, WA 98507-1844

South Texas Voice
P.O. Box 120123
San Antonio, TX 78212
Gene Blake, Editor

Southern California Gay & Lesbian Times
3636 Fifth Ave., Suite 101
San Diego, CA 92103

Southern Voice
P.O. Box 18215
Atlanta, GA 30316
Richard Shumate, Media

SPANK
P.O. Box 1092
Wilkes-Barre, PA 18702
Ed Lupico, Editor / Ron Beck, Publisher

Stonewall Union Lesbian and Gay Pride Report
Cable Channel 21
P.O. Box 10814
Columbus, OH 43201

Stonewall Union Reports Newspaper
P.O. Box 10814
Columbus, OH 43201

The Stranger
1202 E. Pike St., Suite 1225
Seattle, WA 98122
S. T. Miskowski, Editor-in-chief

Tacoma Sounds
P.O. Box 110816
Tacoma, WA 98411-0816
Edward Goldberg, Editor

Talmadge
P.O. Box 533655
Orlando, FL 32853-3655

Taste of Latex
P.O. Box 460122
San Francisco, CA 94146

TenPercent
112-B Kerkhoff Hall
308 Westwood Plaza
Los Angeles, CA 90024
Eric Lynxwile

Texas Triangle
1615 W. 6th St.
Austin, TX 78703
Kay Longco, Editor-in-chief

This Week in Texas
3300 Reagan St.
Dallas, TX 75219
Richard Hebert, Editor

Triangle Journal News
Printers' Ink
P.O. Box 11485
Memphis, TN 38111-0485

Trikone Magazine
P.O. Box 21354
San José, CA 95151-1354
Sandip Roy, Editor

Tulsa Family News
P.O. Box 4140
Tulsa, OK 74159-0140
Tom Neil

TulsaXTRA
P.O. Box 3503
Tulsa, OK 74191-3503

TWN
901 N.E. 79th St.
Miami, FL 33138

Two In Twenty
P.O. Box 105
Somerville, MA 02144

U Report
P.O. Box 2327
Phoenix, AZ 85002-2327

Update
P.O. Box 33148
San Diego, CA 92163-3148
Peter Pronsati, Editor

Uranian Publishing
35 South 600 W.
Salt Lake City, UT 84101
Brandon Creer, Publisher

Urban Fitness
4505 University Wy., N.E. #40
Seattle, WA 98105
Kimberly French, Editor

Us Magazine
1290 Ave. of the Americas
New York, NY 10104-0298
Peter McQuaid, Senior Editor

Valentine News
P.O. Box 81259
Cleveland, OH 44181-0259
Dennis Chaney, Editor

Victory!
2312 North St.
Sacramento, CA 95816
MJ McKean-Reich, Editor

Victory!
First MCC
156 S. Kansas Ave.
Wichita, KS 67211

Village Voice
36 Cooper Square
New York, NY 10003

Voices Out Front
2103 N. Decatur Rd., Suite 185
Decatur, GA 30033

Volume
P.O. Box 106
Bidwell Station
Buffalo, NY 14222

Washington Blade
1408 "U" St., N.W., 2nd Fl.
Washington, DC 20009-3916
Lisa Keen, Editor

WAVES
P.O. Box 684
Windsor, CT 06095

The Western Express
P.O. Box 5317
Phoenix, AZ 85010-5317

What!!!Quears!!!
831 Scott St.
San Francisco, CA 94117
Deaf gay and lesbian magazine

The Wilde Society
InterAmerica
P.O. Box 25008
Fort Wayne, IN 46825
Richard Reynolds, Director

Windy City Times
970 W. Montana, Suite 2F1
Chicago, IL 60614

The Wire
1638 Euclid Ave.
Miami Beach, FL 33139
Andrew De La Plaine

Wisconsin InStep
225 S. 2nd St.
Milwaukee, WI 53204
Ron Geiman

Wisconsin Light
1843 N. Palmer St.
Milwaukee, WI 53212-3718

With a Growing Voice
360 Grand Ave., Suite 385
Oakland, CA 94610

Women Centered News
P.O. Box 3057
Albany, NY 12203

Women's Building News
79 Central Ave.
Albany, NY 12206-3001
Drea Leanza

Women's Educational Media
2017 Mission St., 2nd Fl.
San Francisco, CA 94110
Publisher/Production Company

WomenSpace
P.O. Box 24712
Omaha, NE 68124-0712

Womyn's Vineline
P.O. Box 178079
Toledo, OH 43615

The Word Is Out! Lesbian Voices of Columbus
P.O. Box 02106
Columbus, OH 43202
Jan Solari

Xenogeny
P.O. Box 60716
Nashville, TN 37206
Kenneth Athon, Editor

XTRA!
P.O. Box 7289, Station A
Toronto, Ontario MSW 1X9
Canada

Your Children Too!
222 E. Leith St.
Fort Wayne, IN 46806

YOUTH Magazine
P.O. Box 34215
Washington, DC 20043-4215

Publishing Industry

Alyson Publications, Inc.
40 Plympton St.
Boston, MA 02118
Sasha Alyson, Editor

Avon
1350 Ave. of the Americas
New York, NY 10019
Charlotte Abbott, Editor

Malaga Baldi
P.O. Box 529
New York, NY 10101
Literary agent

Cleis Press
P.O. Box 14684
San Francisco, CA 94114
Frederique Delacoste, Editor

Columbia University Press
562 W. 113th St.
New York, NY 10025
Ann Miller, Editor, "Between Men/Between Women" series

Crown Publishers
201 E. 50th St.
New York, NY 10011
Michael Denneney, Editor

Diane Cleaver
55 5th Ave.
New York, NY 10003
Literary agent

Duke University Press
Box 90660
Durham, NC 27708-0660
Ken Wissocker, Acquisitions Editor, "Series Q"

Firebrand
141 The Commons
Ithaca , NY 14850
Nancy K. Bereano, Editor

Gay Sunshine Press
P.O. Box 410690
San Francisco, CA 94141
Winston Leyland, Editor

Peter Ginsberg
Curtis Brown
10 Astor Pl.
New York, NY 10003
Literary agent

Frances Goldin
305 E. 11th St.
New York, NY 10003
Literary agent

HarperCollins
10 E. 53rd St.
New York, NY 10022-5299
Robert Jones, Christopher Schelling, Editors

HarperCollins San Francisco
1160 Battery St.
San Francisco, CA 94111-1213

Hyperion
114 5th Ave.
New York, NY 10011
Rick Kot, Craig Nelson, Editors

Indiana University Press
601 N. Morton St.
Bloomington, IN 47404-3797
Joan Catapano, Editor

Ira Silverberg & Associates
401 W. Broadway
New York, NY 10012
Literary agent

Kitchen Table: Women of Color Press
P.O. Box 908
Latham, New York 12110
Barbara Smith, Editor

Stephanie Laidman
Jane Rotrosen Agency
318 E. 51st St.
New York, NY 10022
Literary agent

The Lambda Literary Awards (LAMMIES)
c/o Lambda Book Report
1625 Connecticut Ave. N.W.
Washington, DC 20009-1013
Jim Marks, Deacon MacCubbin

Gloria Loomis
150 E. 35th St.
New York, NY 10016
Literary agent

Jed Mattes
200 W. 72nd St. #50
New York, NY 10023
Literary agent

NAIAD Press, Inc.
P.O. Box 10543
Tallahassee, Florida 32302
Barbara Grier, Editor

NAL / Dutton
375 Hudson St.
New York, NY 10014
Peter Borland, Carole DeSanti, Matthew Carnicelli, Editors

New York University Press
P.O. Box 1235
New York, NY 10008-1235
Karla Jay, Editor, "The Cutting Edge: Lesbian Life and Literature"

PEN Gay and Lesbian Committee
PEN American Center
568 Broadway
New York, NY 10012
Stephen Friedman

Publishing Triangle
P.O. Box 114
Prince Street Station
New York, NY 10012
Matt Sartwell, networking group of gays and lesbians in publishing industry

The Putnam Berkley Publishing Group
200 Madison Ave.
New York, NY 10016
John Duff, Publisher, Perigee Books

Routledge, Chapman & Hall
29 W. 35th St.
New York, NY 10023
Bill Germano, Editor

Charlotte Sheedy
611 Broadway, Room 428
New York, NY 10012
Literary agent

St. Martin's Press
175 Fifth Ave.
New York, NY 10011
Keith Kahla

Recovery

Pride in Recovery
800-252-7533

Pride Institute
800-54-PRIDE

Live & Let Live AA
P.O. Box 55372
Birmingham, AL 35255

New Creations
1029 E. Turney
Phoenix, AZ 85014

Women's Project
2224 Main St.
Little Rock, AR 72206

Gay / Lesbian Alcoholics Anonymous
c/o MCC
Box 30357
Bakersfield, CA 93385-1357

Alcoholics Anonymous / People of Color
5149 W. Jefferson Blvd.
Los Angeles, CA 90016

Alcoholics Together Center
1773 Griffith Park Blvd.
Los Angeles, CA 90026

National Association of Lesbian & Gay Alcoholism Professionals
1147 S. Alvarado St.
Los Angeles, CA 90006

Spencer Recovery Center
343 W. Foothill Blvd.
Monrovia, CA 91016

Alcoholics Anonymous / Al-Anon
North Hall Group
c/o MCC
Box 20125
Sacramento, CA 95820

Stepping Stone
Hillcrest Community Recovery Service
3425 5th Ave.
San Diego, CA 92103

Stepping Stone: Central Residential Recovery Services
3767 Central Ave.
San Diego, CA 92105-2506

18th St. Services
217 Church St.
San Francisco, CA 94114

Acceptance Place
673 San José Ave
San Francisco, CA 94110

Al-Anon for Black Gays and Lesbians
1268 Sanchez St.
San Francisco, CA 94114

Crisis & Information Help Line
107 Cameron Dr.
Fort Collins, CO 80525

Project 100
1841 Broad St.
Hartford, CT 06114-1780

Gay Alcoholics Anonymous
185 Cook Ave.
Meriden-Wallingford Hospital
Mental Health Services
Meriden, CT 06450

International Advisory Council for Homosexual Men & Women in AA
P.O. Box 90
Washington, DC 20044

Triangle Club
2030 "P" St. N.W.
Washington, DC 20036

Florida Roundup
P.O. Box 7273
Fort Lauderdale, FL 33338-7273

Lambda South
P.O. Box 030456
Fort Lauderdale, FL 33303

Getting It Together (AA)
Good Samaritan
6085 Park Blvd. N.
Pinellas Park, FL 34665

Go After Your Sobriety (GAYS)
King of Peace MCC
3150 5th Ave. N.
Saint Petersburg, FL 33713

Gay Alcoholics Anonymous
500 C. Amsterdam Ave.
P.O. Box 7005
Atlanta, GA 30306

Lambda Group/Narcotics Anonymous
P.O. Box 77613
Atlanta, GA 30357

Lesbian Alcoholics Anonymous
Midtown YWCA
957 Highland Ave.
Atlanta, GA 30306

Overeaters Anonymous
(Gay/Lesbian Group)
1935 Cliff Valley Way
Atlanta, GA 30329

Survivors of Incest Anonymous
P.O. Box 2502
Decatur, GA 30031

AAAA/AA Positive
4407 N. Clark St.
Chicago, IL 60640

Alcoholics Anonymous, Gay Groups
621 W. Belmont Ave.
Chicago, IL 60657

Alcoholics Anonymous / New Town Alano Club
4407 N. Clark St.
Chicago, IL 60640

Chicago Recovery Alliance
P.O. Box 470688
Chicago, IL 60647

Sexual Compulsives Anonymous
4407 N. Clark St.
Chicago, IL 60640

Kinheart Women's Center
2214 Ridge Ave.
Evanston, IL 60201

Alcoholics Anonymous / Gay & Lesbian
Holy Covenant Metropolitan Community Church
17 W. Maple
Hinsdale, IL 60521-3495

West Suburban 12+12
300 W. Madison Ave.
Oak Park, IL 60302

Juggernauts AA Group
MCC
124½ N. 5th St.
Quincy, IL 62301

Crisis Center for Human Understanding
101 N. Montgomery St.
Gary, IN 46403

Live & Let Live AA Group
Box 213
Muncie, IN 47308

AA (Gay Group)
First Unitarian Church
101 E. Northshore Dr.
South Bend, IN 46617

Gay & Lesbian Alcoholics Anonymous
c/o Drake University Ministries
Education Building
28th & University Aves.
Des Moines, IA 50311

Women's Cultural Collective
P.O. Box 22063
Des Moines, IA 50325

Crisis Center
321 E. 1st St.
Iowa City, IA 52240

Gay Men's Alcoholics Anonymous
511 Melrose Ave.
Iowa City, IA 52246

Lesbian Alcoholics Anonymous
P.O. Box 992
Louisville, KY 40201

Gay Alcoholics Anonymous
Lambda Center
2106 Decatur
New Orleans, LA 70116

Lesbian Alanon / ACOA Meeting
UU Church Annex
7 Middle St.
Brunswick, ME 04011

Alcohol & Drug Intervention Services
74 State Rd., #210
Kittery, ME 03904

Gay / Lesbian Alcoholics Anonymous
Williston West Church
32 Thomas St.
Portland, ME 04102

Intown Counseling Center
477 Congress St.
Portland, ME 04101

Boston Bisexual Women's Network
P.O. Box 639
Cambridge, MA 02140

Lesbian Al-Anon
Women's Center
46 Pleasant St.
Cambridge, MA 02139

Gay & Lesbian AA
175 Wendell Ave.
Pittsfield, MA 01201

Chase & Brexton Gay Group AA
241 W. Chase St.
Baltimore, MD 21201

Live & Let Live Group / Alcoholics Anonymous
St. Vincent DePaul Church
120 N. Front St.
Baltimore, MD 21202

Narcotics Anonymous
GLCC
241 W. Chase St.
Baltimore, MD 21201

Lesbian & Gay Alcoholics Anonymous
c/o St. Augustine Church
600 W. Michigan
Kalamazoo, MI 49007

Brothers & Sisters Al-Anon / Lesbian Al-Anon Group
Plymouth Congregational Church
1900 Nicollet Ave.
Minneapolis, MN 55403

Live & Let Live AA Group
265 Oneida St.
St. Paul, MN 55102

Camp Sister Spirit
P.O. Box 12
Ovett, MS 39464

Live & Let Live AA
P.O. Box 411111
Kansas City, MO 64141-1111

Lambda/Alano Club
1612 E. Charleston
Las Vegas, NV 89104

Pink Triangle Group: Gay & Lesbian AA
District 19AA
P.O. Box 1669
Cheshire Medical Center
Keene, NH 03431

Gay Alcoholics Anonymous
Unitarian Universalist Church
669 Union St.
Manchester, NH 03101

Women's Center of Monmouth County
1 Bethany Rd., Suite B3A42
Hazlet, NJ 07730-1606

Live & Let Live AA
P.O. Box 674
Santa Fe, NM 87504

Gay Alcoholics Anonymous
P.O. Box 131
Albany, NY 12201

Open Mind Group AA
P.O. Box 395
Ellicott Station
Buffalo, NY 14205

Flushing Gays and Lesbians in Recovery
Unitarian Universalist Church
147-54 Ash Ave.
Flushing, NY 11355

Cornell Women's Center
P.O. Box 71
Willard Straight Hall
Ithaca, NY 14853

Al-Anon
Lesbian/Gay Community Services Center
208 W. 13th St.
New York, NY 10011

Alcoholics Anonymous
Lesbian/Gay Community Services Center
208 W. 13th St.
New York, NY 10011

Alcoholics Anonymous New Group
657 Washington St.
New York, NY 10014

Identity House
P.O. Box 572
Old Chelsea Station
New York, NY 10011-0572

Lambda West AA group
Rutgers Presbytarian Church
236 W. 73rd St.
New York, NY 10023

Nar-Anon
Lesbian and Gay Community Services Center
208 W. 13th St.
New York, NY 10011

Narcotics Anonymous
Lesbianand Gay Community
Services Center
208 W. 13th St.
New York, NY 10011

Overeaters Anonymous
Lesbian and Gay Community
Services Center
208 W. 13th St.
New York, NY 10011

Overeaters Anonymous / East Side Gay Group
Gracie Square Hospital
420 E. 76th St.
New York, NY 10021

Project Connect
Lesbian/Gay Community Services
Center
208 W. 13th St.
New York, NY 10011

Pyramid Place
814-816 Amsterdam Ave.
New York, NY 10036

Realization Center
121 E. 18th St.
New York, NY 10003

Spirit Crossroads
P.O. Box 1133
Peter Stuyvesant Station
New York, NY 10009

Response of Suffolk County
P.O. Box 300
Stony Brook, NY 11790-0300

Lambda Acceptance Group, Alcoholics Anonymous
First Presbytarian Church
1605 Genessee St.
Utica, NY 13501

West Nyack Gay & Lesbian AA Group
West Nyack Church of Religious
Science
96 Straw Town Rd.
West Nyack, NY 10994

Live & Let Live AA
1 Edwin Pl.
Asheville, NC 28802

Bisexual Women's Support Group
106 Laurel Hill Rd.
Chapel Hill, NC 27514

Gay Alcoholics Anonymous
160 Windsor Circle
Chapel Hill, NC 27516-1207

The Women's Center
P.O. Box 1057
Chapel Hill, NC 27514

Gay / Lesbian Alcoholics Anonymous
714 9th St.
Durham, NC 27705

Live & Let Live AA
914 Glenwood Ave.
Greensboro, NC 27403-2307

Crisisline
RR 2, Suite 439D
Roanoke Rapids, NC 27870

Crisisline
415 Grace St.
Wilmington, NC 28401

Lambda Alcoholics Anonymous
4313 Lake Ave.
Wilmington, NC 28403

Quest Recovery
1341 Market Ave. N.
Canton, OH 44714

Lambda North
P.O. Box 8427
Columbus, OH 43201

Bi Women's Support Group
P.O. Box 594
Northfield, OH 44067

Live & Let Live Club
P.O. Box 11261
Portland, OR 97211-0261

Lambda Group / AA
P.O. Box 15602
Harrisburg, PA 17105-5602

Gay Alcoholics Anonymous
Dignity
252 S. 12th St.
Philadelphia, PA 19107

Narcotics Anonymous
2125 Chestnut St.
Philadelphia, PA 19103

Here's a Place for Us Group / West Chester 307 Club
1311 West Chester Pike
West Chester, PA 19380

Gay / Lesbian Primary Purpose Alcoholics Anonymous
St. Martins in the Field Church
5220 Clemson Ave.
Columbia, SC 29206

Gay Alcoholics Anonymous
P.O. Box 1462
Greenville, SC 29602

Memphis Lambda Center
241 N. Cleveland St.
Memphis, TN 38104-7148

Suicide & Crisis Intervention
P.O. Box 40068
Memphis, TN 38174

Lambda Lesbian / Gay AA
Unitarian Church
1808 Woodmont Blvd.
Nashville, TN 37215

Live & Let Live AA
2700 W. Anderson Ln., #412
Austin, TX 78757-1132

Adult Children of Alcoholics, Lambda
P.O. Box 191025
Dallas, TX 75219

Lambda AA
2727 Oak Lawn, #101
Dallas, TX 75219

Stonewall Narcotics Anonymous
P.O. Box 567622
Dallas, TX 75356

Lambda Center for Alcoholics
P.O. Box 66703
Houston, TX 77266-6703

Lambda Club AA
8546 Broadway St. #255
San Antonio, TX 78217-6340

Lambda AA
c/o St. Gabriel's Church
13904 City Rd. 193
Tyler, TX 75701

Gay Alcoholics Anonymous
c/o GLA-CV
UMC 0100 Box 119
Tagart Student Center
Logan, UT 84322-0100

Gay Alcoholics Anonymous
c/o St. Mark's Episcopal Church
231 E. 100 South
Salt Lake City, UT 84111

Gay Lesbian Alcoholics Anonymous
P.O. Box 5653
Burlington, VT 05402

Chit Chat AA Group
3401 Tidewater Dr.
Norfolk, VA 23509

Triangle Services Recovery Center
1610 Meadowlake Dr.
Norfolk, VA 23518

Sex Addicts Anonymous
2204 Lashley Ln.
Richmond, VA 23233

AA Group
828 Campbell Ave. S.W.
Roanoke, VA 24016

Crisis Clinic - Teen Line
P.O. Box 2463
Olympia, WA 98507

Crisis Line
1515 Dexter Ave. N.
Seattle, WA 98109

Seattle Bisexual Women's Network
P.O. Box 30645
Greenwood Station
Seattle, WA 98103-0645

Stonewall Recovery Service
430 Broadway E.
Seattle, WA 98102

12 Step Recovery Group
317 Dodge St.
Janesville, WI 53545

Galano Club
2408 N. Farwell Ave.
Milwaukee, WI 53211

Religious

Birmingham Community Church
P.O. Box 130221
Birmingham, AL 35213

Covenant Metropolitan Community Church
P.O. Box 101473
Birmingham, AL 35210-6473
Cliff Morrison

Integrity / Alabama
P.O. Box 530785
Birmingham, AL 35253-0785
Frank Romanowicz, Convener; Episcopal

Metropolitan Community Church
P.O. Box 10021
Huntsville, AL 35810
Rev. Janet Suess-Prince

Metropolitan Community Church
P.O. Box 6311
Mobile, AL 36660-6311
Rev Helen Loper

Metropolitan Community Church
P.O. Box 603
Montgomery, AL 36101-0603
Bev Stephenson

Lamb of God Metropolitan Community Church
P.O. Box 142095
Anchorage, AK 99514-2095
Rev. James Morgan

Presbyterians for Lesbian & Gay Concerns, Arizona
710 W. Los Lagos Vista
Mesa, AZ 85210

Dignity-Integrity / Phoenix
P.O. Box 21091
Phoenix, AZ 85036
Elinor Crocker, Convener
Catholic-Episcopal

Evangelicals Concerned / Western Region
P.O. Box 66906
Phoenix, AZ 85082-6906
Linda Taunt

Gentle Shepherd Metropolitan Community Church
3425 E. Mountain View Rd.
Phoenix, AZ 85028
Rev. Charlotte Strayhorn, Rev. Patrick Stout

Lutherans Concerned / Phoenix
P.O. Box 7519
Phoenix, AZ 85011

Mishpachat Am
P.O. Box 7731
Phoenix, AZ 85011

Oasis Metropolitan Community Church
2405 E. Coronado Rd.
Phoenix, AZ 85006
Rev. Katie Cassidy

Affirmation
P.O. Box 26601
Tempe, AZ 85285
Gay and Lesbian Mormons

Integrity / Tucson
Grace St. Paul's Church
2331 E. Adams St.
Tucson, AZ 85719
Chris Eastoe, Convener
Episcopal

Metropolitan Community Church
3269 N. Mountain Ave.
Tucson, AZ 85719
Rev. Eduard Perry

Metropolitan Community Church of the Living Spring
P.O. Box 365
Eureka Springs, AR 72632
Cheryl Sorrels

Metropolitan Community Church of the Ozarks
P.O. Box 92
Fayetteville, AR 72702-0092
Rev. Teri DiMarco

Dignity / Little Rock
P.O. Box 3015
Little Rock, AR 72203
Catholic

Metropolitan Community Church of the Rock
P.O. Box 1964
Little Rock, AR 72203-1964
Rev. Barbara Freeman

Spiritsong Metropolitan Community Church
P.O. Box 586
Little Rock, AR 72203
Rev. Angela Peace

Metropolitan Community Church of the Harvest
P.O. Box 30357
Bakersfield, CA 93385

New Life Metropolitan Community Church
1823 9th St.
Berkeley, CA 94710-2102
Rev. Barry Wichmann

St. John's Presbyterian Church
2727 College Ave.
Berkeley, CA 94705
A More Light Church

United Lesbian / Gay Christian Scientists
P.O. Box 2171
Beverly Hills, CA 90212-2171

Free Spirit Metropolitan Community Church
1297 S. Spruce Ave.
Bloomington, CA 92316

Metropolitan Community Church at California Men's Colony
1065 Casitas Pass Rd., Suite 208
Carpenteria, CA 93013

Diablo Valley Metropolitan Community Church
P.O. Box 139
Concord, CA 94522-0139

Dignity / Riverside
P.O. Box 9000-153
Corona, CA 91720A.
Garduno;
Catholic

Metropolitan Community Church Ocean of Life
1547D Adams Ave.
Costa Mesa, CA 92629
Rev. Susan Deitrick and
Rev. C. Jane Carl

Shalom Chavurah
P.O. Box 11686
Costa Mesa, CA 92627

Metropolitan Community Church
P. O. Box 388
Culver City, CA 90232
Rev. Nancy Wilson

Response for Gays, Lesbians and Their Families
15739 Ventura Blvd.
Encino, CA 91436

Metropolitan Community Church of the Vineyard
P.O. Box 5511
Fresno, CA 93755-5511
Rev. Jim Ulisse

Divine Redeemer Metropolitan Community Church
346 Riverdale Dr.
Glendale CA 91204-2019
Rev. Joseph Picari

Metropolitan Community Church of the Central Coast
P.O. Box 1117
Grover City, CA 93483-1117
Rev. Randy Lester

Russian River Metropolitan Community Church
P.O. Box 1055
Guerneville, CA 95446
Rev. Jodi Safier

West Hollywood Presbyterian Church
7350 Sunset Blvd.
Hollywood, CA 90046-3411
A More Light Church

Evangelicals Concerned
P.O. Box 1452
Laguna Beach, CA 92651-1452
Kevin Kirby and Todd Souza

Integrity / Southland-Orange County
P.O. Box 1896
Laguna Beach, CA 92652-1896
Alvin T. Ethington, Jr., Convener; Episcopal

Kol Simcha
P.O. Box 1444
Laguna Beach, CA 92652

Seventh Day Adventist Kinship International
Hal Jobe
P.O. Box 7320
Laguna Niguel, CA 92607

Sunrise Metropolitan Community Church of the High Desert
P.O. Box 886
Lancaster, CA 93535
Rev. Christen Chew

Dignity / Long Beach
P.O. Box 93375
Long Beach, CA 90809-2375
Catholic

Long Beach Lesbian and Gay Havurah
Jewish Community Center
3801 E. Willow St.
Long Beach, CA 90815

Metropolitan Community Church
1231 Locust Ave.
Long Beach, CA 90813-3114
Rev. Dusty Pruitt

Affirmation / National Offices
Tere LaTuisa
P.O. Box 46022
Los Angeles, CA 90046
Gay and Lesbian Mormons

Archdiocese of Los Angeles, Pastoral Ministry to the Lesbian and Gay Community
1520 W. 9th
Los Angeles, CA 90015
Father Peter Liuci; Catholic

Beth Chayim Chadashim
6000 W. Pico Blvd.
Los Angeles, CA 90035

Dignity / Los Angeles
P.O. Box 42040
Los Angeles, CA 90042-0042
Catholic

Evangelicals Together
7985 Santa Monica Blvd.
Suite 109, Box 16
Los Angeles, CA 90046

Gay Men's Buddhist Group
928 S. New Hampshire
Los Angeles, CA 90006

Lesbian Zen Group
928 S. New Hampshire
Los Angeles, CA 90006

Holy Trinity Community Church
4209 Santa Monica Blvd.
Los Angeles, CA 90006

Metropolitan Community Church (Silverlake)
3621 Brunswick Ave.
Los Angeles, CA 90039
Rev. Joseph Gilbert

United University Church
817 W. 34th St.
Los Angeles, CA 90007
A More Light Church

Unity Fellowship Church
5149 W. Jefferson Blvd.
Los Angeles, CA 90016
Bishop Carl Bean

Universal Fellowship of Metropolitan Community Churches
5300 Santa Monica Blvd., #304
Los Angeles, CA 90029
Troy Perry, Moderator

Universal Fellowship of Metropolitan Community Churches (International Offices)
5300 Santa Monica Blvd., # 304
Los Angeles, CA 90029
Ravi Verma, Director of Administration

St. Andrew United Church
1 Drake Ave.
Marin City, CA 94965
A More Light Church

Metropolitan Community Church
P.O. Box 3092
Modesto, CA 95353-3092
Rev. Paul Shoopman

Metropolitan Community Church of the Pomona Valley
P.O. Box 226
Montclair, CA 91763
Rev. David Gillentine

Presbyterians for Lesbian / Gay Concerns—Los Angeles
1232 Dell Dr.
Monterey Park, CA 91754

Metropolitan Community Church in the Valley
5730 Cahuenga Blvd.
N. Hollywood, CA 91601-2105
Mr. Duan Wong

American Baptists Concerned
872 Erie St.
Oakland, CA 94610-2286

Montclair Presbyterian Church
5701 Thornhill Dr.
Oakland, CA 94611
A More Light Church

Chevrat 'Or
c/o Temple Sinai
43435 Monterey Ave.
Palm Desert, CA 92260

Integrity of the Desert
125 W. El Alameda
Palm Springs, CA 92263
Carl Neumeister, Convener; Episcopal

Metropolitan Community Church of the Peninsula
P.O. Box 70
Redwood City, CA 94064-0070
Rev. Teri Roderick

Dignity / Sacramento
P.O. Box 161765
Sacramento, CA 95816
Catholic

River City Metropolitan Community Church
P.O. Box 245125
Sacramento, CA 95824
Rev. Elder Freda Smith

Integrity / El Camino Real
Church of the Good Shepherd
301 Corral de Tierra
Salinas, CA 93908
Loudene Grady, Coordinator; Episcopal

Integrity of the Sierra
P.O. Box 110
San Andreas, CA 95249
Ian Snider, President; Episcopal

Affirmation
P.O. Box 86469
San Diego, CA 92138
Mormons

Dignity / San Diego
P.O. Box 33367
San Diego, CA 92163
Catholic

Integrity / San Diego
P.O. Box 34253
San Diego, CA 92163-0801
Robert Heylmun and Chuck Killingworth, Presidents

Metropolitan Community Church in the Country
3901C Manzanita Dr.
San Diego, CA 92105-4503
Rev. Yvette Dube

Metropolitan Community Church
P.O. Box 33291
San Diego, CA 92163
Rev. David Farrell

Yachad
P.O. Box 3457
San Diego, CA 92163

Dignity / San Francisco
Seventh Avenue Presbytarian
1329 7th Ave.
San Francisco, CA 94122-2507
Catholic

Golden Gate Metropolitan Community Church
1600 Clay St.
San Francisco, CA 94109
Rev. Roy Birchard

Lutherans Concerned / San Francisco
566 Vallejo St., #25
San Francisco, CA 94133-4033

Metropolitan Community Church San Francisco
150 Eureka St.
San Francisco, CA 94114-2492
Rev. James Mitulski

The Parsonage
555A Castro St.
San Francisco, CA 94114
Ministry of the Episcopal Church of California

Presbyterians for Lesbian / Gay Concerns
P.O. Box 14653
San Francisco, CA 94114

Sha'ar Zahav
220 Dancers St.
San Francisco, CA 94114

Voice & Vision: Lutheran Lesbian & Gay Ministry
152 Church St.
San Francisco, CA 94114

Hosanna Church of Praise
24 N. 5th St.
San José , CA 95112

Metropolitan Community Church
P.O. Box 388
San José, CA 95103-0388
Rev. Denis Moore

Metropolitan Community Church of Greater Hayward
P.O. Box 247
San Lorenzo, CA 94580
Rev. Michael England

Christ Presbyterian Church in Terra Linda
620 Del Ganado Rd.
San Rafael, CA 94903
A More Light Church

Emergence International: Christian Scientists Supporting Lesbians, Gay Men, and Bisexuals
P.O. Box 9161
San Rafael, CA 94912-9161

Mother River Spirit Metropolitan Community Church
P.O. Box 151171
San Rafael, CA 94915
Rev. Yolanda Vierra-Allen and
Rev. Claudia Vierra-Allen

Christ Chapel Metropolitan Community Church
720 N. Spurgeon St.
Santa Ana, CA 92701-3722
Mr. Hal Nesbitt

Grace Chapel Metropolitan Community Church
230 Lighthouse Rd.
Santa Barbara, CA 93109-1905
Rev. Steven Moore

Dignity / San José
P.O. Box 2177
Santa Clara, CA 95055-2177
Catholic

Lavender Road Metropolitan Community Church
P.O. Box 1764
Santa Cruz, CA 95060
Rev. Jean Hart

New Hope Metropolitan Community Church
P.O. Box 11278
Santa Rosa, CA 95406
Rev. Earl Lewis

Spirit Eagle Metropolitan Community Church
P.O. Box 746
Spring Valley, CA 91976-0746
Rev. Diane Miller

Delta Harvest Metropolitan Community Church
116 W. Willow St.
Stockton, CA 95202-1045
Rev. Sean-Patrick MacMillan

Metropolitan Community Church
P.O. Box 25610
Ventura, CA 93002-5610
Rev. Judy Dahl

Metropolitan Community Church of the Sequoias
P.O. Box 4223
Visalia, CA 93278
Rev. Slade Childers

Affirmation / Los Angeles
P.O. Box 691283
West Hollywood, CA 90069
Methodist

Congregation Kol Ami
8400 Sunset Blvd., Suite 2A
West Hollywood, CA 90069

Integrity / Los Angeles
7985 Santa Monica Blvd. #109-113
West Hollywood, CA 90046

Good Samaritan Metropolitan Community Church
11931 Washington Blvd.
Whittier, CA 90606
Rev. Gina Chapman

Gay and Lesbian Concerned Catholics
St. Thomas Aquinas University Parish
904 14th St.
Boulder, CO 80302

Dignity / Southern Colorado
P.O. Box 1172
Colorado Springs, CO 80901-1172
Catholic

Pikes Peak Metropolitan Community Church
730 N. Tejon St.
Colorado Springs, CO 80903-1012
Rev. Nori Rost

Capitol Heights Church
1100 Fillmore St.
Denver, CO 80206
A More Light Church

Dignity / Denver
P.O. Box 3072
Denver, CO 80201-3072
Catholic

Lutherans Concerned / Denver
P.O. Box 300343
Denver, CO 80203

Metropolitan Community Church of the Rockies
980 Clarkson St.
Denver, CO 80218-2703
Rev. Dr. Charlie Arehart

Tikvat Shalom
P.O. Box 6694
Denver, CO 80206

Metropolitan Community Church Family in Christ
805 S. Shields
Fort Collins, CO 80521
Rev. Mark Lee

Metropolitan Community Church
P.O. Box 1918
Pueblo, CO 81002
Marianne McPherson

Dignity / Hartford
P.O. Box 72
Hartford, CT 06141
Catholic

Metropolitan Community Church
1841 Broad St.
Hartford, CT 06114-1780
David Jaris

Dignity / New Haven
P.O. Box 8581
New Haven, CT 06531
Catholic

Metropolitan Community Church
566 Whalley Ave., Suite 1D
New Haven, CT 06511
Rev. Jim Burrs

Presbyterians for Lesbian / Gay Concerns—Southern New England
23 Sherman St., #2
New London, CT 06320

Integrity / Waterbury Area
St. John's Church
16 Church St.
Waterbury, CT 06702
Ronald H. Davis, President; Episcopal

Am Segulah
P.O. Box 271522
West Hartford, CT 06127

Dignity U.S.A
Marianne Duddy
1500 Massachusetts Ave. N.W., Suite 11
Washington, DC 20005
Lesbian and Gay Catholics

Dignity / Washington
P.O. Box 53001
Washington, DC 20009
Catholic

Bet Mishpachah
P.O. Box 1410
Washington, DC 20013

Brethren / Mennonite Council for Lesbian and Gay Concerns
P.O. Box 65724
Washington, DC 20035

Catholics for a Free Choice
1436 "U" St. N.W.
Washington, DC 20009

Inner Light Unity Fellowship
P.O. Box 2045
Washington, DC 20013

Integrity
P.O. Box 19561
Washington, DC 20036
Lesbian and Gay Episcopalians

Metropolitan Community Church of the Disciples
1638 "R" St. N.W., Suite 1
Washington, DC 20009
Rev. Harry Stock

Metropolitan Community Church
474 Ridge St. N.W.
Washington, DC 20001
Rev. Candace Shultis

Mid-Atlantic Affirmation
P.O. Box 23636
Washington, DC 20026

Presbyterians for Lesbian and Gay Concerns
Westminster Presbyterian Church
400 "I" St., N.W.
Washington, DC 20024

Washington Friends for Lesbian and Gay Concerns
2111 Florida Ave., N.W.
Washington, DC 20008

World Congress of Gay & Lesbian Jewish Organizations
P.O. Box 18961
Washington, DC 20036
William Wahler, Executive Director

Church of Our Savior Metropolitan Community Church
4770 Boca Raton Blvd., Suite C
Boca Raton, FL 33431
Rev. John Jacobs

Breaking the Silence Metropolitan Community Church
P.O. Box 1585
Cocoa, FL 32923
Rev. Linda Bean

Hope Metropolitan Community Church
P.O. Box 15151
Daytona Beach, FL 32115
Rev. Steve Steele

Dignity / Fort Lauderdale
P.O. Box 22884
Fort Lauderdale, FL 33335
Catholic

Sunshine Cathedral Metropolitan Community Church
330 S.W. 27th St.
Fort Lauderdale, FL 33315
Rev. Grant Ford

St. John the Apostle Metropolitan Community Church
P.O. Box 2107
Fort Myers, FL 33902-2107
Em Jay Williams

Trinity Metropolitan Community Church
P.O. Box 140535
Gainesville, FL 32614-0535
Rev. Jerry Seay

Spirit of Life Metropolitan Community Church
4810 Mile Stretch Dr.
Holiday, FL 34690
Rev. Andy Sidden

St. Luke's Metrpolitan Community Church
126 E. 7th St.
Jacksonville, FL 32206-4510
Rev. Frankye White

Metropolitan Community Church
1215 Petronia St.
Key West, FL 33040
Rev. Steven Torrence

Christ Metropolitan Community Church
7701 S.W. 76th Ave.
Miami, FL 33143
Rev. Michael Nikolaus

Grace Metropolitan Community Church
10390 N.E. 2nd Ave.
Miami Shores, FL 33138-2055
Rev. David Park

Etz Chaim
19094 W. Dixie Hwy.
North Miami Beach, FL 33180
Ray Levi

Dignity / Orlando
P.O. Box 530003
Orlando, FL 32853-0003
Catholic

Integrity / Central Florida
P.O. Box 530031
Orlando, FL 32853-0031
Warren Carlson, President; Episcopal

Joy Metropolitan Community Church
P.O. Box 3004
Orlando, FL 32802-3004
Rev. James Brock

Metropolitan Community Church
1139 Everitt Ave.
Panama City, FL 32401
Rev. Thomas Gashlin

Holy Cross Metropolitan Community Church
415 N. Alcaniz
Pensacola, FL 32501
Rev. Zaida Rivera

Beth Rachameem
3817 Creek Way Ct.
Plant City, FL 33567

Church of the Trinity Metropolitan Community Church
7225 N. Lockwood Ridge Rd.
Sarasota, FL 34243
Rev. T. Edward Helms

King of Peace Metropolitan Community Church
3150 5th Ave. N.
St. Petersburg, FL 33713
Rev. Fred Williams

Integrity / Big Bend
P.O. Box 10731
Tallahassee, FL 32302
Episcopal

Dignity / Tampa Bay
P.O. Box 24806
Tampa, FL 33623
Catholic

John Calvin Presbyterian Church
6501 N. Nebraska Ave.
Tampa, FL 33604
A More Light Church

Metropolitan Community Church
2904 Concordia Ave.
Tampa, FL 33629-7013
Rev. Karen Ducham

Dignity / Palm Beach
P.O. Box 3014
Tequesta, FL 33469
Catholic

Metropolitan Community Church of the Palm Beaches
P.O. Box 18527
West Palm Beach, FL 33416
Rev. Marion Harrison

Yeladim Shel Yisrael / Children of Israel
2677 Forest Hill Blvd., Suite 106
West Palm Beach, FL 33406
Jeff Rosenberg

All Saints Metropolitan Community Church
P.O. Box 13968
Atlanta, GA 30324
Rev. Paul Turner

Bet Haverim
P.O. Box 54947
Atlanta, GA 30308

Clifton Presbyterian Church
369 Connecticut Ave. N.E.
Atlanta, GA 30307
A More Light Church

Dignity / Atlanta
P.O. Box 14342
Atlanta, GA 30324
Catholic

First Metropolitan Community Church of Atlanta
1379 Tullie Rd. NE
Atlanta, GA 30329
Rev. Reid Christensen

Gay Catholics of Georgia and Friends
P.O. Box 14342
Atlanta, GA 30324

Integrity / Atlanta
P.O. Box 13603
Atlanta, GA 30324-0603
Mark Stevens, Convener; Episcopal

Lutherans Concerned / Southeast
P.O. Box 13673
Atlanta, GA 30324

Presbyterians for Lesbian / Gay Concerns
P.O. Box 8362
Atlanta, GA 31106-0362

Family of God Metropolitan Community Church
P.O. Box 2201
Columbus, GA 31902
Rev. Liz Leach

Metropolitan Community Church
P.O. Box 14624
Savannah, GA 31416

Christ Covenant Metropolitan Community Church
798 Ray's Rd., Suite 100
Stone Mountain, GA 30083
Glenna Shepherd

Affirmation
P.O. Box 75131
Honolulu, HI 96836-0131

Dignity / Honolulu
P.O. Box 3956
Honolulu, HI 96812-3956
Catholic

Ke Anuenue O Ke Aloha Metropolitan Community Church
P.O. Box 23334
Honolulu, HI 96823
Rev. Maggie Tannis and
Rev. John Bullock

New Liberation Metropolitan Community Church
P.O. Box 347
Puunene, Maui, HI 96784-0347
Rev. David Pelletier

Metropolitan Community Church
P.O. Box 1959
Boise, ID 83701
Rev. Tyrone Sweeting

Integrity / Fox Valley
St David's Church
Randall & Illinois Ave.
Aurora, IL 60506
Episcopal

Integrity / East Central Illinois
1011 S. Wright St.
Champaign, IL 61820
Episcopal

McKinley Memorial Church
809 S. 5th St.
Champaign, IL 61820-6299
A More Light Church

Archdiocesean Gay & Lesbian Outreach
(AGLO)
Our Lady of Mt. Carmel Church
690 W. Belmont
Chicago, IL 60657

Catholic Advocates for Gay & Lesbian Rights
5249 N. Kenmore
Chicago, IL 60640

Church of Resurrection Metropolitan Community Church
5540 S. Woodlawn
Chicago, IL 60637-1623
Rev. Gordon McCoy

Congregation Or Chadash
656 W. Barry Ave.
Chicago, IL 60657

Dignity / Chicago
3023 N. Clark St., Suite 237
Chicago, IL 60657
Catholic

Gentle Spirit Metropolitan Community Church
P.O. Box 597350
Chicago, IL 60659-7350
Rev. Ralph Conrad

Good Shepherd Metropolitan Community Church
615 W. Wellington Ave.
Chicago, IL 60657-5305
Wayne Bradley

Integrity / Chicago
P.O. Box 2516
Chicago, IL 60690
Daniel Wall, President; Episcopal

Lutherans Concerned / Chicago
P.O. Box 10197
Chicago, IL 60610

Lutherans Concerned / North America
P.O. Box 10461
Ft. Dearborn Station
Chicago, IL 60610

Presbyterians for Lesbian / Gay Concerns
600 W. Fullerton Pkwy.
Chicago, IL 60614

United Church of Christ Coalition for Lesbian & Gay Concerns
6171 N. Sheridan Rd., Suite 701
Chicago, IL 60660

North Shore Unitarian Church
2100 Half Day Rd.
Deerfield, IL 60015-1298
Unitarian Universalist

Affirmation / National Offices
P.O. Box 1021
Evanston, IL 60204
United Methodists for Lesbian and Gay Concerns

Christ the Redeemer Metropolitan Community Church
P.O. Box 6146
Evanston, IL 60204-6146
Rev. Lee Campbell

Dignity / Fort Wayne
P.O. Box 11988
Fort Wayne, IN 46862
Catholic

Holy Covenant Metropolitan Community Church
17 W. Maple
Hinsdale, IL 60521-3495
Rev. Karon Van Gelder

Joy of Life Metropolitan Community Church
P.O. Box 1161
North Chicago, IL 60064
Rev. Peter Trabaris

South Suburban Fellowship Metropolitan Community Church
70 Sycamore Dr.
Park Forest, IL 60426
Rev. Hal Hasse

Spirit of Life Metropolitan Community Church
P.O. Box 1614
Peoria, IL 61656-1614

Metropolitan Community Church Illiamo
123-1/2 N. 5th Ave.
Quincy, IL 62301
Mike Howard

Metropolitan Community Church of the Quad Cities
1001 18th Ave.
Rock Island, IL 61201
Rev. Roy Lenington

Faith Eternal Metropolitan Community Church
P.O. Box 4824
Springfield, IL 62708
Rev. Jim Lynch

Spinoza
P.O. Box 6112
Bloomington, IN 47407

Tri-State Metropolitan Community Church
P.O. Box 3382
Evansville, IN 47732
Rev. Neil Biggers

New World Church & Outreach Center
P.O. Box 11553
Fort Wayne, IN 46859

Affirmation
33 E. 32nd St.
Indianapolis, IN 46205
Methodist

Dignity / Central Indiana
P.O. Box 431
Indianapolis, IN 46206
Catholic

Gay, Lesbian, and Affirming Disciples Alliance (Disciples of Christ)
P.O. Box 19223
Indianapolis, IN 46219

Jesus Metropolitan Community Church
P.O. Box 19392
Indianapolis, IN 46219-0392
Rev. Marilyn Marr

Dignity / Lafayette
P.O. Box 4665
Lafayette, IN 47903
Catholic

Dignity / Muncie
P.O. Box 2111
Muncie, IN 47307
Catholic

Lutherans Concerned / Bettendorf
P.O. Box 773
Bettendorf, IA 52722

Church of the Holy Spirit Metropolitan Community Church
P.O. Box 21010
Des Moines, IA 50321
Paul Rupelt and Sharon Sloat

Presbyterians for Lesbian / Gay Concerns of Eastern Iowa
P.O. Box 3202
Iowa City, IA 52244

Metropolitan Community Church
P.O. Box 361
Sioux City, IA 51102
Rev. Margaret Hutchens

Church of New Hope Metropolitan Community Church
P.O. Box 34
Waterloo, IA 50704
John Wilson

L'Cha Dodi
c/o JCRB/AJC
5801 W. 115th St., Suite 203
Oakland Park, KS 66211
Phil Meltzer

Metropolitan Community Church of Johnson County
12510 W. 62nd Terr., Suite 106
Shawnee, KS 66216
Rev. Celena Duncan

Metropolitan Community Church
P.O. Box 4776
Topeka, KS 66604-0776
Rev. Paul Evans

First Metropolitan Community Church of Kansas
156 S. Kansas Ave.
Wichita, KS 67211
Rev. Bill Peckham

Dignity / Lexington
533 Cane Run Rd.
Lexington, KY 40405-1434
Catholic

Integrity / Central Kentucky
P.O. Box 355
Lexington, KY 40584-0355
Episcopal

Lexington's Metropolitan Community Church
1013 Reilue Ct.
Lexington, KY 40517
Rev. Rex Van Alstine

Affirmation / Louisville
1014 S. 2nd St., Suite 901
Louisville, KY 40202-2858
Methodists

B'Nai Shalom
c/o Jacobs
P.O. Box 4012
Louisville, KY 40204

Central Presbyterian Church
318 W. Kentucky St.
Louisville, KY 40203
A More Light Church

Dignity / Louisville
P.O. Box 4778
Louisville, KY 40204
Catholic

Honesty: Southern Baptists Advocating Equal Rights for Gays & Lesbians
P.O. Box 7331
Louisville, KY 40257

Lutherans Concerned / Louisville
P.O. Box 7692
Louisville, KY 40257-0692

Metropolitan Community Church
P.O. Box 32474
Louisville, KY 40232-0474
Rev. Dee Dale

Presbyterians for Lesbian / Gay Concerns—Louisville
522 Belgravia Ct., #2
Louisville, KY 40208

Metropolitan Community Church in Paducah
P.O. Box 176
West Paducah, KY 42002-0188
Kevin Boyd and Susan Walter

Dignity / Baton Rouge
P.O. Box 4181
Baton Rouge, LA 70821
Catholic

Joie de Vivre Metropolitan Community Church
P.O. Box 64996
Baton Rouge, LA 70896-4996
Rev. Nancy Horvath

Presbyterians for Lesbian / Gay Concerns
2285 Cedardale
Baton Rouge, LA 70808

Metropolitan Community Church of Lafayette
P.O. Box 92682
Lafayette, LA 70509

Metropolitan Community Church of Lake Charles
P.O. Box 384
Lake Charles, LA 70602
Rev. R.A. Webber

Dignity / New Orleans
2048 Camp St.
New Orleans, LA 70130
Catholic

First Unitarian Church for the Gay & Lesbian Task Force
1800 Jefferson Ave.
New Orleans, LA

Integrity / New Orleans
Trinity Episcopal Church
1339 Jackson Ave.
New Orleans, LA 70130
Brian Sykes, Convener; Episcopal

Jewish Gay & Lesbian Alliance
1228 Bourbon St., Apt. D
New Orleans, LA 70116-2554

Vieux Carre Metropolitan Community Church
1128 St. Roch Ave.
New Orleans, LA 70117
Dexter Brecht

Victory Fellowship Metropolitan Community Church
P.O. Box 4200
Shreveport, LA 71134
Rev. Charlene Bock

Dignity / Maine
P.O. Box 8113
Portland, ME 04104
Catholic

Am Chofshi
RR1, Box 686
South Harpswel, ME 04079
Susan Horowitz; Maine's lesbian, gay and bisexual Jewish organization

Adath Rayoot
c/o GLCC
Box 22575
Baltimore, MD 21203
Jewish Gays of Central Maryland

Dignity / Baltimore
P.O. Box 1243
Baltimore, MD 21203-1243
Catholic

Integrity / Baltimore
Emmanuel Church
811 Cathedral St.
Baltimore, MD 21201
Teri Lamay, President; Episcopal

First & Franklin Street Church
210 W. Madison St.
Baltimore, MD 21201-4693
A More Light Church

Lutherans Concerned / Baltimore - Washington
P.O. Box 23271
Baltimore, MD 21203-5271

Metropolitan Community Church
3401 Old York Rd.
Baltimore, MD 21218
Rev. Joseph Totten-Reid

Open Door Metropolitan Community Church
P.O. Box 127
Boyds, MD 20841-0127
Rev. Ken Ehrke

New Ways Ministry
4012 29th St.
Mt. Rainier, MD 20712

Rockville Presbyterian Church
215 W. Montgomery Ave.
Rockville, MD 20850
A More Light Church

Church of the Covenant
67 Newbury St.
Boston, MA 02116
A More Light Church

Dignity / Boston
91 Berkeley St., Suite 610
Boston, MA 02116-6203
Catholic

Metropolitan Community Church
P.O. Box 15590, Kenmore Station
Boston, MA 02215
Tim Koch

Office of Lesbian, Bisexual, and Gay Concerns / Unitarian Universalist Association
25 Beacon St.
Boston, MA 02108-2800

Am Tikva
P.O. Box 11
Cambridge, MA 02238

Morning Star Metropolitan Community Church
231 Main St.
Cherry Valley, MA 01611-3143
Rev. Ron Anderson

Dignity / Fall River
P.O. Box 627
Fall River, MA 02722
Catholic

Jewish Lesbian Daughters of Holocaust Survivors
P.O. Box 75
Hadley, MA 01035

Presbyterians for Lesbian / Gay Concerns—Boston
28 9th St., #403
Medford, MA 02155

Integrity / Boston Metro
Christ Church, Episcopal
12 Quincy Ave.
Quincy, MA 02169
The Rev. James Campbell-Young, Initial Convener;
Episcopal

Integrity / Western Massachusetts
P.O. Box 5051
Springfield, MA 01101-5051
Jim Barnes, President;
Episcopal

Lutherans Concerned / New England
8 1/2 Chestnut St.
Waltham, MA 02154-0404

United Church Coalition for Lesbian / Gay Concerns Youth and Young Adult Outreach Program
69 Monadnock Rd.
Worcester, MA 01609-1714

Beit Chayim
P.O. Box 7292
Ann Arbor, MI 48107

Huron Valley Community Church of Ann Arbor
2145 Independence
Ann Arbor, MI 48104

Tree of Life Metropolitan Community Church
P.O. Box 2598
Ann Arbor, MI 48106
Rev. Thomas Carone

Dignity / Detroit
P.O. Box 32874
Detroit, MI 48232
Catholic

Full Truth Unity Fellowship
4458 Joy Rd.
Detroit, MI 48204

Intregity / Detroit
Christ Church
960 E. Jefferson Ave.
Detroit, MI 48207
Rosemary Hogan; Episcopal

Dignity / Greater Lansing
P.O. Box 1265
East Lansing, MI 48826
Catholic

Redeemer Metropolitan Community Church
1665 N. Chevrolet Ave.
Flint, MI 48504
Rev. Lin Stoner

Dignity / Grand Rapids
P.O. Box 1373
Grand Rapids, MI 49501
Catholic

Reconciliation Metropolitan Community Church
300 Graceland N.E.
Grand Rapids, MI 49505-6201
Rev. Martie Casmero

Phoenix Community Church
P.O. Box 2222
Kalamazoo, MI 49003-2222
United Church of Christ

Divine Peace Metropolitan Community Church
P.O. Box 71938
Madison Heights, MI 48071
Teri Stidham

Muskegon Metropolitan Community Church
P.O. Box 132
Muskegon, MI 49443-0132
Rev. Daniel Brauer

Metropolitan Community Church
P.O. Box 836
Royal Oak, MI 48068
Mark Bidwell

Presbyterians for Lesbian / Gay Concerns—Detroit
P.O. Box 1004
Royal Oak, MI 48068-1004

Simcha
P.O. Box 652
Southfield, MI 48037

Lutherans Concerned-Integrity / Southwest Minnesota
1418 State St.
Marshall, MN 56258
Ray Ogdahl, President

Affirmation
101 E. Grant St.
Minneapolis, MN 55403
Methodist

Affirmation
P.O. Box 3878
Minneapolis, MN 55403
Mormon

All God's Children Metropolitan Community Church
3100 Park Ave.
Minneapolis, MN 55407
Clark Bufkin

Dignity / Twin Cities
P.O. Box 3565
Minneapolis, MN 55403
Catholic

Integrity / Twin Cities
University Episcopal Center
317 17th Ave., S.E.
Minneapolis, MN 55414
Thomas Kane, Convener; Episcopal

Keshet
3500 Holmes Ave.
Minneapolis, MN 55408

Lutherans Concerned / Twin Cities
100 N. Oxford St.
St. Paul, MN 55104-6540

Presbyterians for Lesbian / Gay Concerns
3538 22nd Ave. S.
Minneapolis, MN 55407

The Wingspan Ministry of St. Paul-Reformation Lutheran Church
100 N. Oxford St.
St. Paul, MN 55104

St. Luke Presbyterian Church
3121 Groveland School Rd.
Wayzata, MN 55391
A More Light Church

Metropolitan Community Church of the Gulf Coast
P.O. Box 1182
Biloxi, MS 39533
Rev. Tom Schult

Integrity / Mississippi
P.O. Box 68314
Jackson, MS 39286-9998
Episcopal

Metropolitan Community Church
P.O. Box 5304
Jackson, MS 39296

St. Stephen's United Community Church
P.O. Box 7654
Jackson, MS 39284-7654

Dignity / Columbia
701 Maryland
Columbia, MO
Catholic

United Covenant Mission Church
P.O. Box 7152
Columbia, MO 65205

Affirmation
5709 Virginia Ave.
Kansas City, MO 64110-2855
Methodist

All Souls Unitarian Church
4500 Warwick Rd.
Kansas City, MO 64111

Integrity / Kansas City
P.O. Box 414164
Kansas City, MO 64141
Episcopal

Lutherans Concerned / Kansas City
1104 N.E. Vivian Rd.
Kansas City, MO

Spirit of Hope Metropolitan Community Church
P.O. Box 10087
Kansas City, MO 64111-0087
Rev. John Barbone

United Church Coalition for Lesbian and Gay Concerns
5933 Holmes
Kansas City, MO 64110

Van Brunt Boulevard Presbyterian Church
5205 E. 23rd St.
Kansas City, MO 64127
A More Light Church

Metropolitan Community Church in the Ozarks
P.O. Box 2782
Springfield, MO 65801

Agape Church
2026 Lafayette Ave.
St. Louis, MO 63104-2528

Dignity / St. Louis
P.O. Box 23093
St. Louis, MO 63156
Catholic

Gibson Heights Presbyterian Church
1075 S. Taylor St.
St. Louis, MO 63110
A More Light Church

Metropolitan Community Church of Living Faith
6501 Wydown Blvd.
St. Louis, MO 63105
Rev. Ken Pilot

Metropolitan Community Church
P.O. Box 7226
St. Louis, MO 63177-7226
Rev. Bradley Wishon

St. Louis Gay and Lesbian Chavurah
Central Reform Congregation
77 Maryland Plaza
St. Louis, MO 63108
Gay and Lesbian Jewish Congregation

Family of God Metropolitan Community Church
P.O. Box 23003
Billings, MT 59104
Sherrie Pantle

Affirmation / Bozeman
1000 N. 17th Ave., #29
Bozeman, MT 59715
Lesbian and Gay Mormons

Metropolitan Community Church Shepherd of the Plains
P.O. Box 2162
Great Falls, MT 59403
Gina Hartung

Lutherans Concerned / Omaha
First Lutheran Church
31st & Jackson Sts.
Omaha, NE 68105

Metropolitan Community Church
P.O. Box 3173
Omaha, NE 68103-0173
Rev. Matthew Howard

Mishpachat Chaverim
c/o Emenitove
959 S. 51st St.
Omaha, NE 68106

Presbyterians for Lesbian / Gay Concerns
3810 S. 13th St., #26
Omaha, NE 68107

Dignity / Las Vegas
P.O. Box 70424
Las Vegas, NV 89170
Catholic

Metropolitan Community Church
1119 S. Main St.
Las Vegas, NV 89104-1026
Rev. B.J. McDaniels

Metropolitan Community Church of the Sierras
P.O. Box 21192
Reno, NV 89515-1192
Rev. Roy Cole

Metropolitan Community Church in the Mountains
P.O. Box 53
Hanover, NH 03755-0053
Rev. Lisa Dawn McCabe

Dignity / New Hampshire
P.O. Box 7
Manchester, NH 03105-0007
Catholic

Integrity / New Jersey
Trinity Episcopal Church
Asbury & Grand Aves.
Asbury Park, NJ 08404
Episcopal

Dignity / Metro New Jersey
550 Ridgewood Rd., Box M
Maplewood, NJ 07040
Catholic

New Jersey Lesbian and Gay Havurah
P.O. Box 2576
Menlo Park, NJ 08818

Christ the Liberator Metropolitan Community Church
P.O. Box 10494
New Brunswick, NJ 08906-0494
Rev. Arthur Runyan II

Dignity / New Brunswick
P.O. Box 10781
New Brunswick, NJ 08906
Catholic

Presbyterians for Lesbian and Gay Concerns (New Jersey)
P.O. Box 38
New Brunswick, NJ 08903-0038

Presbyterians for Lesbian / Gay Concerns (National)
P.O. Box 38
New Brunswick, NJ 08903-0038
Jim Anderson

Dignity / New Mexico
P.O. Box 27294
Albuquerque, NM 87125
Catholic

Emmanuel Metropolitan Community Church
P.O. Box 80192
Albuquerque, NM 87108
Rev. Donna Lockridge

Kinship
P.O. Box 26012
Albuquerque, NM 87125
Seventh Day Adventists

Metropolitan Community Church
2404 San Mateo Pl. N.E.
Albuquerque, NM 87110
Rev. Phil Wolfe

Integrity / Albany
Grace & Holy Innocents
498 Clinton Ave.
Albany, NY 12206
Sylvia Rieth;
Episcopal

St Ann's Church of Morrisania
295 St. Ann's Ave.
Bronx, NY 10454

Old South Haven Church
S. Country Rd., P.O. Box 203
Brookhaven, NY 11719
A More Light Church

Dignity / Brooklyn
P.O. Box 021313
Brooklyn, NY 11202-1313
Catholic

Lafayette Avenue Church
85 S. Oxford St.
Brooklyn, NY 11217
A More Light Church

The Church of Gethsemane
1012 8th Ave.
Brooklyn, NY 11215
A More Light Church

Unity Fellowship Church
230 Classon Ave.
Brooklyn, NY 11205
Rev. Zachary Jones

Dignity / Buffalo
P.O. Box 75
Ellicott Station
Buffalo, NY 14205
Catholic

Integrity / Western New York
Church of the Ascension
16 Linwood Ave.
Buffalo, NY 14209
James Estep, Convener;
Episcopal

Westminster Presbyterian Church
724 Delaware Ave.
Buffalo, NY 14209-2294
A More Light Church

Dignity / Nassau
P.O. Box 48
East Meadow, NY 11554
Catholic

John Calvin Church
50 Ward Hill Rd.
Henrietta, NY 14467
A More Light Church

Dignity-Integrity / Mid-Hudson
P.O. Box 356
LaGrangeville, NY 12540-0356
Linda Brandt;
Catholic-Episcopal

Metropolitan Community Church of the Hudson Valley
40 Duncan Dr.
Latham, NY 12110
Rev. Jane Jerome

Dignity / Capital District
P.O. Box 11204
Loudonville, NY 12211
Catholic

Axios: Eastern and Orthodox Christians
328 W. 17th St., #4F
New York, NY 10011

Central Presbyterian Church
593 Park Ave.
New York, NY 10021
William Pindar;
A More Light Church

Conference for Catholic Lesbians
P.O. Box 436, Planetarium Station
New York, NY 10024

Congregation Beth Simchat Torah
57 Bethune St.
New York, NY 10014-1791
Rabbi Sharon Kleinbaum

Dignity / Big Apple
P.O. Box 1028
New York, NY 10011
Catholic

Dignity / New York
P.O. Box 1554
FDR Station
New York, NY 10150
Catholic

Evangelicals Concerned
311 E. 72nd St., Suite 1G
New York, NY 10021
Dr. Ralph Blair

Gay and Lesbian Committee of Congregation B'nai Jesurua
270 W. 89th St.
New York, NY 10024

Good Shepherd-Faith Church
152 W. 66th St.
New York, NY 10023
Choon Koo;
A More Light Church

Integrity / New York
P.O. Box 5202
New York, NY 10185-0043
Nick Dowen, President;
Episcopal

International Association of Lesbian and Gay Children of Holocaust Survivors
c/o CBST
57 Bethune St.
New York, NY 10013

Jan Hus Presbyterian Church
351 E. 74th St.
New York, NY 10021
Jan Orr-Harter;
A More Light Church

Metropolitan Community Church
446 W. 36th St.
New York, NY 10018
Rev. Patricia Bumgardner

Presbyterians for Lesbian / Gay Concerns
56 Perry St., #3R
New York, NY 10014

Radical Faeries
P.O. Box 1251
Canal Street Station
New York, NY 10013

Rutgers Presbyterian Church
236 W. 73rd St.
New York, NY 10023
Robert Doyle;
A More Light Church

World Congress of Gay and Lesbian Jewish Organizations
P.O. Box 3345
New York, NY 10008-3345
William Wahler

Dignity / Suffolk
P.O. Box 1336
Patchogue, NY 11772-0794
Catholic

Calvary St. Andrews Church
68 Ashland St.
Rochester, NY 14620
A More Light Church

Dignity-Integrity / Rochester
17 S. Fitzhugh St.
Rochester, NY 14614
Catholic-Episcopal

Nayim
P.O. Box 18053
Rochester, NY 14618

Open Arms Metropolitan Community Church
875 E. Main St.
Rochester, NY 14605
Rev. Cathy Elliott

Third Presbyterian Church
4 Meigs St.
Rochester, NY 15607
A More Light Church

National Gay Pentecostal Alliance
P.O. Box 1391
Schenectady, NY 12301-1391

Ray of Hope Metropolitan Community Church
P.O. Box 6955
Syracuse, NY 13217-6955
Keith Herrick

Dignity / Mid-New York
P.O. Box 352
Utica, NY 13503
Catholic

The Gay and Lesbian Catholic Community
P.O. Box 352
Utica, NY 13503-0352

Integrity / Westchester
P.O. Box 2038
White Plains, NY 10602-2038
Bruce Betts, President;
Episcopal

Lutherans Concerned / Triangle
P.O. Box 665
Apex, NC 27502

Metropolitan Community Church
P.O. Box 25278
Asheville, NC 28813
Rev. Frank Scott

Unitarian Universalist Church
1 Edwin Pl.
Asheville, NC 28813

Gay Baha'i Fellowship
P.O. Box 2623
Asheville, NC 28802

Metropolitan Community Church of the High Country
P.O. Box 504
Boone, NC 28607
Cindy Long

The Church of Reconciliation
110 N. Elliott
Chapel Hill, NC 27514
A More Light Church

Lutherans Concerned
1900 The Plaza
Charlotte, NC 28205

Metropolitan Community Church
4037 E. Independence Blvd.
Suite 726
Charlotte, NC 28205
Rev. Randy Votsch

New Life Metropolitan Community Church
2644 Chesterfield Ave.
Charlotte, NC 28205
Rev. Robert Darst

Dignity / Triangle
P.O. Box 51129
Durham, NC 27727
Catholic

Eno River Unitarian-Universalist Church
4907 Garrett Rd.
Durham, NC 27707

Lesbian / Gay Shabbat
807 Onslow St.
Durham, NC 27705
Lesbian and Gay Jewish Congregation

St. Mary's Metropolitan Community Church
P.O. Box 5808
Greensboro, NC 27435-0808
Rev. Christine Oscar

Metropolitan Community Church
216 2nd St. N.W., Suite 200
Hickory, NC 28603
Rev. Nancy Brown

Affirmation / Raleigh
P.O. Box 5691
Raleigh, NC 27650
Methodists

Integrity / Raleigh
Church of the Good Shepard
P.O. Box 28024
Raleigh, NC 27611
Episcopal

Lutherans Concerned
9508 Kirkhill Dr.
Raleigh, NC 27615

St. John's Metropolitan Community Church
P.O. Box 5626
Raleigh, NC 27650-5626
Rev. W. Wayne Linsey

Unitarian Universalist Church
3313 Wade Ave.
Raleigh, NC 27607
Triangle Lesbian & Gay Concern

St. Jude's Metropolitan Community Church
4326 Market St., Suite 170
Wilmington, NC 28403
Kathi Beall

Unity Christ Church
717 Orchard Ave.
Wilmington, NC 28403

United Church Coalition for Lesbian / Gay Concerns (United Church of Christ)
18 N. College St.
Athens, OH 45701

Dignity / Cincinnati
P.O. Box 983
Cincinnati, OH 45201
Catholic

Integrity / Greater Cincinnati
4905 Chalet Dr., #11
Cincinnati, OH 45217-1445
Jeffrey L. Dey and Charles Walker; Episcopal

New Spirit Metropolitan Community Church
65 E. Hollister St.
Cincinnati, OH 45219-1703
Rev. Bonnie Daniel

Chevrei Tikva
P.O. Box 18120
Cleveland, OH 44118

Dignity / Cleveland
P.O. Box 91697
Cleveland, OH 44101
Catholic

Dignity / Greater Columbus
P.O. Box 02001
Columbus, OH 43202
Catholic

Integrity / Central Ohio
P.O. Box 292625
Columbus, OH 43229
Episcopal

New Creation Metropolitan Community Church
P.O. Box 10009
Columbus, OH 43201
Margaret Hawk

Community Gospel Church
P.O. Box 1643
Dayton, OH 45407

Spirit of the Rivers Community Church
P.O. Box 10333
Columbus, OH 43207

Dignity / Dayton
P.O. Box 55
Dayton, OH 45401
Catholic

Metropolitan Community Church (Dayton Parish)
P.O. Box 4021
Dayton, OH 45401-4021
Raeanna Biddle

Integrity / Northeast Ohio
P.O. Box 0397
Oberlin, OH 44074-0397
Episcopal

Central United Methodist Church
701 W. Central
Toledo, OH 43610
Support services

Dignity / Toledo
P.O. Box 1388
Toledo, OH 43603
Catholic

Good Samaritan Parish Metropolitan Community Church
P.O. Box 4907
Toledo, OH 43620
Bill Dannelly

Integrity / Toledo
2272 Collingwood Blvd.
Toledo, OH 43620
Jorge Perez and Kelly Termin, Co-conveners;
Episcopal

Family of Faith Metropolitan Community Church
P.O. Box 382
Jenks, OK 74037
Rev. Marian Fink

Great Plains Metropolitan Community Church
P.O. Box 63
Lawton, OK 73502
Carla Howerton

Church of Christ for Gays
P.O. Box 75481
Oklahoma City, OK 73147

Dignity-Integrity / Oklahoma City
P.O. Box 25473
Oklahoma City, OK 73125
Catholic/Episcopal

Lighthouse Metropolitan Community Church
P.O. Box 26221
Oklahoma City, OK 73126
Rev. John Nicholas

New Horizons Metropolitan Community Church
P.O. Box 12457
Oklahoma City, OK 73157
Rev. Kaye Lee

Dignity-Integrity / Tulsa
P.O. Box 701044
Tulsa, OK 74170-1044
Susi Timi;
Catholic-Episcopal

Metropolitan Community Church of Greater Tulsa
P.O. Box 4187
Tulsa, OK 74159-0187
Rev. Alice Jones

Metropolitan Community Church of the Siskiyous
8165 Gold Rey Rd.
Central Point, OR 97502

Metropolitan Community Church
P.O. Box 10091
Eugene, OR 97440-2091
Rev. Marguerite Scroggie

Presbyterians for Lesbian / Gay Concerns—Oregon
P.O. Box 3391
Eugene, OR 97403

Affirmation
P.O. Box 12673
Portland, OR 97212
Methodist

Dignity / Portland
P.O. Box 6708
Portland, OR 97228-6708
Catholic

Integrity / Columbia-Willamette
c/o AFSC
2249 E. Burnside
Portland, OR 97214
Bruce Mason, Co-Convener;
Episcopal

Metropolitan Community Church
1644 N.E. 24th Ave.
Portland, OR 97232-1630
Rev. Dennis Chappell

Metropolitan Community Church (Roseburg)
P.O. Box 2125
Roseburg, OR 97470
Jim Hopper

Dignity / Willamette Valley
P.O. Box 532
Salem, OR 97308
Catholic

Sweet Spirit Metropolitan Community Church
P.O. Box 13969
Salem, OR 97309-1969
Patricia Jackson

Metropolitan Community Church of the Lehigh Valley
1345 Linden, Suite 3
Allentown, PA 18102

Integrity / Bethlehem
P.O. Box 5181
Bethlehem, PA 18015-5181
Dixie Dugan White;
Episcopal

Dignity / Erie
P.O. Box 3746
Erie , PA 16508
Catholic

Integrity / Northwest Pennsylvania
P.O. Box 1782
Erie, PA 16507-0782
Dorothy Konyha, Convener;
Episcopal

Dignity / Northeast Pennsylvania
P.O. Box 379
Hamlin, PA 18427
Catholic

Dignity / Central Pennsylvania
P.O. Box 297
Harrisburg, PA 17108-0297
Catholic

Dignity / North Central Pennsylvania
94 Kinsey St.
Montgomery, PA 17752
Catholic

Vision of Hope Metropolitan Community Church
130 E. Main St.
Mountville, PA 17554
Rev. Peter Helt

Beth Ahavah
P.O. Box 7566
Philadelphia, PA 19101

Dignity / Philadelphia
P.O. Box 53348
Philadelphia, PA 19105
Catholic

Integrity / Philadelphia
Holy Trinity Church
1904 Walnut St.
Philadelphia, PA 19103
William Dobkowski and Martha Dooley, Co-conveners;
Episcopal

Metropolitan Community Church
P.O. Box 8174
Philadelphia, PA 19101-8174
Rev. Herbert Evans

Tabernacle United Church
3700 Chestnut St.
Philadelphia, PA 19104
A More Light Church

Bet Tikva
c/o Persad Center
5150 Penn Ave.
Pittsburgh, PA 15224-1627
Synagogue and community for lesbian, gay and bisexual Jews and their friends

Affirmation
P.O. Box 10104
Pittsburgh, PA 15232-0104
Methodist

Dignity / Pittsburgh
P.O. Box 362
Pittsburgh, PA 15230
Catholic

Integrity / Pittsburgh
P.O. Box 5619
Pittsburgh, PA 15207-0619
William Camp, Chairperson; Episcopal

Lutherans Concerned / Pittsburgh
P.O. Box 81866
Pittsburgh, PA 15217-0866

Metropolitan Community Church
4836 Ellsworth Ave.
Pittsburgh, PA 15213
Rev. Roberta Dunn

Presbyterians for Lesbian / Gay Concerns
P.O. Box 9022
Pittsburgh, PA 15224

Friends for Lesbian & Gay Concerns
P.O. Box 222
Sumneytown, PA 18084
Quakers

Dignity / Providence
P.O. Box 2231
Pawtucket, RI 02861
Catholic

Metropolitan Community Church
2010 Hawthorne Dr., Suite 10
Charleston, SC 29418
Mary Moore

Community Fellowship Metropolitan Community Church
P.O. Box 8753
Columbia, SC 29202

Lutherans Concerned / South Carolina
P.O. Box 8828
Columbia, SC 29202-8828

St. Jude Community Church
309 Heyward St.
Columbia, SC 29202

Metropolitan Community Church
P.O. Box 6322
Greenville, SC 29606-6322
Rev. Mich Hinson

Metropolitan Community Church
P.O. Box 3032
Myrtle Beach, SC 29578
Rev. Buddy Vess

Unitarian Universalist Church
251 E. Henry St.
Spartanburg, SC 29303

United Church Coalition for Lesbian / Gay Concerns
Route 1, Box 76
Lake Preston, SD 57249-9718

St. Francis & St. Claire Metropolitan Community Church
P.O. Box 266
Sioux Falls, SD 57101-0266
Rev. Don Reush

Integrity / East Tennessee
P.O. Box 4956
Chattanooga, TN 37405
Michael E. Thompson, Convener; Episcopal

Metropolitan Community Church
P.O. Box 80183
Chattanooga, TN 37414
Rev. Polley Ireland

Metropolitan Community Church (Tri-Cities)
P.O. Box 1612
Johnson City, TN 37605-1612
Chuck Thompson

Metropolitan Community Church
P.O. Box 2343
Knoxville, TN 37901-2343
Rev. W. James Richards

Gays Rejoicing & Affirmed in a Catholic Environment
(GRACE)
6 S. McLean, #402
Memphis, TN 38104

Holy Trinity Community Church
1559 Madison Ave.
Memphis, TN 38104

Integrity / Memphis
Calvary Church
102 N. 2nd St.
Memphis, TN 38103
Howard Wiggins, Convener; Episcopal

Integrity / Middle Tennessee
P.O. Box 121172
Nashville, TN 37212
Fred H. Ellis III and Sue Ross, Co-Conveners; Episcopal

Metropolitan Community Church
P.O. Box 60406
Nashville, TN 37206
Rev. Buddy Truluck

Exodus Metropolitan Community Church
P.O. Box 3274
Abilene, TX 79604
Rev. George Allen

Metropolitan Community Church of the Rio Grande Valley
Route 1, Box 53
Alamo, TX 78516
Richard Ford

Metropolitan Community Church
P.O. Box 1276
Amarillo, TX 79105-1276
Rev. Robert Finch

Trinity Metropolitan Community Church
331 Aaron Ave., Suite 125
Arlington, TX 76012
Rev. Jo Crisco

Affirmation / Austin
7403 Shoal Creek Blvd.
Austin, TX 78757
Methodist

Dignity / Austin
P.O. Box 2666
Austin, TX 78768
Catholic

Integrity / Austin
P.O. Box 4327
Austin, TX 78765-4327
Mark Casstevens and Dorothy Ruhl, Co-conveners; Episcopal

Metropolitan Community Church
425 Woodward Ave.
Austin, TX 78704
Rev. Wendy Foxworth and Rev. Ken Martin

Seventh-Day Adventist Kinship
P.O. Box 110116
Carrollton, TX 75011-0116
Gay and Lesbian Seventh Day Adventist

Christ's Temple Metropolitan Community Church
1315 Craig St.
Corpus Christi, TX 78404-3330
Sherry Hilliard

Affirmation / Dallas
P.O. Box 190987
Dallas, TX 75219-0987

Beth El Binah
P.O. Box 191188
Dallas, TX 75219

Cathedral of Hope Metropolitan Community Church
P.O. Box 35466
Dallas, TX 75235-0466
Rev. Michael Piazza

Congregation Beth El Binah
P.O. Box 191188
Dallas, TX 75219
Jewish congregation

Dignity / Dallas
P.O. Box 190133
Dallas, TX 75219-0133
Catholic

Harvest Metropolitan Community Church
5900 S. Stemmons Fwy.
Denton, TX 76205
Rev. Colleen Darraugh

Integrity / Dallas
P.O. Box 190351
Dallas, TX 75219-0351
Keith Carney, Treasurer; Episcopal

Presbyterians for Lesbian / Gay Concerns
Bethany Presbyterian Church
4523 Cedar Springs Rd.
Dallas, TX 75219

Metropolitan Community Church
P.O. Box 3121
El Paso, TX 79903
Rev. Rick Schisler

Cathedral of Hope Metropolitan Community Church
Mel White
P.O. Box 609
Ennis, TX 75120

Agape Metropolitan Community Church
P.O. Box 15247
Fort Worth, TX 76119
Rev. Brenda Hunt

Dignity / Houston
P.O. Box 66821
Houston, TX 77266
Catholic

Houston Mission Church
P.O. Box 131371
Houston, TX 77219-1371

Integrity / Houston
P.O. Box 66008
Houston, TX 77266-6008
Dale McNeill, Convener; Episcopal

Kingdom Community Church
614 E. 19th Ave.
Houston, TX 77008

Maranatha Fellowship Metropolitan Community Church
P.O. Box 667032
Houston, TX 77266-7032
Rev. Janet Parker

Metropolitan Community Church of the Resurrection
1919 Decatur St.
Houston, TX 77007-7636
Rev. John Gill

Mishpachat Alizim
P.O. Box 960136
Houston, TX 77298

Church With a Vision Metropolitan Community Church
P.O. Box 1287
Longview, TX 75606-1287
Rev. Mary Jean Hinsey

Metropolitan Community Church
5501 34th St.
Lubbock, TX 79407-3309
Rev. Renae Phillips

Dignity / San Antonio
P.O. Box 12484
San Antonio, TX 78212-0484
Catholic

Metropolitan Community Church
1136 W. Woodlawn Ave.
San Antonio, TX 78201-5791
Rev. James Lewey

River City Living Metropolitan Community Church
202 Holland
San Antonio, TX 78212

St. Gabriel Community Church
(ICCC)
13904 County Rd. 193
Tyler, TX 75703

Central Texas Metropolitan Community Church From the Heart
P.O. Box 22043
Waco, TX 76702-2043
Durrell Watkins

Affirmation / Tarrant County
P.O. Box 48382
Watauga, TX 76148-0382
Methodist

Wichita Falls Metropolitan Community Church
P.O. Box 8094
Wichita Falls, TX 76307
Rev. Margaret Walker

Metropolitan Community Church (Bridgerland)
P.O. Box 4285
Logan, UT 84321
Kelly Byrnes

Affirmation / Wasatch
P.O. Box 526175
Salt Lake City, UT 84152

Presbyterians for Lesbian / Gay Concerns (Wasatch)
412 E. 3400 South, #1
Salt Lake City, UT 84115
Rev. L. Dean Hay

Reconciliation
P.O. Box 1501
Salt Lake City, UT 84110

Restoration Church
P.O. Box 511316
Salt Lake City, UT 84151-1316

Sacred Light of Christ Metropolitan Community Church
P.O. Box 11321
Salt Lake City, UT 84147-0321
Larry Adams

Christ Church Presbyterian
Red Stone Campus
Burlington, VT 05401
A More Light Church

Dignity / Vermont
P.O. Box 782
Burlington, VT 05402-0782
Catholic

Presbyterians for Lesbian / Gay Concerns—Northern New England
10 Winter St.
Montpelier, VT 05602

Affirmation / Virginia
P.O. Box 19334
Alexandria, VA 22320

Dignity / Northern Virginia
P.O. Box 10037
Main Station
Arlington, VA 22210
Catholic

Dignity-Integrity / Charlottesville
P.O. Box 3670
Charlottesville, VA 22903
Edward Strickler, Jr.; Catholic-Episcopal

Metropolitan Community Church in Charlottesville
P.O. Box 3275
University Station
Charlottesville, VA 22903
Rev. Judy Gingerich

Metropolitan Community Church of Northern Virginia
(NOVA)
7245 Lee Hwy.
Falls Church, VA 22046
Rev. Elder Darlene Garner

Dignity / Norfolk
P.O. Box 434
Norfolk, VA 23501
Catholic

New Life Metropolitan Community Church of Tidewater
P.O. Box 1026
Norfolk, VA 23501-1026
Leon Arrington

Central Virginia Affirmation
P.O. Box 25615
Richmond, VA 23260-5615

Dignity-Integrity / Richmond
P.O. Box 5207
Richmond, VA 23220
Joseph Hilterman; Catholic

Metropolitan Community Church
2501 Park Ave.
Richmond, VA 23220
Rev. J. Dwayne Johnson

Metropolitan Community Church of the Blue Ridge
P.O. Box 20495
Roanoke, VA 24018
Rev. Thomas Bohache

Integrity / Tidewater
P.O. Box 1086
Yorktown, VA 23692
Dr. Ann Carlson, Spokesperson; Episcopal

Overlake Metropolitan Community Church
P.O. Box 6612
Bellevue, WA 98008

Song of Messiah Metropolitan Community Church
P.O. Box 4389
Bellingham, WA 98227
Rev. Sue Stackhouse

New Creation Metropolitan Community Church
P.O. Box 2463
Everett, WA 98203-0463
Rev. Michelle Carmody

Affrmation
2115 N. 42nd St.
Seattle, WA 98103
Methodist

Angels Among Us Metropolitan Community Church
P.O. Box 2081
Mount Vernon, WA 98237
Rev. Anne Hulse

Eternal Light Metropolitan Community Church
207 N. Washington
Olympia, WA 98501
Rev. Clain Lust

River of Life Metropolitan Community Church
P.O. Box 1678
Richland, WA 99352-0059
Rev. Gary Wilson

Dignity / Seattle
P.O. Box 20325
Seattle, WA 98102-1325
Catholic

Integrity / Puget Sound
P.O. Box 20663
Seattle, WA 98102
Alan Quigley and Diane Stipp, Co-conveners; Episcopal

Metropolitan Community Church
1202 E. Pike St., Suite 930
Seattle, WA 98122-3934
Rev. Cheri Starchman

Presbyterians for Lesbian / Gay Concerns
1900 Western Ave., #1107
Seattle, WA 98107-1037

Tikvah Chadashah
P.O. Box 2731
Seattle, WA 98111

Affirmation / Spokane
3 N. 9th St.
Cheney, WA 99004

Emmanuel Metropolitan Community Church
P.O. Box 769
Spokane, WA 99210
Rev. Gary Wilson

Unitarian Universalist Church
321 W. 8th Ave.
Spokane, WA 99204

New Heart Metropolitan Community Church
2150 S. Cushman
Tacoma, WA 98405
Rev. Janice Skaggs

Metropolitan Community Church of the Gentle Shepherd
P.O. Box 5094
Vancouver, WA 98668
Rev. Teresa Nunn

Seventh Day Adventist Kinship International
P.O. Box 2360
Walla Walla, WA 99362
Seventh Day Adventist

Metropolitan Community Church North Pines
P.O. Box 1269
Yelm, WA 98597
Rev. Lynn Hallett

University Congregational United Church of Christ
4515 16th Ave. N.E.
Seattle, WA 98105-4201
Rev. Dave Shull and Rev. Peter Ilgenfritz

Freedom Fellowship Christian Workshop for Lesbians, Gays & Bisexuals
P.O. Box 1552
Morgantown, WV 26505

Angel of Hope Metropolitan Community Church
P.O. Box 672
Green Bay, WI 54305
Thomas Schuh

Integrity-Dignity / Madison
P.O. Box 730
Madison, WI 53701
Andrew Stuart and Paulette Quick; Episcopal-Catholic

Dignity / Milwaukee
P.O. Box 597
Milwaukee, WI 53201
Catholic

Lutherans Concerned
P.O. Box 11864
Milwaukee, WI 53211

Metropolitan Community Church
P.O. Box 1421
Milwaukee, WI 53201-1421
Rev. Lew Broyles

LDS Brotherhood
P.O. Box 152
Wasau, WI 54402

Women's Health

AAPHR: American Association of Physicians for Human Rights
(Gay and Lesbian Medical Association)
273 Church St.
San Francisco, CA 94114
Kate O'Hanlan

AAPHR / Lesbian Health Fund
201 E. Gorgas Ln.
Philadelphia, PA 19119
Dr Sallyann M. Bowman

ACT UP Women's Safer Sex Working Group
ACT UP Workspace
135 W. 29th St.
New York, NY 10010

Atlanta Lesbian AIDS Project
P.O. Box 5409
Atlanta, GA 30307

Boston Women's Health Book Collective
Amigas Latinas en Accion Pro-Salud (ALAS)
240A Elm St.
Somerville, MA 02144

Chicago Lesbian Community Cancer Project
P.O. Box 46352
Chicago, IL 60646

Emma Goldman Clinic for Women
227 N. Dubuque
Iowa City, IA 52245
Gail Sand, Co-director

Fenway Community Health Project
7 Haviland St.
Boston, MA 02115
Deborah Ruhe

Iris House
Women & AIDS Women's Center
2271 2nd Ave.
New York, NY 10035
Marie St. Cyr

Lesbian AIDS Project
129 W. 20th St.
New York, NY 10010
Amber Hollibaugh

Lesbian Cancer Support Group
The Lavender Project
Presbyterian-St. Luke's Medical Center
1719 E. 19th Ave.
Denver, CO 80218
Terri O'Hara, Health Educator

Lesbian Health Initiative
P.O. Box 130158
Houston, TX 77219-0158
Dr. Norri Collier

Lesbian Health Program
Community Health Project
The Lesbian and Gay Community Services Center
208 W. 13th St.
New York, NY 10011
Dana Greene

Lesbian Health Project
Office of Gay and Lesbian Health Concerns
New York City Department of Health
125 Worth St., Box 67
New York, NY 10013
Marj Plumb, Director

Lesbian Health Project
The Center
P.O. Box 3357
San Diego, CA 92163-3357

Lesbian Health Project / LA
8240 Santa Monica Blvd.
West Hollywood, CA 90046
Suzann Gage

Lesbian's Educational AIDS Resource Network
14002 Clubhouse Circle, #205
Tampa, FL 33524

Lesbians with HIV & AIDS
New York Hospital
525 E. 68th St.
New York, NY 10012
Michelle Russell

Lesbians with HIV Support Group
Bronx Lebanon Hospital Center
165-Selwyn Ave.
Milstern Building, Apt 7B
Bronx, NY 10457
Lisa Winters/Risa Denenberg

Lesbians Working in AIDS
Open monthly meeting in New York City; call 212-742-8726 for information

Lyon-Martin Clinic
1748 Market St., Suite 201
San Francisco, CA 94102
Selena Green/Lani Kaahumanu

Mautner Project for Lesbians with Cancer
P.O. Box 90437
Washington, DC 20090
Susan Hester/Deb Morris

National Cancer Institute
EPN-22
9000 Rockville Pike
Bethesda, MD 20892
Suzanne Haynes

PONY
(Prostitutes of New York)
25 W. 45th St.
New York, NY 10036

San Francisco Office of Lesbian & Gay Health
Department of Health
101 Grove St., #204
San Francisco, CA 94102

Seattle Lesbian Cancer Project
2732 N.E. 54th St.
Seattle, WA 98105
Liz Illg

St. Marks Women's Health Collective
P.O. Box A711
New York, NY 10163-0711

The Lavender Project at Presbyterian -St. Luke's Medical Center
1719 E. 19th Ave.
Denver, CO 80218
Terri O'Hara, Health Educator

Whitman Walker Clinic
1407 "S" St. N.W.
Washington, DC 20009
Amelie Zurn

Women in Crisis
360 W. 125th St.
New York, NY 10027

Women Organized to Respond to Life-Threatening Diseases
(WORLD)
P.O. Box 11535
Oakland, CA 94611

Women's AIDS Network
San Francisco AIDS Foundation
P.O. Box 426182
San Francisco, CA 94142-6182
Alina Ever

Women's Cancer Resource Center
3023 Shattuck Ave.
Berkeley, CA 94705

Women's Community Cancer Project
c/o The Women's Center
46 Pleasant St.
Cambridge, MA 02139

Women's Project
Health Crisis Network
5050 Biscayne Blvd.
Miami, FL 33137-3241

Writers

Linsey Abrams
Sarah Lawrence College
Bronxville, NY 10708

Paul Alexander
c/o Villard Books
201 E. 50th St.
New York, NY 10022
Author, Boulevard of Broken Dreams

Dorothy Allison
141 The Commons
Ithaca, NY 14850
Author, Bastard Out of Carolina

Hilton Als
The New Yorker
20 W. 43rd St.
New York, NY 10036

John Ashbery
George Borchardt Agency
136 E. 57th St.
New York, NY 10022
Author, Flowchart

Bruce Bawer
c/o William Morrow
1230 Ave. of the Americas
New York, NY 10020
Author, A Place at the Table

John Berendt
c/o Random House Publicity
201 E. 50th St.
New York, NY 10022
Author, Midnight in the Garden of Good and Evil

Blanche McCrary Boyd
Vintage
201 E. 50th St.
New York, NY 10022
Author, The Revolution of Little Girls

David Brock
c/o American Spectator
2020 N. 14th St., P.O. Box 549
Arlington, VA 22216-0549

Rita Mae Brown
c/o Bantam Books
1540 Broadway
New York, NY 10036
Author, Venus Envy, Dolly

Frank Browning
c/o Random House
201 E. 50th St.
New York, NY 10022
Author, Culture of Desire

Chandler Burr
c/o Hyperion
114 5th Ave.
New York, NY 10011

William S. Burroughs
P.O. Box 147
Lawrence, KS 06044

Peter Cameron
c/o Irene Skolnick
121 W. 27th St.
New York, NY 10001
Author, The Weekend

George Chauncey, Jr.
c/o Harper Collins Publishers, Inc.
10 E. 53th St.
New York, NY 10022
Author, Gay New York

Michelle Cliff
c/o Dutton
375 Hudson St.
New York, NY 10014
Author, Free Enterprise

Blanche Wiesen Cook
c/o Charlotte Sheedy Agency
611 Broadway, Rm. 428
New York, NY 10012

Bernard Cooper
c/o Viking/Penguin Books
375 Hudson St.
New York, NY 10014
Author, A Year of Rhymes

Dennis Cooper
c/o Grove/Atlantic Inc.
841 Broadway
New York, NY 10003

Quentin Crisp
c/o St. Martin's Press
175 5th Ave., 15th Fl.
New York, NY 10010
Author, The Naked Civil Servant

Michael Cunningham
c/o Gail Hochman
1501 Broadway
New York, NY 10036

Frank De Caro
c/o New York Newsday
2 Park Ave.
New York, NY 10016

Samuel Delaney
c/o University Press of New England
23 S. Main St.
Hanover, MA 03755-2048

Mark Doty
c/o Beacon Press
Horticultural Hall
300 Massachusetts Ave.
Boston, MA 02115
Poet, My Alexandria

David Drake
1540 Broadway, 18th Fl.
New York, NY 10036
Author, The Night Larry Kramer Kissed Me

Stuart Elliott
c/o NewYork Times
229 W. 43th St.
New York, NY 10036
Advertising Columnist

Lily Eng
The Seattle Times
Fairview Ave. N. & John St.
P.O. Box 70
Seattle, WA 98111
Staff Writer

Lillian Faderman
c/o Dutton/NAL
375 Hudson St.
New York, NY 10012
Author, Odd Girls and Twilight Lovers

Leslie Feinberg
141 The Commons
Ithaca, NY 14850

Allen Ginsberg
Box 582
Stuyvesant Station
New York, NY 10009
Author

Brad Gooch
156 5th Ave., Suite 617
New York, NY 10010
Writer, City Poet

Renee Graham
The Boston Globe
P.O. Box 2378
Boston , MA 02107-2378
Staff Writer

Jesse Green
c/o Cynthia Cannell
Janklow & Nesbit
598 Madison Ave.
New York, NY 10022

Jim Grimsley
P.O. Box 2225
Chapel Hill, NC 27515

Thom Gunn
c/o Farrar, Straus, Giroux
19 Union Square W.
New York, NY 10009

Marilyn Hacker
c/o Fran Collin
P.O. Box 33
Wayne, PA 19087-9998

E. Lynn Harris
c/o Doubleday
1540 Broadway
New York, NY 10036
Author, Just As I Am.

Essex Hemphill
4325 Baltimore Ave., 3rd Fl.
Philadelphia, PA 19104

Andrew Hollcran
P.O. Box 577
Keystone Heights, FL 32656
Author, The Dancer From the Dance

Alan Hollinghurst
c/o Pantheon
201 E. 50th St.
New York, NY 10022
Author, The Folding Star

Richard Howard
Creative Writing Program
Department of English
University of Houston
Houston, TX 77204-3012

Janis Ian
P.O. Box 4371
Los Angeles , CA 90078
Columnist, The Advocate

Gary Indiana
c/o High Risk Books
180 Varick St., 10th Fl.
New York, NY 10014

Richard Isay
c/o Simon & Schuster
1350 Ave. of the Americas
New York, NY 10019
Author, Being Homosexual

Randall Kenan
c/o Harcourt, Brace & Co.
15 E. 26th St., 15th Fl.
New York, NY 10010
Author, Let the Dead Bury Their Dead

Wayne Koestenbaum
60 Madison Ave.
New York, NY 10010
Author, The Queen's Throat

Larry Kramer
c/o St. Martin's Press
175 5th Ave.
New York, NY 10010

Tony Kushner
c/o Joyce Ketay Agency
1501 Broadway, Suite 1910
New York, NY 10036

Arthur Laurents
P.O. Box 582
Quogue, NY 11959

David Leavitt
65 Dayton Ln.
East Hampton, NY 11937
Author, Lost Language of Cranes, While England Slept

Jenifer Levin
c/o Dutton
375 Hudson St.
New York, NY 10014
Author, Sea of Light, Waterdancer

Heather Lewis
Doubleday
1540 Broadway
New York, NY 10036
Author, House Rules

Eric Marcus
Jed Mattes Inc.
200 W. 72nd St. # 50
New York, NY 10023
Author, Making History: The Struggle for Gay & Lesbian Equal Rights, 1945-1990

April Martin
c/o Harper Collins Publishers, Inc.
10 E. 53rd St., 7th Fl.
New York, NY 10022

Armistead Maupin
c/o Harper Collins Publishers, Inc.
10 E. 53rd St., 7th Fl.
New York, NY 10022
Author, Tales of the City

Terrence McNally
Manhattan Theatre Club
453 W. 16th St.
New York, NY 10011

James Merrill
c/o Alfred A. Knopf
201 E. 50th St.
New York, NY 10022
Author, A Different Person, et.al.

Kate Millett
c/o Anne Borchardt
136 E. 57th St.
New York, NY 10022

Donna Minkowitz
36 Cooper Sq.
New York, NY 10003

Richard D. Mohr
25 Beacon St.
Boston, MA 02108

Michael Musto
c/o The Village Voice
36 Cooper Sq.
New York, NY 10003
Columnist, The Village Voice

Michael Nava
c/o St. Martin's Press
175 5th Ave., 15th Fl.
New York, NY 10010

Joan Nestle
P.O. Box 1258
New York, NY 10116
Author, The Persistent Desire

Leslea Newman
c/o Charlotte Raymond
32 Bradlee Rd.
Marblehead, MA 01945

Torie Osborn
P.O. Box 4371
Los Angeles, CA 90078
Columnist, The Advocate

Camille Paglia
c/o Vintage
201 E. 50th St.
New York, NY 10022
Author, Vamps and Tramps

Dale Peck
c/o Irene Skolnick
121 W. 27th St.
New York, NY 10001
Author, Martin and John

Degen Pener
1633 Broadway
New York, NY 10019
Staff Writer, Elle magazine

Felice Picano
P.O. Box 294
Village Station
New York, NY 10014
Author

Deb Price
Detroit News
321 W. Lafayette
Detroit, MI 48226

Adrienne Rich
c/o W. W. Norton
500 5th Ave.
New York, NY 10110

Ned Rorem
c/o Simon & Schuster
1230 6th Ave.
New York, NY 10020

Gabriel Rotello
2 Park Ave.
New York, NY 10016
Columnist, Newsday

Paul Rudnick
c/o Dutton/NAL
375 Hudson St.
New York, NY 10014

Doug Sadownick
c/o St. Martin's Press
175 5th Ave., 15th Fl.
New York, NY 10010

Diane Salvatore
224 W. 57th St.
New York, NY 10019

Sapphire
401 W. Broadway, Suite 2
New York, NY 10012
Author, American Dreams

Mark Schoofs
36 Cooper Square
New York, NY 10003

Sarah Schulman
208 W. 13th St.
New York, NY 10011
Activist, Author

David Sedaris
c/o Little, Brown
54 Beacon St.
Boson, MA 02108

Kevin Sessums
c/o Vanity Fair
350 Madison Ave.
New York, NY 10017

Michelangelo Signorile
c/o Out
110 Greene St., Suite 600
New York, NY 10012
Columnist

Barbara Smith
P.O. Box 908
Latham, NY 12110

WRITERS

Liz Smith
c/o New York Newsday
2 Park Ave.
New York, NY 10016
Columnist

David Trinidad
401 W. Broadway
New York, NY 10012
Author, Answer Song; Monday, Monday

Gore Vidal
c/o Random House
201 E. 50th St.
New York, NY 10022

Linda Villarosa
c/o Essence
1500 Broadway
New York, NY 10036
Senior Editor

Patricia Nell Warren
8306 Wilshire Blvd., Suite 8306
Beverly Hills, CA 90211

Eric K. Washington
P.O. Box 250150
New York, NY 10025

John Weir
6922 Hollywood Blvd., 10th Fl.
Hollywood, CA 90028

Edmund White
c/o Maxine Groffsky
2 5th Ave.
New York, NY 10011

Jeannette Winterson
c/o Suzanne Gluck
ICM
40 W. 57th St.
New York, NY 10019
Author, Written on the Body; The Passion

Youth

Phoenix Gay and Lesbian Youth Group
P.O. Box 80174
Phoenix, AZ 85060

Voit Valley One in Ten
3136 N. 3rd Ave
Phoenix, AZ 85013
Darren Whallon

23 and Under Support Group
Pacific Center for Human Growth
2712 Telegraph Ave.
Berkeley, CA 94705

Lambda Youth Network
P.O. Box 7911
Culver City, CA 90233

Eagle Center
7051 Santa Monica Blvd.
Hollywood, CA 90038
Jerry Battey, Director

Youth Outreach
c/o Gay & Lesbian Community Services Center
1625 N. Schrader Ave.
Hollywood, CA 90028-9998

Family Workshops
10861 Queensland St.
Los Angeles, CA 90034
Barbara Bernstein/Marilyn Lebow

Gay and Lesbian Youth Talkline
c/o Gay & Lesbian Community Services Center
1625 N. Hudson Ave.
Los Angeles, CA 90028-9998
Helpline

The Pen Pal Program
c/o Gay & Lesbian Community Services Center
1625 N. Hudson Ave.
Los Angeles, CA 90028-9998
Pen Pal Program

Project 10
Fairfield High School
7850 Melrose Ave.
Los Angeles, CA 90046
Virginia Uribe

Rainbow's End
Spectrum
1000 Sir Francis Drake Blvd.
Rm. 10
San Anselmo, CA 94960

Gay Youth Alliance/San Diego
P.O. Box 83022
San Diego, CA 92138-3022

18th St. Services
217 Church St.
San Francisco, CA 94114
Camille Anacabe; outpatient drug and alcohol counseling for gay and bisexual men

Bay Area Sexual Minority Youth Network
P.O. Box 460268
San Francisco, CA 94146-5012

Bay Positives
518 Waller St.
San Francisco, CA 94117
Antigone Hodgins; HIV-positive youth

Central City Hospitality House Youth Program
146 Leavenworth St.
San Francisco, CA 94102

Cole St. Youth Clinic
555 Cole St.
San Francisco, CA 94117
Erica Bisgyer

Diamond St. Youth Shelter
536 Central Ave.
San Francisco, CA 94117

Gay and Lesbian Youth Advocates
1095 Market St., Suite 201
San Francisco, CA 94103

Gay Youth Community Coalition (GYCC) of the Bay Area
P.O. Box 846
San Francisco, CA 94101-0846

Larkin St. Youth Center
1044 Larkin St.
San Francisco, CA 94109

Lavender Youth Recreation & Information Center
1853 Market St.
San Francisco, CA 94103

National Gay Youth Network
P.O. Box 846
San Francisco, CA 94101-0846

Pro Active Youth Job Training Program
c/o Community United Against Violence
973 Market St., Suite 500
San Francisco, CA 94103

Special Programs for Youth
Youth Guidance
375 Woodside Ave.
San Francisco, CA 94127
Janet Shawitz

Support Services for Gay & Lesbian Youth
San Francisco Unified School District
1512 Golden Gate Ave.
San Francisco, CA 94115
Kevin Gogin, MFCC

Youth Advocates Teen HIV Program
555 Cole St., Suite 6
San Francisco, CA 94117
Susan Castillo, Program Director

Youth Empowerment Services
1242 Market St.
San Francisco, CA 94102

Youth Networks
2215 Market St., Suite 479
San Francisco, CA 94114-1612

Youth Visibility Project
The Gay & Lesbian Alliance Against Defamation
1360 Mission St., Suite 200
San Francisco, CA 94103

Legal Advocates for Children and Youth
111 W. St. John, Suite 315
San José, CA 95113

National Coalition for Gay, Lesbian & Bisexual Youth
P.O. Box 24589
San José, CA 95154-4589

Peninsula Family YMCA
Project FOCYC, Gay & Lesbian Teen Intervention Program
240 N. El Camino Real
San Mateo, CA 94401

Youth and Family Assistance
Community Living Room
28 W. 37th Ave.
San Mateo, CA 94403

Contra Costa Youth Group
Pacific Center for Human Growth
1250 Pine St., Suite 301
Walnut Creek, CA 94596

Walnut Creek Youth Group
1250 Pine St., Suite 301
Walnut Creek, CA 94596

Gay and Lesbian Adolescent Social Services
8901 Melrose Ave., #202
West Hollywood, CA 90069-5613
Group homes for lesbian and gay and HIV-positive adolescents. Licensed foster family agency for lesbian and gay teens and for infants, toddlers and young children who have been abused.

Youth Services Program
P.O. Drawer 18-E
Denver, CO 80218-0140
Cheryl Schwarz, Youth Services Coordinator

Danbury Gay, Lesbian & Bisexual Youth Group
105 Garfield Ave.
Danbury, CT 06810
Pam Gilmartin, Facilitator

Inner City Youth Project
1841 Broad St.
Hartford, CT 06114-1780

AIDS Project New Haven
254 College St., Suite 200
New Haven, CT 06510
Ruben Rivera, Director of Education

Bisexual Gay Lesbian Active Dialogue for Youth
c/o AIDS Project New Haven
P.O. Box 636
New Haven, CT 06503

International Gay & Lesbian Youth Organization
American Secretariat
P.O. Box 42463
Washington, DC 20015-0463

National Advocacy Coalition on Youth and Sexual Orientation
1025 Vermont Ave. N.W., Suite 200
Washington, DC 20005

National Network of Runaway & Youth Services, Inc.
1319 "F" St. N.W., Suite 401
Washington, DC 20004

Rehoboth Institute
326 S. Carolina Ave. S.E.
Washington , DC 20003
Dan Byrne, Clinical Director

Sexual Minority Youth Assistance League
333½ Pennsylvania Ave. S.E.
3rd Fl.
Washington, DC 20003-1148

YOUTH Magazine
P.O. Box 34215
Washington, DC 20043-4215

Queer Youth—Gainesville Gay Switchboard
P.O. Box 12002
Gainesville, FL 32604-0971
Doug Dankle, Switchboard Coordinator

Jacksonville Area Sexual Minority Youth Network
P.O. Box 23778
Jacksonville, FL 32241-3778
Keif Schleifer

Delta Youth Alliance
P.O. Box 533446
Orlando, FL 32853

Your Turf
c/o Gay and Lesbian Community Services of Central Florida
P.O. Box 533446
Orlando, FL 32853-3446

Florida Sexual Minority Youth Service Providers
712 Tropical Circle
Sarasota, FL 34242
Betsy Nelson

COMPASS Youth Program
2677 Forest Hill Blvd.
West Palm Beach, FL 33406
Sheila Bewsee, Coordinator

Young Adult Support Group
c/o Atlanta Gay and Lesbian
Community Center
63 12th St.
Atlanta, GA 30309

Resources for Gay, Lesbian & Bisexual Youth
740 Fletcher St.
Cedartown, GA 30125

Youth Outreach Services
1154 Fort St. Mall, Rm. 415
Honolulu, HI 96813

Iowa Gay Youth Helpline
800-332-8182

Horizons Youth Services
961 W. Montana St.
Chicago, IL 60614

Neon St. Center for Homeless Youth
Travelers & Immigrant Aid
327 S. LaSalle St.
Chicago, IL 60604-3471

Pride Youth
1779 Maple St.
Northfield, IL 60093

Indianapolis Youth Group
P.O. Box 20716
Indianapolis, IN 46220

Gay & Lesbian Youth in Discussion & Education
c/o Gay & Lesbian Resource
Center
4211 Grand Ave.
Des Moines, IA 50312

Young Women's Resource Center
554 28th St.
Des Moines, IA 50312-5222

United Action for Youth
410 Iowa Ave.
Iowa City, IA 52240

Louisville Youth Group
P.O. Box 4664
Louisville, KY 40204

Boston Alliance of Gay and Lesbian Youth
P.O. Box 814
Boston, MA 02103

Framingham Regional Alliance of Gay & Lesbian Youth
P.O. Box 426
Framingham, MA 01701-0003

Pioneer Valley Youth Support Group
P.O. Box 202
Hadley, MA 01035

Northfield Mt. Hermon School Homosexual-Bisexual-Heterosexual Alliance
Northfield Mt. Hermon School
Northfield, MA 01360
High school group

Governor's Commission on Gay & Lesbian Youth
c/o Health Awareness Services
71 Elm St.
Worcester, MA 01609

Supporters of Worcester Area Gay and Lesbian Youth
P.O. Box 592
Westside Station
Worcester, MA 01602

United Church Coalition for Lesbian / Gay Concerns Youth and Young Adult Outreach Program
69 Monadnock Rd.
Worcester, MA 01609-1714

Cape and Islands Gay and Lesbian Youth Group
Drawer 78
Yarmouth Port, MA 02675

Ozone House Gay and Lesbian Youth Group
608 N. Main St.
Ann Arbor, MI 48104

Affirmations Lesbian & Gay Community Center
195 W. Nine Mile Rd., # 110
Ferndale, MI 48220

Windfire / Grand Rapids
c/o Lesbian & Gay Community Network of Western Michigan
909 Cherry S.E.
Grand Rapids, MI 49506
Todd VerBeek

Kalamazoo Resource Center Youth Group
P.O. Box 1532
Kalamazoo, MI 49005-1532

Windfire / Kalamazoo
c/o WMU Alliance for Lesbian and Gay Support
Faunce Student Services
Kalamazoo, MI 49008

Michigan Alliance for Lesbian and Gay Youth Services
617 N. Jenison
Lansing, MI 48915

Windfire / Traverse City
P.O. Box 562
Traverse City, MI 49685

Lesbian & Gay Student Support Group
Minnesota Center for Arts Education
6125 Olson Memorial Highway
Golden Valley, MN 55422
High school group

The Marshal GLBT Youth Group
Minnesota AIDS Project
109 S. 5th St.
Marshall, MN 56258

Lesbian, Gay and Bisexual Student Support Group
South High School
3131 19th Ave. S.
Minneapolis, MN 55407
High school group

Minnesota Task Force for Gay and Lesbian Youth
P.O. Box 8588
Minneapolis, MN 55408

So What If I Am?
2200 Emerson Ave.
Minneapolis, MN 55405

University of Minnesota's Youth and AIDS Project
428 Oak Grove St.
Minneapolis, MN 55403

Youth Intervention Project
Hennepin County Red Door Clinic
525 Portland Ave. S., Lower Level
Minneapolis, MN 55415
HIV/AIDS Services

Northwest Youth & Family Services
1775 Old Highway 8, Suite 101
New Brighton, MN 55112

Triangle Group
St. Louis Park High School
c/o Lenox Community Center
6715 Minnetonka Blvd.
St. Louis Park, MN 55426-3488
High school group

Gay, Lesbian and Bisexual Student Support Group
Central High School
275 N. Lexington Parkway
St. Paul, MN 55104

Gay, Lesbian & Bisexual Student Support Group
Health Start
590 Park St., Suite 208
St. Paul, MN 55103-1843
High school group

Hennepin County Home School
1074 Selby Ave.
St. Paul, MN 55104
High school group

Lesbian and Gay Youth Together
Wingspan Ministry of St. Paul-Reformation Lutheran Church
100 N. Oxford St.
St. Paul, MN 55104
Leo Treadway, Ministry Associate

St. Paul School District Program for Lesbigay Youth
St. Paul School District
360 Colbourne Ave.
St. Paul, MN
High school group

Growing American Youth
c/o Our World Too, Inc.
11 S. Vandeventer
St. Louis, MO 63108

Gay and Lesbian Youth Talkline
P.O. Box 94882
Lincoln, NE 68509

Burke High School Guidance Department
12200 Burke Blvd.
Omaha, NE 68154-2399
High school group

Gay Youth Outreach Program
University of Nevada
Mailstop 058
Reno, NV 89557

Gay and Lesbian Youth in New Jersey
P.O. Box 137
Convent Station, NJ 07961-0137

Identity Acceptance Movement
Middle Earth Crisis Center
2740 Martin Ave.
Bellmore, NY 11710

Young Adults Against Drugs and Alcohol
2488 Grand Concourse, Rm. 317
Bronx, NY 10458

Gay and Lesbian Youth Services of Western New York
190 Franklin St.
Buffalo, NY 14202

Youth Environmental Services Inc.
30 Broadway
Massapequa, NY 11758

Bisexual, Gay and Lesbian Youth of New York
Lesbian and Gay Community Services Center
208 W. 13th St.
New York, NY 10011-7799
Hadar Dubowsky

Harvey Milk School
2 Astor Pl., 3rd Fl.
New York, NY 10003
Christopher Rodriguez

Hetrick Martin Institute
2 Astor Pl., 3rd Fl.
New York, NY 10003
Frances Kunreuther

National Advocacy Coalition for Sexual Minority Youth
Hetrick Martin Institute
2 Astor Pl., 3rd Fl.
New York, NY 10003
Frances Kunreuther

Youth Education Life Line
135 W. 29th St., 10th Fl.
New York, NY 10001
Tom Beer; HIV/AIDS Services

Youth Enrichment Services
Lesbian and Gay Community Services Center
208 W. 13th St.
New York, NY 10011-7799
Barbara Bickart

Gay, Lesbian & Bisexual Youth Group
c/o AIDS Center of Queens County
9745 Queens Blvd.
Rego Park, NY 11374

Lesbian & Gay Youth of Rochester
c/o Gay Alliance of Genessee Valley
179 Atlantic Ave.
Rochester, NY 14607-1255

Lighthouse
Downtown United Presbyterian Church
121 N. Fitzhugh St., Rm. 441
Rochester, NY 14614

Lesbian Gay Youth Program of Central New York
Echo Center
826 Euclid Ave.
Syracuse, NY 13210

Syracuse Lesbian Gay Youth Program
c/o Lambda Youth Services
P.O. Box 6103
Syracuse, NY 13217
Raymond Stoffel, Director

OutRight!
P.O. Box 3203
Durham, NC 27715-3203

Time Out Youth
1431 Armory Dr.
Charlotte, NC 28204

Gay & Lesbian Adolescent Support System
(GLASS)
Alternative Resources of the Triad
P.O. Box 4442
Greensboro, NC 27404

A Safer Place Youth Network
P.O. Box 12831
Raleigh, NC 27605-2831

Cincinnati Youth Group
P.O. Box 19852
Cincinnati, OH 45224

Moore and Associates
6611 Rockside Rd., Suite 215
Cleveland, OH 44131
Douglas J. Moore, Ph.D.

Presence and Respect for Youth in Sexual Minority
1418 W. 29th St.
Cleveland, OH 44113

Kaleidoscope Youth Coalition
P.O. Box 8104
Columbus, OH 43201

Northwest Ohio Gay / Lesbian Youth Group
Central United Methodist Church
701 W. Central Ohio
Toledo, OH 43610

Lesbian, Gay & Bisexual Youth Support Program
Youth Services of Tulsa
302 S. Cheyenne
Tulsa, OK 74103

National Resource Center for Youth Services
202 W. 8th St.
Tulsa, OK 74119-1419
Gay Phillips, Program Manager

Metropolitan Community Church / Eugene
The Koinonia Center
1414 Kincaid St.
P.O. Box 10091
Eugene, OR 97440

Oregon Sexual Minority Youth Network
P.O. Box 162
Portland, OR 97207-0162

Outreach to Rural Youth Project
P.O. Box 25791
Portland, OR 97225
Scott Thiemann

Park Ave. Social Club
P.O. Box 2294
Portland, OR 97208

Phoenix Rising
620 S.W. 5th Ave., #710
Portland, OR 97204
Valerie Whittlesey, Executive Director

Eagles Perch
P.O. Box 11543
Harrisburg, PA 17108

Gay and Lesbian Youth Alliance
P.O. Box 31
Lancaster, PA 17603-0031

Bridges Project of American Friends Service Committee
1501 Cherry St.
Philadelphia, PA 19102

Penguin Place Youth Group
201 S. Camac St.
Philadelphia, PA 19107

Sexual Minority Youth Roundtable
c/o Philadelphia County Health Department
1642 Pine St.
Philadelphia, PA 19103

Voyage House
1431 Lombard St.
Philadelphia, PA 19146
Susan Pursch, Director

Growing Alternative Youth
4120 Brownsville Rd.
Suite 16-1416
Pittsburgh, PA 15229

One in Teen Youth Services
c/o The Center for Lesbian & Gay Community Services
703 Berry Rd.
Nashville, TN 37204-2803

National Youth Advocacy Alliance
P.O. Box 121690
Arlington, TX 76012

Inside OUT YOUTH
University YWCA
2330 Guadalupe St.
Austin, TX 78705
Newsletter

Out Youth Austin
University YWCA
2330 Guadalupe St.
Austin, TX 78705

LAMBDA Services—Youth OUTreach
P.O. Box 31321
El Paso, TX 79931-0321
Community center

National Gay Alliance for Young Adults
P.O. Box 190426
Dallas , TX 75219-0426

Houston Area Teen Coalition for Homosexuals
P.O. Box 66574
Houston, TX 77266-6574

Houston Institute for the Protection of Youth, Inc.
811 Westheimer, Suite 102
Houston, TX 77006

Positive Choices
5429 W. Orem
Houston, TX 77045
Jimmy Braun

Cache Valley Gay and Lesbian Youth
P. O. Box 4285
Logan, UT 84323-4285

Stonewall Youth Services
Utah Stonewall Center
770 South 300 West
Salt Lake City, UT 84101

Utah Gay and Lesbian Youth Group
Utah Stonewall Center
770 South 300 West
Salt Lake City, UT 84101

Outright Vermont
P.O. Box 5235
Burlington, VT 05402
Karin Eade

Whitman-Walker Clinic—Northern Virginia
3426 Washington Blvd., #102
Arlington, VA 22201
Jody Wheeler, Youth Outreach/Health Educator

Richmond Organization for Sexual Minority Youth
P.O. Box 5542
Richmond, VA 23220

Youth Out United
485 S. Independence Blvd.,
Suite 111
Virginia Beach, VA 23452

Youth Eastside Services
16150 N.E. 8th
Bellevue, WA 98008

Snohomish County GLB Youth Support Group
Snohomish County Health District
3020 Rucker Ave., Suite 206
Everett, WA 98201-3971

Stonewall Youth
P.O. Box 7383
Olympia, WA 98507

Center for Human Services
17011 Meridian Ave. N.
Seattle, WA 98133
Bookda Gheisar

Gay and Lesbian Youth Info Line
814 N.E. 40th St.
Seattle, WA 98105

Gay, Lesbian and Bisexual Youth Program and Infoline
American Friends Service Committee
814 N.E. 40th St.
Seattle, WA 98105

Lambert House Gay, Lesbian & Bisexual Youth Center
1818 15th Ave.
Seattle, WA 98122

Seattle Counseling Service for Sexual Minorities
200 W. Mercer, Suite 300
Seattle, WA 98119

Youth Advocates, Inc.
2317 E. John St.
Seattle, WA 98112

Oasis Gay, Lesbian and Bisexual Youth Association
Tacoma-Pierce County Health Department
3629 S. "D" St.
Tacoma, WA 98408-6897
Nancy Mellor

Vashon Youth and Family Services
P.O. Box 237
Vashon, WA 98070

Young Gay and Proud
P.O. Box 3642
Charleston, WV 25336-3642

Madison Community United
P.O. Box 310
Madison, WI 54701
Social service agency for gay and lesbian youth providing counseling, referral, information and advocacy.

Gay Youth Milwaukee
P.O. Box 09441
Milwaukee, WI 53209

Gay & Lesbian Oriented Youth
P.O. Box 9725
Casper, WY 82609-0721